Sociology

The Study of Social Life in the UK and Kenya

By

David Spurling

AuthorHouse™ UK Ltd.
500 Avebury Boulevard
Central Milton Keynes, MK9 2BE
www.authorhouse.co.uk
Phone: 08001974150

First published by AuthorHouse 4/8/2010

ISBN: 978-1-4490-9625-0 (sc)

Front cover: Photo of Ngong Market, Kenya
Back cover: Photo of Rochester castle and cathedral, UK

This book is printed on acid-free paper.

Contents

Chapter One

Science of Sociology

There are a number of different definitions of 'sociology', which all have the fundamental idea of "the ways in which society operates". Sociology is unlike some other sciences, such as mathematics, where a series of propositions will usually lead to definite conclusions. It is often defined as a *social science* because it deals with the ways in which human beings interact with each other .It looks at the ways in which people make decisions about other people and why they interact in that way. In society, there is often room for disagreement because of differences and unpredictability in the ideas and behaviour of individuals. Even where sociologists agree on ideas about what is wrong; they may not necessarily be in agreement on how to remedy the situation. For example, all sociologists regard most crime as undesirable but there are a host of different potential remedies recommended.

Part of the problem, in many cases, is that sociologists do not have adequate data for the purposes, which they would wish to investigate. In many cases, as we discuss elsewhere in this book, we need to look at both primary and secondary data. Secondary data means information, which has been used and collected for other purposes, for instance, information from government surveys. Primary data means data we collect for our own purpose. While primary data would fully serve the purpose of intended research, it is expensive to obtain, unlike secondary data which is often cheaper and more readily accessible.

Schools of thought in Sociology

There are a variety of points of view about sociology, which include; structural functionalism, Marxism and Weberian, modernism, post modernism and more recently, feminism. Functionalism means looking at society in the same way that we would look at the human body, that is, if each part of the body is functioning correctly then the body, as a whole will work well.

Karl Marx (1818 –1883) was very interested in the economic conditions of the age and assumed that the economic ideas were the most important factors governing people's behaviour. Karl Marx is often said to be one of the early sociologists but he also wrote on many other subjects as well.

Max Weber (1864 –1920), also regarded as one of the early sociologists, looked at the ways in which bureaucracy functioned as well as organisations as a whole.

Modernism looks at the way society has grown, particularly with so-called scientific management. This is where people associated with F.W. Taylor (popularly referred to as the father of scientific management) tried to break down processes into small parts and then tried in turn to see how productivity could be improved. This school of thought is also sometimes called Fordism since Henry Ford was the best known of the managers who tried to improve production in his firm in a scientific way. He followed previous ideas on the division of labour more thoroughly than most previous managers and managed to satisfy both workers and customers by giving them higher wages and better productivity, respectively. Henry Ford was also interested in the private lives of his employees since he wanted them to be respectable and not to indulge overmuch in alcohol or tobacco.

Post Modernists would suggest that there is no one easy idea, which would help us to understand society and even less to eliminate the faults of any one society.

Sociology is a comparatively new subject; the term was not used until the 19th century, by Auguste Comte (1789 –1857). Most of the well-known sociologists such as Marx and Comte thought that sociology was important and would rely on scientific method. Comte believed that sociology would be an important science, which would help the human race as a whole. In other words it was not just an academic discipline but was important for its applicability. The bias in sociology has been towards looking at capitalist economies and to a lesser extent, socialist or communist ones. Sociology started in an era when there was rapid industrial change particularly in the U.K. Sociological theory set out to investigate why this occurred and what would be the consequences.

Karl Marx was also very concerned with the political consequences as well. He assumed that there would always be conflicts in society, and that this would end in revolution. Other sociologists have been more interested in how society can function in the most efficient manner. They too have tended to look at the present capitalist or mixed economy society. Weber was very interested in what he regarded as the protestant ethic and in how far it was the cause of economic growth and change. He assumed that Puritanism and also the idea that wealth should be reinvested in many cases would lead to prosperity. Other people would suggest that this was not unique to Protestantism; one of the many causes of the rise of Japan as a major economy in the post war periods was that they tended to reinvest profits in the companies rather than simply indulging in profits for personal consumption.

Traditional Economies compared with Capitalist Economies

Traditional economies refer to economies where life continues in the same old way. These kinds of economies are mainly found in rural areas of some third world countries, and it is likely that their systems are quite different in that the emphasis is often on co-operation rather than on competition. In many cases as J.K.Galbraith (1909-2006), the well known economist suggests, the local population is likely to resist change since there is little scope for risk taking, as most of the population is poor. There is also less specialisation than in the modern economies.

It is however a very loose term since whilst for many it is associated with a tribal society, for others it could be a feudal system and so on.

Problems of trying to determine who belongs to a particular school within sociology

Part of the problem in sociology is that while there are these different schools of thought, not all writers will agree even within these schools of thought. The term 'liberal' may mean or be associated with freedom of the individual to some people, but have a completely different meaning to others. Some Liberals would not wish to restrict the use of pornography, whilst other sociologists such as the late Andrea Dworkin would regard pornography as part of the exploitation of women. Differences of opinion are also true of other social sciences such as economics.

The other practical problem is that most people will look at their immediate problems when they are writing and it is difficult therefore to get an overall view of a certain issues. Even feminism can be subdivided into a variety of points of view. This reflects the idea that we are influenced by our surroundings. Some Black feminists will be aware of the struggles of many of the poor people in third world countries and will conclude that the basic issue about poverty is the most important. Unsurprisingly Marxists are more likely to look for causes of crime in terms of poverty and alienation of youth, feminists will point out correctly that men are much more likely to commit crimes. The religious right will probably attribute poverty to family breakdown and lack of faith.

It is not the purpose of this book to try convince you of the correctness of any one of these but to enable you to understand basic theories and also as far as possible how to test their conclusions. Unlike the physical sciences it is often difficult to carry out experiments, and there may be ethical reasons why we would wish not to do so. There have been exceptions about experiments for example in Nazi Germany where scientists could often carry out experiments. This was also the case in South Africa, where the apartheid system applied from the late 1940's to the early 1990's and the results of separation of different racial groups could be well seen. In the former Soviet

Union there were also experiments in different family patterns, especially immediately after the Russian revolution in 1917. There was for a short while more experiments with groups of families living together but in the longer term the Russian family structure was very similar to many other western European nations.

Problems of distinguishing correlation and causality

We are all conditioned by a number of different factors such as religion or quasi religions such as Marxism or fascism, the people who we mix with, and the media. Given that the average viewing time for television in the U.K. is about 20 hours per week to say that we are unaffected by it seems unlikely. It is however more difficult to judge whether or not such factors as violence on TV is the sole cause of violence in the home as so many other factors come into account. We need to distinguish between correlation and causation.

Correlation means that we can establish a statistical link between one variable and another. In very few cases do we get a perfect correlation (which is represented by plus 1 or minus 1), so that in most cases there must be more than one variable, which influences the other factors. In correlation, we have to be careful to ensure that there is some evidence that one variable affects another. In some cases it is not obvious which variable affects which one.

Causality means that one variable causes another. The fact that there may be more violence on television does not necessarily mean that it causes more violence. It could be argued the other way around that if we become more aware of violence generally then we are more willing to watch it on television.

Extent of Inequality

Sociologists have been interested in inequality since the time of Karl Marx. How far differences are due to inherent differences of talents and other factors has been a matter of debate for a long time. In Victorian times, 1837 –1901, what is sometimes called Social Darwinism was a common view held by Spencer (1820 –1903) that the principle of natural selection which Darwin thought applied to evolutionary principles generally also applied to societies as a whole. Thus if natural selection worked for the common good then the current position was always likely to be the best one possible. Thus if the British position was predominant both politically and commercially, as it was in Victorian times, then this was likely to be because British society was best. Even more importantly from our general viewpoint was that, if people were at the top of their society it was because they had more ability than the other members of society did. Social Darwinist viewpoints are no longer generally held by sociologists but they may be held explicitly or implicitly by other people. Such people would hold the view that the existing patterns of inequality were necessary for a country such as the U.K.

to function at its best. This would have been true of many of the monetarist group of economists and also of the New Right group of sociologists.

Changes in patterns of inequality within the U.K

There was a rapid increase in inequality in 1980s in the U.K. ,those who were almost at the bottom of the income ladder had their incomes after inflation rising only by 7%. On the other hand those who were almost on the top of the income ladder found that their salaries rose by 38%. The Institute for Fiscal Studies has suggested that in the 1980s that wage growth played a part in this, since in rapid wage growth people already doing well will do even better as there is a scarcity of skilled labour. By contrast the poorest households are likely to contain non-working individuals and therefore will gain relatively little with wage inflation especially if state benefits are not increased over and above that of inflation. There has been an increase in interest in equality, partly because sociologists such as Marx and his followers have made various predictions about inequality and partly because inequality affects the ways in which people live.

Sources of information for Inequality

When looking at inequality, sociologists will in most cases want data to be able to formulate theories or to refute existing ones. Here they can obtain information from sources such as the Government survey reports about the different levels of income and wealth. However sociologists and other social scientists will not necessarily agree about how to remedy the situation. It is possible to see a relationship between educational attainment and income. This can clearly be seen in the relationship between graduating from university and associated jobs and incomes in many countries. In 2003 Bristol University, in the U.K., was criticised by the private schools about its entry requirements being lower for some people e.g. those from deprived backgrounds. It was claimed that such people might have lower grades than those from the private schools (often confusingly called public schools). Bristol University, said that it was doing this in some departments since “A levels” were not necessarily good predictors of educational attainment. One might wonder why it is so often used, given that it does not seem to have been a good indicator of grades at final university level.

Relationships between inequality and other indicators

Sociologists will be interested in equality sometimes in its own right but also because there is often a direct or indirect relationship between inequality and income or other factors. Many people would suggest that poverty would lead to certain types of crimes. It would seem plausible that the unemployed will have more time to commit certain types of crimes, such as robberies, than people who are at work. On the other hand, white-collar crimes such as fraud would seem to be easier to commit by people in the workplace than people outside it are. How far official statistics of crimes increase with inequality will partly be determined by what crime police give priority to researching and investigating.

Effect of changes in house prices on inequality

In a period of rapid house price changes such as those in the early 2000s, there is likely to be increase in disparities between wealth of rich and poor .This is because people at the lowest percentiles of the income distribution are not gaining much, as they are likely to be tenants, while people at the upper end gain considerably. There is also likely to be an age divide. In U.K. in 2007 when house prices rose rapidly first time buyers formed a smaller part of the total market than usual. On the whole first time buyers were likely to be younger than people who already had homes. The increase in house prices is therefore likely to have meant that older people as a whole had more wealth in comparison with younger people.

Major sociological problems

Crime

Crime is one of the major sociological problems. It is always difficult to be certain about crime figures since in most countries, reported cases of crime are not necessarily representative of the true/actual crime numbers. Instances of sexual harassment and domestic violence are rarely reported to the authorities. Even murders are generally under reported. This was shown by the case of the late Dr Harold Shipman, in the U.K., who was convicted of 15 murders in 2003, but who was suspected of carrying out over 200 murders. This estimate was obtained by looking at likely death rates for patients of other general physicians and comparing it with his.

Race

Racism has been a problem for many years. Hostile attitude towards other races had perhaps its best known effect in the Second World War with Nazi Germany when about 6,000,000 Jews were killed in concentration camps along with other groups such as homosexuals and gypsies. It is, however, not just an old problem.

This means that everyone not of the right race has to be either killed or at least removed from the area. Whilst it is easy to see that some people are racist, there has been less attention paid as to why people might be racist in the first place.

Is it just people who are authoritarian who are likely to be racist? Some people would suggest that the media play a major part in stimulating racism by dwelling on any problem, which asylum seekers might cause. Sociologists might therefore be interested not only in the views, which people hold but also on the basis of the information from which people get their views.

Social exclusion

Sociologists have been interested in social exclusion, partly because it has been realised that in many cases social exclusion may well cause problems for society as a whole. After the Brixton riots in the early 1980's the then Conservative government looked at some of the causes. Sociologists in particular have looked at the effects of social exclusion, which can be measured by several factors including; income levels, education, training, health and living environments. We can look at social exclusion in terms of lack of basic facilities in housing, such as exclusive use of bathroom and availability of toilets. It would also include overcrowding in residential areas as well as the homelessness.

Social exclusion could also include looking at the neighbourhood as a whole and assess its access to parks and open spaces, libraries as well as local health facilities. We can also see how different types of houses are subject to excessive levels of pollution or noise. There have been several studies about links between cancer and the location especially near nuclear power stations.

We can look at social exclusion in education such as where people cannot get children into local schools, and also children who are excluded for one reason or another from certain schools. We may also find some categories of children such as the visually impaired or the physically handicapped, who cannot get the educational facilities, which they need. Social exclusion might also include the inability to get into university or other forms of education.

Sociologists have investigated the difference in infant mortality and life expectancy between one social class and another to know what causes the differences. It might also include living in so-called sink areas where risks of vandalism and mugging are common. There have also been suggestions that the very poor might not have access to good food at reasonable prices, especially when local shops close early, and the supermarkets are some distance away. In the U.K., the then Minister of Health - John Reid - in 2004 suggested that for some poor people cigarettes were the only forms of relaxation although most people disagreed with this. Other people suggested that there were other forms of relaxation including watching television and playing sports on publicly owned grounds, which would provide a healthy alternative.

We may find that social exclusion may be partly caused by the people themselves, if we were to accept the right wing views of a controversial American sociologist Charles Murray, but other sociologists would dispute this. Social exclusion does not just deal with families. The old very often suffer from hypothermia in the winter months. The number of deaths will vary from one year to another partly because of the weather conditions but a reasonable estimate in the U.K. would be about 20,000 deaths per year. Social exclusion policy should look at such issues as well.

Poverty

Sociologists are well aware of Maslow's hierarchy of needs which is detailed in many books including those written by Simon Cruickshank, James Gachihi and David Spurling. The hierarchy has at its base the most basic physiological needs that people need; food and shelter. Once these needs are satisfied other needs including social needs can then be satisfied for most people.

Sociologists usually distinguish between relative and absolute poverty. We can find absolute poverty in much of the third world where people do not have access to adequate pure water, food or shelter. In many third world countries mortality rates are very high for children under the age of five years. This is comparatively rare in most of the western world. It could be argued that the homeless have been on the increase in the U.K. and that their life expectancy is often as low as in parts of the third world. Some social scientists have therefore used the term fourth world to denote the very poor in the developed countries.

Sociologists have also been interested in what is often called relative poverty. There is no one definition of relative poverty, but one generally accepted measure is that people below 60% of the median disposable income are poor. Disposable income means the amount that people get after direct taxation. Median means the middle value when placed in order of size. The national minimum wage, which came into force in April 1999 in the U.K., was a measure, which was meant to help the 'working poor'. However it was not always well targeted. Some people on low wages may be part of a richer family earning what is called sometimes 'pin money'. Also, the national minimum wage was not available to people in the 16-17 age range, which may have been reasonable for people living within families, but would not be helpful to people who for whatever reason cannot live at home. From October 2004 the national minimum wage was applied to lower age groups although they would not receive the standard minimum pay. In particular, however, the minimum wage was helpful to women who perhaps unsurprisingly tend to suffer more from poverty than men.

Sociologists would also be interested in the minimum wage because children are much more likely to be present in low-income households than in high-income households. This in turn may be for a number of different reasons; it may be more difficult to obtain well-paid jobs where there are family ties and it will often be difficult to travel too far, necessitating the need to take up local jobs rather than getting the more highly paid jobs in the city.

Low income may also be related to ethnic group. The U.K. publication Social Trends suggests that that being part of a large family of Pakistani or Bangladeshi origin is likely to lead to poverty. Although in 2009 there was a lot of discussion by the Labour and Conservative parties about choice of schools, in many cases people without cars do not really have access to other secondary schools particularly in the rural areas where public transport is often poor. In any case schools will not be able to take everyone who applies. The poorer people including those from ethnic groups might well be left with the 'sink schools'. Sink schools is the name given to those schools where no one else wants to go to. It is usually assumed that these schools will be mainly in the poorer areas.

Common Sense and Limitations

Non-academics when discussing sociology would sometimes suggest that it is merely an application of common sense. One of the problems is that even if we agree that one thing causes another we would want to know which of the influences are important and which are less important. This is very important for public policy debates in discussions on crime or on why some people with the same intelligence levels seem to do much better when it comes to taking examinations and getting jobs. This is particularly true when looking at men and women where only some of the differences at work occur because of differences in qualifications.

However, even if we ignore the fact that common sense is not necessarily that common we would find if you were looking at the topic of television viewing and how far it might lead to crime debate that there would be different schools of thought amongst the general public. The first may be that most people can distinguish between the screen and the reality and therefore, the violence which occurs in cartoons is unlikely to lead people to go out to hit someone as a result. Other people, particularly those who may have been mentally unstable (one estimate is as high as 25 % of the U.K. population), or of trying to cope with the mentally unstable would sometime try to prove the opposite; that television will lead to de-sensitisation. They would therefore suggest that watching television would mean that at least they become immune to real life violence, in war time and that even worse it may lead to more violence. Many sociologists will therefore suggest that they need a more empirical approach. This means, that we would look at people who watch television for different periods including those who have no television at all. We could therefore try testing our hypothesis by testing if those who regularly watch television, particularly television with a lot of violence, do have a higher propensity to violence than those who don't watch any television at all. However, even this would not necessarily prove anything. It could be argued that we need, as mentioned before, to distinguish between correlation and causality. If we found that people who watch a lot of television particularly with gratuitous violence rather than news items which may show violence are themselves violent; it might be that this merely proves people who are violent watch a lot of violent television rather than it accentuates the process. There have been occasional examples of copycat violence where people (usually younger) will carry out a crime in the same way as seen on the screen. Sociologists may often be frustrated because they cannot necessarily carry out experiments. For instance, if they wished to investigate the effect of what happens if people were not be allowed to watch so much television particularly violence. This is not usually possible though it might be made possible to make some sort of international investigations to see if there is still a clear-cut correlation. Sociologists (and psychologists) often use the term 'conditioning' to denote the ways in which these influences have their effect upon us.

In 2004, in the U.K., there was considerable debate about violent pornography and its influence, following the murder of a schoolteacher, by a murderer who seemed to be obsessed with such films.

People's main objectives

Though modern developed society tends to think of money and its scarcity as being the main objective in life, a little thought will show that most of the time we are concerned with what money will buy. It is not even obvious why we buy some goods rather than others. Is it rational to buy personalised number plates for cars? Is it rational to buy paintings or jewellery, which will spend most of their time in a safe? We may also buy items for the prestige value sometimes called goods of ostentation. Such goods are called *Veblen goods* named after the 19th century economist, Veblen, since people buy more of them irrespective of the rise in price. We can see the way that the advertising industry uses this in the sale of houses, which are often called exclusive. We might assume from the advertisements that many people are interested in status as well as in money. This may also affect the jobs which people will put in for. There has been a lot of debate from sociologists such as John Goldthorpe about the position of clerks and higher paid manual workers and their status. The usual assumption has been that white collar workers have been in a higher social class than manual workers. Marx assumed that economic ideas are paramount but not all sociologists such as the post modernists would accept this.

Within our work, our values will show in the ways in which offices are placed often to give an indication of seniority and so on. It is not obvious, on a purely rational basis, to see why a more important manager needs a bigger office. Status may also affect the job titles. This is not confined to the middle class. Many people have been amused by the way that the *rat catchers* are now termed *rodent operatives*. There have been disputes between sociologists about the effects of the class system. It is often assumed that white-collar workers have a higher status even if they get paid less compared with blue-collar workers.

Use of money and the impersonal nature of society

In modern society money is used as the main medium of exchange. This occurs once we move into a society of specialisation, where no one individual is producing all goods for ourselves. Exchanging goods for other goods is possible but it would make life difficult. Use of money leads to specialisation of labour which some sociologists, notably Max Weber and Emile Durkheim, were very interested in. Bartering does, however, still take place in areas such as international trade, particularly where exchange rates do not perform their underlying function. It also can be seen taking place in such areas as the transfer of council houses or housing association houses in the U.K.

Some of the earlier economists thought it good that people did not need to know whom they were dealing with when buying and selling goods and services. Adam Smith referred to the 'invisible hand' and assumed that competition would solve most problems. This is somewhat ironic as he worked for the government as a customs officer. It might be noted however that this was not the same as supporting all private enterprise since he assumed that if tradesmen for example, talked together they were often conspiring against the public interest.

The effect of using money rather than having a bartering system means that we are often several steps removed from the people producing goods and services for us. This is likely to give us a different sort of society from one in which the owner manager made all the major decisions. Some sociologists have suggested that we now have to trust the institution rather than the individual. This is one of the many reasons why firms spend so much money on branding. For a long while St Michael's the brand name for Marks and Spencer was assumed to mean good quality at a reasonable price for clothing. However, this trust can be misplaced as has been shown with some of the spectacular bankruptcies such as Enron in the U.S.A. Michael Moore in his book suggests that Enron executives in several instances managed to get large sums of money from the company in spite of this bankruptcy. (Enron was the case of bankruptcy that involved the biggest amount in history so far in the early 2000s and most people would probably agree with his conclusions that this seemed unfair.)

Specialisation leading to alienation

Specialisation partly gave rise to increased monopoly power leading to greater class conflicts. It may also have led to alienation since workers as well as many lower grade managers may have felt that they were working for an impersonal organisation. Sociologists have concentrated most on the worker/employer relationship but the effects on consumers as well as on the supplier's relationship with the impersonal firms may also be important. Specialisation has led to tasks becoming simpler as seen in some of the car firms. This would explain why in many countries car firms have had high strike rates, even though wages are higher in many cases than in other jobs. In September 2004 Fords announced that they would be closing the car plant in East London, which had been in existence for over 50 years. This was in spite of the fact that the management had given an assurance about the company a few months earlier. This shows the problems of specialisation but also that specialisation has other indirect effects, leading to global companies whose interest is the particular company and not any one country.

To over simplify Marx he defined two major classes, that is, capitalists and workers. Capitalists were the people who owned the land, the factories and other major resources. The workers were the people producing the goods and services.

Critics of Marx would say that he was writing in the 19th century and did not foresee the rise in the middle class who do not regard themselves as part of the oppressed. Marxists would say that the problems might have been postponed. They, along with some other sociologists, might suggest that the problems have been displaced, that is, people in the third world suffer from the increasing gap between rich and poor especially those in sub-Saharan African countries.

The effects of specialisation

Adam Smith, the well-known economist in 1776 produced the book called *'The Wealth of Nations'* which looked at the effects of specialisation even in such an activity as pin making. Pin making was possibly chosen, as it is difficult to imagine that there are that many processes to go through. Specialisation has two opposite effects on employment. The first is it creates the specialist who is confident of potentially high earnings, particularly if they are in scarce occupations. We can easily see this with the effect of very high wages paid to sport stars and to pop stars. This will be very true if it is impossible to find substitutes for such people in the eyes of the consumers. The second effect is that if the activity suddenly goes out of fashion, or if there is a new substitute such as greater automation, then there is a high risk of unemployment. This can readily be seen, with railway signalling personnel who have a very limited choice of who to work for. Apart from the effects on the workers, there is also an effect on the business as a whole since in many cases people may find it difficult to communicate with other specialists, especially when a great deal of jargon is used. Perhaps more importantly for the sociologists than psychologists is that it means that people at work have very clearly defined but small roles. In many cases they do not know very much about other people even when working in the same set of offices, let along people working for the same firm.

Sociologists and the Woodfordisation process

Wilmott and Young did a survey in 1957, where they studied people living in

Bethnal Green in the East End of London and Woodford - then a prosperous suburb of London. Unsurprisingly they found there were a number of differences. Some sociologists and others have therefore used the word Woodfordisation to describe what happens if people move from poor areas to richer areas. The word *embourgeoisement* has been used to describe this process. In the poorer areas people will often live closer to each other and have relatives within easy reach. The extended family is the name given to people and their immediate relatives such as aunts, uncles, cousins, and grandparents, and is much more likely to be important in closer knit areas than in the suburbs and town areas where children will tend away to seek better jobs. The patterns have probably been accentuated even more since the time of the study as more young people have moved away to University. The pattern may have been slightly reversed where many young people move from their homes to University during the term and in many cases are more likely to return to home during the vacation period.

Differences in class behaviour

Sociologists since the time of Karl Marx have been interested in the class system. However, even non-Marxists would be interested in the patterns of economic and social behaviour. Both economists and sociologists would wish to know what would happen if, say, there was an economic growth rate of perhaps 2 ½% - 3% that has been the norm since World War 2 in the United Kingdom. If the people who are currently on an income of £20 000 per year have an income rise to £30 000 per year do they have the same pattern of spending social behaviour as those who are currently on £30 000 per year? We can find data about how people spend their money from both Social Trends and Economic Trends and in some cases this will show not just the present pattern, but also how it has varied over time. However, the past is not always a very reliable guide to the future, especially when new products come in.

This is important not just to sociologists and economists but also to government officials when wishing to predict the effects of changes in incomes. This aspect of class behaviour will be important to the government for taxation purposes, since the government needs to know what goods will lead to more revenue and the amount of money that will be raised. They may also need to know how people wish to spend the money: will they require more universities or will they merely want to spend money on goods and services for their homes. The Chancellor of the Exchequer will try to predict what will happen before making any major changes in the taxation policy. However, private firms will also be interested in this area to estimate demand. In many cases larger firms try to build up their own patterns of finding out what happens with changes in incomes.

The patterns of behaviour are important when planning new developments, for example most people have criticised Becontree in East London/Essex, which was built in the 1930s on what was then open land for workers mainly for the Ford plant manufacturing cars. The criticisms were that there were rows of houses with few, if any, social amenities such that adequate social interaction could not really take place. Sociologists have been interested in what is often called the pattern of urbanism or urbanisation. Some sociologists assume that the West may be getting to a pattern of non urbanisation as with new technology people are free to live where they wish.

The Government tried to improve on the Becontree experience with the new towns in the immediate post war period when building Basildon in Essex, Stevenage, and Milton Keynes. The idea was that the towns should be reasonably self-contained so that people would not need to travel to work. In practice the main line trains from Fenchurch Street to Southend on Sea and Shoeburyness went within a few metres of Basildon town centre and many people therefore commuted by car to the nearest station at Laindon which was inconvenient.

The housing in Basildon has often been condemned as un-imaginative but for people with young children the crossing of roads was fairly easy with underpasses and the wider pavements were very helpful compared with other more picturesque places. Thamesmead, which was built in Southeast London, had high-rise flats, which were not necessarily suitable for parents with young children. The lakes and water were pleasant features but Thamesmead lacked shops and adequate bus routes. Unlike most other places the roads are rarely full since the car ownership is much lower than most other places. However Thamesmead suffered from being between two Boroughs, that is Greenwich and Bexley, which did not seem to take much interest. It was sometimes claimed that the former Greater London Council (GLC) tried to get rid of any problem families onto Thamesmead rather than having them in the home boroughs.

Relationship between urban development and sociological theory

Sociology as was said at the beginning of this topic deals with how people interact. Therefore if we are designing new urban development plans, such as the Thames Gateway it would be help if we know both where and how people interact. The Thames Gateway area is the biggest regeneration project in Europe and would be about the size of Tokyo although speakers from the project assured people that it would not look like Tokyo or lead to a concrete jungle.

Some people have commented that we live in a more impersonal age. This has been particularly true of the Communitarians mainly a U.S.A. based movement. It is not always clear how we prove or disprove this although newspaper headlines, say, showing an old person dead in a house for several days or even weeks might suggest that at least for some people this is true.

It is however not just old people who can feel that life is impersonal. Some local authorities have suggested that young people need their own space even within parks so that they can feel that they in effect own a part of the space. Young mothers with small children - especially if they live in flats rather than houses - may also need to communicate with other young mothers and feel that they have few opportunities to do so. The moves towards smaller nuclear families will in many cases make the mothers feel more isolated perhaps than in the past. The young mothers may therefore need part of a community centre where they have room to bring their children to play while still having access to talk to other people.

As the population gets more elderly and there are an increasing number of people who are no longer in full time employment, there may be a need for places for them to have somewhere to meet Apart from formal places, it could be helpful if we knew how people meet other people outside their family groups. In some cases this may be fairly obvious e.g. typically mothers used to meet outside the school playgrounds at the end of the day. The growth of the use of cars to and from schools would suggest that this part of interaction is less common nowadays.

The moves toward temporary rather than permanent full time work may mean that work-based friendships are slightly less likely to develop. The close relations often developed in the very strike prone docks and coal mining industry, perhaps reflected the fact that in many cases as in the old Docklands, in the East of London and even near Tilbury the port on the Thames in Essex a high percent of the local population had their same place of work. This made it more likely for work-based relationships to occur.

Choice and society

Another basic problem in sociology is that of choice or lack of it. Marxists are sometimes said to be deterministic; that people are to a large extent conditioned by the economic circumstances in which they are found. This is often called materialist determinism. Some actions are therefore almost or wholly inevitable.

Whist Marx was opposed to religion there are paradoxically counterparts in some religious beliefs. Many people who subscribe to Calvinism - a part of the Protestant Christian tradition - would believe in predestination; that everything is predetermined though in this case by God rather than by economic considerations. There has always been a debate in theology about free will and predestination and the same type of debate goes on within sociology. Other people would ague what while we are conditioned by circumstances, we also do have freedom of choice. They would suggest that though nurture and nature are important we also have freedom of choice. This idea might be tested for example by looking at twins brought up in the same household who might be thought to have both the same nurture and genetic make up to at least have a likelihood of the same circumstances.

Richard Tawney a Christian socialist in his book "*Religion and the Rise of Capitalism*" suggests a theory that capitalism was influenced by the emergence of the Protestant religion. His views are similar to those of Weber. In part of the Roman Catholic heritage there was at least lip service paid to the concept of the just price, that is, what should be paid rather than relying entirely on the 'invisible hand'. This phrase, much beloved of some of the 18th century economists such as Adam Smith is nowadays often referred to as market forces. He used the phrase to mean that the market would co-ordinate the problems of reconciling suppliers and consumers demands without any external interventions. Adam Smith believed in competition and would probably have joined with Marx in condemning monopoly capitalism. Many of the problems of modern society arise less from private sector organisations as such, but relate more to firms that have a great deal of monopoly power. Many sociologists have recently become interested in the concept of globalisation, where the actions of one country or major firm have effects on other people far removed from the original decision making process.

Since the events of September 11th 2001 when the Twin Towers in New York were destroyed there has been increasing realisation that small groups of people can often use their power to create havoc within other countries. This is in line with the post modernist thought that we are living in an age where the distinction between capitalism and communism have become less important. This is sometimes called convergence theory. We need to look much more closely at what causes people to become hostile particularly to the Americans and to a lesser extent to other western countries and their way of life.

Attitudes towards lending

For a long while usury that is, lending money at interest was forbidden in countries such as the U.K. Sociologists have often been concerned about the lack of credit at reasonable prices to poorer communities in the U.K. and to poor countries of the world. Some local authorities have also been concerned about this and have tried to encourage the use of credit unions. Credit Unions are formed when people join together to be able to lend to other members of the Credit Union at reasonable rates of interest. In the U.K. in the early 2000's although base rate has been at its lowest for about 40 years, this has not been reflected in other forms of lending such as shop store cards where a typical rate of interest might be over 20%. This is also true of hire purchase agreements. Even for wealthier individuals there have been concerns on taking mortgages when interest rates are low as things could change when the rates rise. Some of the Muslim community have been concerned as well about usury, and this has affected the choice of some Muslim students when looking at student loans.

Choice

Choices usually have to be made by individuals or by society with incomplete or imperfect information. If an individual, wishes to purchase some washing powder, he is unlikely to have perfect information as to the price charged by every single shop or supermarket in his locality and he may not be aware if a supermarket's own brand of washing powder is as good as a more famous brand among other factors. Furthermore, individuals do not have perfect information about their wants in the future due to its uncertainties. This is to a large extent true in sociology. We may believe that crime is influenced by poverty but we often have no way to absolutely prove it although quantitative research has become part of the sociologist's tools. We are often unable to carry out research for ourselves and so we have to use secondary data, which has often not been designed for our purpose. We have to choose using the best techniques available to us, what information to use and whether - in some cases - we try to go on to carry out further research to make more use of data, relevant to our needs.

Power

In many countries it is fairly obvious who has the formal powers; the Prime Minister or President and the Cabinet as they have the nominal responsibilities of the government.

There is also the power of the media. In most countries, the media is considered powerful because of its sizeable reach to the community or the citizenry. As such it can expose all sorts of things some of which should have remained hidden for both positive and negative reasons. In recent years, the media has especially had an edge due to the ever growing arm of investigative journalism. With technology, media houses are now able to let the people know of things they unearth, as they unearth them.

Similarly some of the chairmen of multinational corporations will often control budgets, which may be larger than that of industrial countries making them very powerful people in society. It is not always clear, especially in the light of Enron - the biggest corporate bankruptcy so far - just how responsibly this power is being exercised. Many people especially in 2009 have become clearer about the effects of globalisation and that people's employment can quickly be changed with the decision by the chairmen of a multinational corporation.

The late Anthony Sampson in 1962 wrote a book called the *"Anatomy of Britain"*, which examined the main people who ran the civil service and the big firms. In many cases the elite groups were predominately from the top public schools such as Eton and Harrow. (The term public school in the U.K. is confusingly used for the major fee paying schools). The top people were mainly educated at Oxford and Cambridge and were pre-dominantly male.

More recently Jeremy Paxman, who is a well-known TV personality, also wrote a book " the English "on much the same lines but drew slightly different conclusions. A capitalist economy will probably have greater extremes of wealth and incomes than other economies. This has been partially proved by the experience of Eastern European countries following the collapse of the Soviet Union.

However sociologists have not just been interested in people with a great deal of power. They have also been interested in the use of power within families. Feminists such as Sylvia Walby have often been concerned with what they would regard as patriarchy being influential almost everywhere.

Nearly all countries provide at least in theory education for children, although in some cases there may be considerable absenteeism. All Western European countries have a National Health Service, although the U.S.A has more of a Health Care System provided through private insurance in contrast to the European countries. There has also been an increase in interest in merit goods, for example health and education, which it is felt should be available to individuals irrespective of their income. More of the economy's resources have been channelled into these fields, and most of these have been within the public sector.

In 2010 there was considerable debate about the lack of student grants as well as charges for tuition fees for students in the U.K. There was also controversy about Government proposals to allow some of the best-known universities to charge topping up fees. Some people felt that it was unfair that students should be likely to face large debts at the end of a degree. At the present time there have been cheap loans, which are not normally repayable until the individual is earning a reasonable amount, so as to repay the money without undue hardship. Very little of the debate centred on whether or not the education could be provided in a different form although there were some suggestions that degrees might be taken in two years rather than the conventional three. There has been, in contrast, much less debate in the same media about the role of pre school provision since this is where some of the wide disparities in income are likely to arise. There seems to be some evidence to show that if we want to reduce inequality we will do better to spend more money on the early years.

There is inequality in training, where successive governments in the United Kingdom have tried to improve the quality of skilled labour available since the original training the Industrial Training Act 1964. Indicative planning has also been used to forecast surpluses and also bottlenecks, where shortages are likely to occur and which in turn will have effects on the rest of the economy.

Government and health spending

In the U.K., health has sometimes been described as a postcode lottery meaning that how well or bad the treatment patients receive depend largely on where they live.

The government has therefore set many quantitative targets without always seeming to realise the limits of statistical data.

One of the criticisms of the NHS was that it was a national sickness service, that is, it gave people care once they were sick but had done comparatively little to try to reduce the potential illness in the first place. The government faces a dilemma since some people resent what they regard as the nanny state that is, telling people what they should do. On the other hand the costs to the NHS of smoking, drinking, drugs and increasingly obesity are very high and many people feel that it would be helpful if such costs could be reduced in the first place. Part of the problem is that in many cases smoking is addictive and many smokers say that they would welcome the opportunity to break their addiction. Few people would suggest that freedom of choice should apply to the very young. There is however no agreement about what age people should be able to make decisions for themselves about smoking and drinking. In the U.K., there are different ages; 18 for drinking in a Public House and 16 for smoking which seems to have no obvious rationale. This has now been raised to 18.

Few people are consistent anyway as the chain smoker who complains about people taking drugs might be thought to be hypocritical. The latest statistics indicate that in the U.K. probably about 120,000 people die annually of smoking related illnesses like lung cancer.

Action on Smoking and Health (ASH) an anti smoking pressure group carried out a very good quantitative analysis on this in the 1970s, showing that the arguments about smoking such as that people were predetermined to die for other reason of personality were invalid.

Education and Income Differences

In the U.K., it has sometimes been said that Higher Education is only provided to people who show that they don't need it. This may sound unkind but what it means is that whereas health provision is provided only to people who show they are sick in some way or another; higher education is usually only provided to people who achieve a very high grade to enter the institutions in the first place. In 2003, the government announced it would in future provide some sort of grant for people over 19 who had less than the basic minimum of 5 GCSEs. Sociologists will be interested in the effects of education on incomes; in 2000 parents from the higher professional groups have 74% of their offspring achieving 5 or more GCSEs Grades A to C whereas for people in routine jobs the figure was only 29%. Some critics of the educational system may also suggest that in the future there is more need for people to be trained, not necessarily in the academic subjects.

The underclass

The underclass includes people, who are unemployed, or those who perhaps only obtain income infrequently from work, or those who work short hours due to such reasons as family problems. It may also refer to the children of people who are deprived in one way or another.

The underclass may well have very limited opportunities for such basic needs as housing. This is particularly true in terms of rapidly rising house prices especially in these current times. Housing associations exist in many areas but have relatively little money to buy new plots of land, or build more houses. They may also be less able to obtain better education as the middle class will be more aware of where the better schools are and will be able to pay to determine this. Secondly, even if members of the underclass are aware of where better schools are, they may well not be able to move house, to take advantage of the better education.

There is also considerable evidence that the middle class or professional class would usually have houses away from environmental problems, such as excessive noise. This means that even if professional people are living on main roads, they are much more likely to live at a distance from the traffic, compared to the people in the underclass who are more likely to have houses abutting the main road. Whereas many of the professional classes will have private medical care, ,if necessary through agencies, the underclass will obviously not have provision for this and will have to put up with lengthy waiting lists when they need medical attention.

Consumer sovereignty

The concept of consumer sovereignty implies that resources are allocated according to consumers' preferences, rather than according to the state's preferences. It may, therefore, be argued that if there is any state intervention (if the price mechanism is not allowed to work completely freely) resources will not always be allocated according to consumers' preferences. However, the degree to which consumers are "sovereign" in a pure capitalist economy depends upon their ability to pay. Individuals with low incomes may not have the ability to buy those items they wish to purchase. It may only be with some state intervention that consumers with low incomes will have their wants satisfied. Consumers may only be able to afford medical attention when they want it if the state provides a health service. These consumers may only be "sovereign" if there is some state intervention. To tell a very poor person faced with an expensive operation for a severe medical problem that they have a choice about which hospital they want is meaningless unless either the State provides health care or by chance they have medical insurance. There are goods sometimes called public goods like the provision of open spaces, which cannot be provided adequately through the price mechanism.

SELF-EXAMINATION QUESTIONS

1. What does a 'subsistence' or 'traditional' economy mean? Are any sociological differences likely to arise from such a system compared with a western style economy? Why does change not occur very much in traditional economies?

2. How far is it true that experimentation is not possible in sociology unlike in the physical sciences? Is it always possible to carry out experiments in all the natural sciences, for example in Astronomy? Why might there be ethical problems in trying to carry out some experiments?

3. What is meant by the term 'merit goods'? Can sociologists provide assistance on how these should be provided? Does sociology provide any help on the effectiveness or otherwise on what is happening at the present time? What advice would sociologists have in common if at all about how to improve the education system?

4. In what ways do modern governments influence the distribution of income? Can sociologists provide assistance on which would be the most effective ways of helping the poor? Would your answer be different about how this could be achieved in a developing country or a modern western economy? Why might capital intensive methods such as providing steel works, not necessarily be helpful to third world countries?

5. What are the comparative merits of 'deductive' and 'inductive' methods of reasoning in sociology? How can we be sure of not using doctored methods when we have representative samples? What, if anything, can we do if we have historical samples, which are not necessarily random?

6. What does the statement 'sociology is a social science' mean? In what ways, if any, do the methods in social sciences differ from those in physical sciences?

7. How far will modern computer methods mean that it is possible to obtain more predictions following from sociological theory?

8. What is meant by the term 'sociological laws'? How far is such a phrase useful?

9. Some sociologists have assumed that people are rational, by which they mean that consumers will maximise their satisfaction from the resources, including money and time, which are available to them. How far is this assumption reasonable in a modern developed country? Explain with reference to the large volume of persuasive advertising in such an economy.

10. Explain what is meant by 'positive sociology ' and 'normative sociology'. Is it possible in practice to have a system of sociology, which is purely positive? Why is the distinction between the two important?

11. Does the fact that most Eastern European countries have moved away from planned economies mean that there are no major sociological problems remaining? Would a Marxist analysis be the same as a Weberian or feminist one on this?

12. How far it is true that sociology is a science, and how far is it an art?

13. Does the fact that there are so many viewpoints in sociology, mean that sociology cannot really help us to understand society

14. What do sociologists mean by 'racism'? How far can the classification of ethnic groups in terms of incomes, class, employment opportunities, help us to find indications of problems? How far does it help us to find solutions to problems?

15. Why might lack of objective information help to distort what is happening with ethnic groups? Where do most people get their perceptions about different ethnic groups from? How can we test the theory that mixing more with different racial groups helps to reduce racism?

16. How can we measure inequality? Does the fact that women are obtaining more jobs prove that inequality between sexes has decreased?

17. What is meant by the term 'social exclusion'? How far is it possible to measure it and can sociologists help to suggest remedies?

18. How far does the national minimum wage help to reduce poverty? Why is it suggested that it has not always been well targeted?

19. How far is poverty linked to ethnic groups, and also to gender and socio economic class? Are these the only likely sources of poverty?

20. What problems might we find in trying to say what peoples' objectives are? Marx thought that economic ideas were the most important. Does the experience of the 21st century help us to agree or disagree on his conclusions on this?

21. Why might the study of specialisation of labour be of importance to sociologists? Which of the major sociologists investigated this? What are the advantages and disadvantages of such a system?

22. If people move from working class areas to middle class areas even while carrying out the same jobs, would we expect their pattern of social behaviour to be the same? Illustrate your answer with reference to any sociological studies.

23. Why might the development of areas such as Becontree in the 1930's - in the U.K. - which was criticised of just being rows of houses be relevant when discussing newer developments such as the Thames Gateway in the early 2000's?

24. Some people have suggested that we do not need more new houses in green field areas. What is meant by this and how far, if at all, can sociologists help to predict what would happen if we build on such sites rather than on brown field sites?

25. High rise flats have been criticised as being unsuitable for families, but in the early 2000's Ken Livingstone then Mayor of London suggested that we need more high-rise buildings. Would sociologists be able to help us understand the arguments for and against such buildings?

26. How far does the movement towards urbanisation mean that we have a move towards an impersonal society? Would the answer given by Marxists and Communitarians be the same?

27. Why might the growing proportion of the elderly population in the U.K. have different social implications compared to other countries such as those in Asia where the majority of the population is young?

28. In the early 2000's it has been suggested that only about 50% of the population in the U.K. have permanent 9-5 jobs. If this were true what would be the effects on relationships at work and also relationships within the community?

29. What is meant by 'deterministic'? Some people have suggested that both Marxist and some puritan Christians are both authoritarian and believe in determinism. How far is this true? Why might it be important to determine this?

30. Sociologists sometimes use the words 'nurture' and 'nature'? What do these two terms mean and why are they important? Why is it in practise often difficult to assess the relative importance of either?

31. How far is it true that religion has played a part in changes in society? Is it true that religion always plays a conservative role?

32. What would be the effects if lending of money at high rates of interest was forbidden? Why might sociologists be interested in the extent of credit facilities particularly in poorer areas?

33. What have been the effects on society of the credit boom on both the poor and the rich?

34. How far is it true that it is very difficult to show whether people are rational or irrational because we do not have perfect information? Which sociologists thought that people would become more rational over time? Have their predictions come true? How could we test this? Why might it be difficult to make predictions in sociology if people are irrational?

35. How far is it true, as Marx thought, that power is mainly concentrated in the same few hands and this is largely due to economic opportunities? Why might the answers to this be important in the study of sociology?

Sociological Concepts

The word 'concept' in sociology is used to mean ideas. One of the most common concepts in sociology is that of *social class*. To show this we might use an indicator such as income or occupation. The two may not have a big correlation and this has given rise to a great deal of controversy over what definition of class we need to use and why. However, this indicates one of the problems of sociology; until recently it was assumed that the man was often the breadwinner and the occupation of head of household was regarded as the important one. In many cases however there are more single parent families so that the women's occupation is the important one. In the case of *Dinkies* (Dual Incomes No Kids Yet) the occupations may be very similar between husband and wife. In this case the dual income is likely to be much higher than the income of one person working and of course the average income per head is also much higher. However, even this is not the whole story since in many cases older people may well have bought their houses so they have less expenditure on housing and even if they have not completed the mortgage they have less money to pay out. Similarly, whilst sociologists have often looked at salaries or manual and non-manual workers and also the differences in hours worked they have not often looked at the time travelling to and from work. There is also the expense of travelling so that to compare these workers with people working locally is obviously not helpful. We ideally, would like to know what the disposable income is and even to modify this to give an idea of what people can afford in many cases

Positivism

Karl Popper 1925 -1999, an Austrian born philosopher who worked for a long while at the London School of Economics, was very keen to criticise both Marxists and followers of Hegel. In his book '*The Open Society and his Enemies*', Popper assumed that we should look for a society in which individuals can to some extent, look after their own destiny and where the future is difficult to predict, rather than one which is inevitable, as Karl Marx suggested. Karl Popper also suggested that rather than having any one overall vision of the society that would be the only possible system, we should look for incremental changes sometimes called piecemeal social engineering. Sometimes we could modify the planning system so that people live in more suitable houses, for instance in the 1960s the use of high rise flats was clearly not suitable if the lifts did not work for many people with children. On the other hand the use of such flats for childless couples might be different.

Although Karl Popper did not state this, it is reasonable to assume that he would have approved of the ideas of trying to change society in small ways, such as better town planning and looking at the needs of individuals, rather than perhaps trying to change society as a whole. As with many other social scientists, Karl Popper drew partly upon evolutionist theory, first advanced by Charles Darwin in his work *'On the Origin of Species'*. He hoped that society would improve in gradual steps rather than in a revolutionary manner. In his book *The Poverty of Historicism* he attacked social theories that claimed that the social sciences were partly historical sciences, and that there was inevitability about what would happen.

The division between people who assume that we have free will and those who believe there is determinism applies both to religion and Marxism. Popper was very much a positivist in suggesting that we need to look to both theories and evidence to support the theories. One of the problems however of the positivist approach is that not all ideas are readily quantifiable and there may be problems of pursuing a positivist approach in only looking to test ideas which can be easily tested. This criticism is not however confined to positivist sociologists.

Not all sociologists would necessarily believe that we should move towards positivism; some feminists have talked about male-stream sociology.

Problems of evidence

There is the point that even a great deal of the 'evidence' itself may have been subject to bias. Also, there may be far too many variables to include them all in the data used as 'evidence'.

If we try to compare men's and women's health some facts are easy to quantify, with a few exceptions such as people being on a life support machine we know whether a person is alive or dead. However if we ask someone whether they are well, the old joke "that women have colds but men have flu" comes to mind; the answer is subject very much to personal judgement. Even diagnoses of illness are subject to fashions, changes in our knowledge and subject to different doctors taking different points of view.

Measures of crime

Social Trends says there are 2 different measures of crime. The first is the measure of crime which is recorded by the police and comes therefore from victims of crime from recording their complaints to the police. The other includes the British Crime Survey, whereby surveys of victims are carried and others are carried out. The other point is that even within these measures there are problems, for example in 2008-2009 about 4.7 million crimes were recorded by the police some of these were due to the methods of recording crime. The British Crime Survey by contrast had suggested much higher figures that of 10.7 million crimes in 2008- 9.

Unreported crimes

There are a number of reasons why crimes are not reported. The first is that in many cases, the incident is regarded as too trivial, or the police couldn't do anything, the victims did not report the crime as it was done in private. The police themselves may not report crimes for the following reasons: they may try to avoid the paperwork involved; they may try to put people off reporting crimes or even suggest they contact other agencies. Therefore, quantitative data that suggest major increases or major decreases in crime are regarded with some degree of caution. It might also be noted that perhaps the most common crimes are those committed by motorists, for example, transgressing speed limits, and these are very unlikely to be recorded by either method.

Even murders are under reported. This was shown in the case of murders by the late Dr Harold Shipman who was convicted of 15 murders in 2003 but who was suspected of carrying out over 200 murders.

Drugs offences and age

There has been considerable debate about the use of drugs. In particular the use of cannabis which is usually held to be the most widely selected drug is changing its classification from class B to class C and the maximum penalty will fall in the U.K.

It is usually assumed that drug offences are more likely to be carried out in certain age groups, for example the young rather than the old. How far drug offences vary from one year to another and possibly even from one area to another may be due to the seriousness with which different police forces regard such crimes. There was considerable comment in the London area where one major policeman seemed to suggest that some drug crimes should be virtually ignored.

Which groups most harm society?

If the logic of looking at case of crime and how much crime there is, is to try to protect society against harm by individuals then it would seem logical to try to work out what the probability of some crimes taking place is and also how harmful they are. Clearly murders are one of the most harmful of crimes but fortunately such crimes are rare. Whilst road accidents are far more of a risk to the young than murders very little research seems to have been done to reduce this. In most cases, the very people who proclaim to be in favour of law and order usually ignore the problems of road accidents.

If the logic of crime prevention is to reduce risk to the individual members of society then it would seem sensible to find out first what causes harm to members of society. The Royal Statistical Society has been pressing to try to find some measures of risk which would be understood by members of the public who are not necessarily numerically literate.

The word 'accident' is a cause of bias since for a long while accident meant something that happened by chance and clearly most road accidents do not fall into this category. The risks to children from road accidents are far greater than that of abduction and other related crimes. In spite of media hyperbole the number of children killed in the way of James Bulger (the young child killed in February 1993 by two young children about the age of 9) has varied slightly from one year to another because of the nature of the crime but has not increased or decreased significantly over the last 50 years. Perceptions of crimes are often said to be almost as important as the crimes themselves. In 2001-2002, two thirds of persons interviewed said that they believed national crime over past few years have increased a lot even though most data suggested that crime levels was falling. The media do not necessarily help since they will report any figures which seem to suggest that crimes are rising.

Why some crimes are likely to be under reported

Most people would regard violent crime as perhaps most important, but reporting of such incidents may vary according to the cause. As one might assume, women are far more likely to suffer domestic violence than men. Domestic violence against men may be under-recorded partly because there is no recourse for social workers for male victims and it may seem a plausible hypothesis that the police are unlikely to take male victims seriously enough.

One major cause of the under-recording of domestic violence is that women may be unwilling to admit that the incident has taken place. It could also be that in some cases the women believe it to be an isolated incident and thus not worth reporting. Research estimates in Social Trends suggested that 1 in 4 women would experience domestic violence at some time during her life. If this is true, it would suggest, (in line with feminist thinking) that such crime should be taken more seriously. The number of deaths from domestic violence is also quite high which seems yet another reason why the investigation of such crimes and preferably measures to prevent them should be more of a priority.

Social workers and sociologists in general may have quite a lot to say about the use of prison, probation and other attitudes towards punishment. The number of people in prison in the United Kingdom has risen rapidly to over 71 000 by mid 2002 which is an increase of over 25 000 since 1990. In early 2010 it was around 83 000 people. It is unlikely that this represents an increase of the number of crimes by this percentage and could reflect a number of different factors, such as, the tendency to give prison sentences when other measures could be used; giving slightly longer sentences or even that the police have been better at catching people in certain categories. Men much more frequently commit crimes than women and therefore there is a much higher proportion of males in prison rather than females. How far this is due to social attitudes and how far due to inherent nature of the male is very much a matter of debate.

Also, the young are much more likely to commit crimes than people of older ages. The peak age is 18 for males and 15 for females. Data shows that theft is by far the most common offence for both male and female. This again has led to much comment by sociologists about the influence at school and at home. The 'nature' versus 'nurture' debate has been one that has been widely debated by sociologists and others. Some sociologists such as Sylvia Walby seem to suggest that men are inherently violent. There is also much debate about whether people are inherently programmed to commit crimes or perhaps commit crimes as a result of their conditioning at home or at school. Clearly there are some other factors that come into play; otherwise everyone in the same social condition would do the same things.

Sociologists may also have views about types of punishment. Evidence suggests that the young are more likely to commit crimes as well as with less educated as opposed to the old and the more educated respectively. Some people have suggested therefore that better education and in particular better education in pre-school ages might well help to reduce the volume of crime. This again can be a matter of quantitative research. There has been some quantitative research into the effect of supervision orders and action plans and that research in 2000 found that there was a reduction in reconviction rates across all offence categories between 1997 and 2000.

Attitudes toward asylum seekers

The debate about where asylum seekers should go and whether they should be allowed into the country in the first place was a problem from 2003. The media were very hostile to asylum seekers. It is not clear whether the readers of the newspapers really understood much about the asylum seekers. In many cases it would seem that hostility towards accommodation for asylum seekers would be linked with racism although the organisers of such protest would often seem to suggest they were not. The extreme right wing parties such as the British National Party would often seek to suggest linkage between asylum seekers and crime.

There are also suggestions that they should be vetted for terrorism, although it is not clear why asylum seekers should be more or less likely to harbour people with terrorist potential than, say, tourists. There is little hard evidence about where people came from. Other people would suggest that asylum seekers are mainly economic migrants and that they come to the U.K. in search of a better life rather than to escape from persecution. Again, without firm evidence we cannot be sure what the facts are. The U.K. Home Office itself may try to get more evidence by testing people's abilities in certain languages if they claim to come from certain countries. However, what countries are unsafe or safe may well depend upon the Home Office's perception of risk in other countries, and it is not quite clear how these too could be factual. It is unlikely that the Home Office has access to all the information about the way some minorities groups, particularly gypsies (sometimes called *roma);* will be treated by the authorities. Few countries are likely to admit the persecutions of minorities, although in the past there have been some exceptions as with the Nazis in Germany.

In many cases, figures of risk are not very certain even where one might reasonably expect them to be so. In Iraq in 2009, following the war, there were no figures of the numbers of total casualties of Iraqi people caught up in clashes, although there were figures for the coalition forces whether from Britain or the U.S.A.

Ethnic groups

The number of people in the United Kingdom who describe themselves as belonging to a minority or ethnic group was about 4 and a half million in 2001-2002, about 8% of the United Kingdom with the proportions varying rapidly between different areas. Leicester and the East Midlands have one of the highest proportions. Minority ethnic groups are generally younger than the white population. 19% of the white population were under 16 whereas for those of mixed origin 55% were under 16. This is important when looking at crime statistics because if the young are the ones who predominantly commit crimes, then even if there are no differences between ethnic groups we would expect to find a higher proportion of mixed groups committing crimes than the white population merely because of the age distribution.

There are differences in size of families between different ethnic groups. Sometimes this is because of differences in religious opinion about family planning; for example in the Kosovan tradition, it would be usual for women to be married as not to be married and have a family would be a disgrace.

The word *immigrant* is frequently used in a hostile fashion it should be noted that there has been differences between the ethnic groups which themselves have followed different trends. For example the new Commonwealth countries such as India, Jamaica and Nigeria following the British nationality act then refugees of the Asian descent following the 60s and 70s from such countries like Kenya, Malawi and Uganda. Contrary to most people's opinions, there was a net loss of people from the United Kingdom during the 1970s whereas by the year 2000 suggestions were that in 2001, there was a net increase in migration of 126 000. Again the total number of asylum seekers remained relatively steady since 1999, although in August 2003 there was a suggestion that there was a fall in applications. It might also be noted that the United Kingdom ranked joint 7th with Luxembourg when looking at relative sizes of country's population and the number of asylum seekers locations.

Education and Income Differences

During 2009, in the U.K., there was considerable debate on education. There has also been debate about provision of education. In March 2004 the then Prime Minister suggested that in future he would like all people under 18 either to be at school or to have some type of training.

Urbanisation

One of the problems in sociological research is getting hold of data, relevant for a given purpose. If we are looking at the problems of urbanisation, we need to define what we mean by 'urban' and 'rural'. Does urban mean whole towns over a certain size? Is it determined by the levels of income of the inhabitants? Is it defined by the rates of crime and unemployment of a given geographical area?

Definitions of the term 'urban' vary somewhat amongst different nations. European countries define urbanized areas on the basis of urban-type land use, not allowing any gaps of typically more than 200 metres, and use satellite photos instead of census blocks to determine the boundaries of the urban area. In less developed countries, in addition to land use and density requirements, a requirement that a large majority of the population, typically 75%, is not engaged in agriculture and/or fishing is sometimes used. An urban area is an area with an increased density of human-created structures in comparison to the areas surrounding it. An urban area is more frequently called a city or town.

Urban areas are created and further developed by the process of urbanization. Measuring the extent of an urbanized area helps in analyzing population density and urban sprawl, and in determining urban and rural populations.

Rural areas (also referred to as "the country", countryside) are sparsely settled places away from the influence of large cities. Such areas are distinct from more intensively settled urban and suburban areas, and also from unsettled lands such as outback, American Old West or wilderness. Inhabitants live in villages, hamlets, on farms and in other isolated houses. In modern usage, rural areas can have an agricultural character, though many rural areas are characterized by an economy based on logging, mining, petroleum and natural gas exploration, or tourism.

If we look at the categories, we can see those who most people would regard as rural are the people who live and work on farms or in forestry commission work. In the South East of England, we have people who live in what might be regarded as the rural area but whose main lifestyle may be urban. Many of the people living in the so called villages in the South East might well work in central London or in the Docklands, watch sport such as cricket or football in the London area, do their clothes shopping in London and probably do all food shopping in one of the out of town or even major town shopping centres.

In the South West of England, which has a very high proportion of elderly people, these people may have their roots in urban culture and may well find it difficult to adjust to rural culture. In some cases they may have seen the rural areas particularly in the seaside mainly in the middle of summer and find it difficult to adjust to living in the rural area especially if they get too old to use their cars.

We sometimes have people who work and will have a flat in a major city during the week but will return to their main homes at the weekend situated in the countryside. In the U.K. the reverse process applies, particularly affecting Wales where people have their main homes in the West Midlands but have a second home in Wales. This annoys the local Welsh people who sometimes find themselves priced out of reasonable priced accommodation as the demand for housing gets greater. In other cases we have people who would regard themselves as almost completely urban, that is, they both work and live in an urban area and use it for the their leisure activities too.

In developed countries, the assumption that there were major differences between urban and rural living seem somewhat unlikely, since in many cases there is a spectrum rather than a clearly defined differences.

In Africa, internal migration - especially rural to urban - takes place in large part in response to existing imbalances and inequalities in development, employment opportunities, income and living conditions between the regions of a country, the dominant direction of such movement being dictated by the location of employment-generating projects. Thus, where public and private investment is concentrated in the major city, as is the case in most African countries, the dominant migration stream will be directed towards the capital. The decision regarding where and when to move is also affected by the experiences of, and information received from, members of the family who have already moved to urban areas. Migrants in Africa take advantage of the network of relatives and friends in the towns to ease the migration and relocation process. The welfare system of the extended family supports newly-arrived migrants and shelters them from the strains and stresses of the urban environment. Indeed, migration in Africa is usually a household rather than an independent, individual decision. In most of Africa, the structure of employment is such that in plantation agriculture, industry, commerce and transportation, the demand is mostly for men. Consequently, men trend to migrate alone, leaving their wives and families behind, at least initially.

Growth of the urban areas

Urban areas are nothing new. We can find examples such as Egypt which had a very sophisticated society during the rule of the Pharaohs. As evidence of this, the pyramids would have required a great deal of engineering knowledge as well as organisational ability to build them. The Greeks in Athens had very clear cut divisions of labour with the slaves doing most of their work, leaving the Athenians free to participate in direct democracy for the free men.

Thus, throughout history, the world has experienced urbanization but the huge rise in the number of people making their homes in towns and cities is a recent phenomenon. The United Nations estimates that about 180,000 people are being added to the urban population every day. North America and Europe's urban areas already account for about 70-80% of the regions' populations, and these are expected to stabilize at these levels.

Developing nations are shouldering the vast majority of this burden, leaving them struggling to cope with the huge influx of people into urban areas. Some cities' populations are 40 times larger than they were in 1950.

Sociologist's explanations of urbanisation

Sociologists have often classified movement towards the urban areas as being either push or pull. By push they mean that the conditions in the rural areas were unattractive, pushing the inhabitants to shift to the urban areas, whilst pull meant that the conditions in the urban areas offered more attractions. In the 18th Century, in the U.K. there was wide scale movement from the rural to the urban areas. There were 2 reasons for this. The agricultural revolution meant that greater productivity in agriculture could be obtained but this did not necessarily mean more people working in the rural areas because greater efficiency could be obtained through the use of machinery. The profits obtained by the big landowners could often be ploughed back into other activities, for example coal mining, and building of factories, which meant there was a greater demand for urban workers. The growth of the factory system as opposed to the people carrying out such activities as weaving at home meant that people needed to be within easy reach of their place of work. Usually we assume that there is an upper limit on the amount of time people would take to get to and from work. Some people have suggested maybe about an hour though in practise in the London area people would take much longer than this to get to and from work. For the poorer people in the 18th Century the distance was likely to be imposed by how far these people could reasonably walk at the end of a shift from the coalmine or factory.

It was also governed by the availability of housing. With long hours there was likely to be a relatively small stock of suitable accommodation. In a few cases such as Saltaire in the Bradford area, there was an enlightened employer, Titus Salt (1803 -1876), who built satisfactory housing within close proximity to the factory. Mostly, accommodation was extremely poor. In some cases, the males in particular would have lived in close proximity to their work but might have returned at frequent intervals to their original homes as often as they could manage.

Even for non-manual work, transport limited how far people would wish to be away from each other. In the London area there were a series of different centres for different occupations. Fenchurch Street, which is near the Tower of London, was a natural magnet for the shipping industry, due to its proximity to the River Thames.

It was also a natural magnet for other related industries such as shipping insurance so that there were clusters of shipping firms plus marine insurance companies within a very short walking distance so that people could easily be in contact with each other. Similar considerations were applied in other areas; most of the banks were within range of the Bank of England or Moorgate.

As transport improved, the size of urban areas became greater. This is partly because people could travel longer distances to and from work and also because of the agricultural revolution where more food could be imported into London from areas such as Gloucester without undue transport cost.

Many people in the U.K. have a romantic view of the rural areas, derived from paintings in the 18th Century by people such as Constable, or some of the TV dramas by Jane Austen - a well known novelist; or due to the present day nostalgic television programmes such as Heartbeat and the James Herriot stories about the life of a vet. In practice, though, in the 18th century, life in the rural areas was very harsh and people preferred to work in factories rather than being in domestic service or trying to be self sufficient with small quantities of land.

In the 21st Century the computer means that people are much more footloose, that is, firms or individuals are not tied to one particular location. In August 2003, it was suggested that about 2 million people worked at home and this increasing number was partly due to the use of the computer.

It remains to be seen whether it might be yet another 'industrial revolution' whereby people may work 2 or 3 days a week in a central office because this gives companionship and face to face contact, then work from home on other days of the week.

SELF-EXAMINATION QUESTIONS

1. What does a subsistence or traditional economy mean? Are any sociological problems likely to arise from such a system compared with a western style economy?

2. How far is it true that experimentation is not possible in sociology unlike in the physical sciences?

3. What is meant by the term 'merit goods'? Can sociologists provide assistance on how these should be provided? Does sociology provide any help on the effectiveness or otherwise on what is happening at the present time?

4. In what ways do modern governments influence the distribution of income? Can sociologists provide assistance on what would be the most effective ways of helping the poor? Would your answer be different about how this could be achieved in a developing country or a modern economy?

5. What are the comparative merits of deductive and inductive methods of reasoning in sociology?

6. What does the statement 'sociology is a social science' mean? In what ways, if any, do the methods in social sciences differ from those in physical sciences?

7. How far will modern computer methods ensure that it is possible to obtain more predictions following from sociological theory?

8. What is meant by the term 'sociological laws'? How far is such a phrase useful?

9. Some sociologists have assumed that people are rational, meaning that consumers will maximise their satisfaction from the resources - including money and time - which are available to them. How far is this assumption reasonable in a modern developed country? Explain with reference to the large volume of persuasive advertising in such an economy.

10. Explain what is meant by 'positive sociology ' and 'normative sociology. Is it possible in practice to have a system of sociology, which is purely positive? Why is the distinction between the two important?

11. Does the fact that most Eastern European countries have moved away from planned economies mean that there are no sociological problems remaining. Would a Marxist analysis be the same as a Weberian or feminist one on this?

Additional Questions

1. How far it is true that sociology is a science, and how far is it an art? (Hint: How far can sociologists use experimentation compared to the physical scientists? How do we know what ideas to test in the first place?

2. Does the fact that there are so many viewpoints in sociology, mean that sociology cannot really help us to understand society? How far do the different viewpoints reflect the differences of the times at which the views were formulated? How far do they reflect the different interests of the researches?

3. Why is it difficult to measure the number of crimes accurately? Why might this make it difficult for us to view social problems accurately? Why would this matter when we are looking at problems of domestic violence?

4. What is meant by a concept? Why might sociologists be interested in the concept of risk? Why might it influence the research methods and also the selection of topics being studied? Why might perceptions of risk be important as well as accurate views of risk? (Hint: Why might the perception of crime be important to many people?)

5. How far can sociologists help us to determine the causes of crime and also the likely remedies of some crimes? In what ways, if at all, can different statistical methods help them? What are the problems of trying to find the number of crimes in the first place?

6. Why might sociologists be interested in the idea of correlation and causality? Why is it often difficult to find out causes of problems? Are there likely to be many different causes of poor or good education? What happens if we have several different variables and want to measure their importance?

7. What do sociologists mean by 'racism'? How far can the classifications of ethnic groups in terms of incomes, class, and employment opportunities help us to find indications of problems? How far does it help to find solutions to problems? What are the limits of using data? (Hint: How far will we have accurate data in terms of educational performance?)

8. Why might lack of objective information help to distort what is happening with ethnic groups? Where do most people get their perceptions about different ethnic groups from? How can we test the theory that mixing more with different racial

groups helps to reduce racism? (Hint: how can we show how much the different ethnic groups mix? Would it be different between different age groups?)

9. How can we measure inequality? What are the problems in trying to measure differences in opportunities for different ethnic groups, genders and classes? Does the fact that women are obtaining more jobs prove that inequality between sexes has decreased? What are the problems in trying to measure incomes?

10. What is meant by the term 'social exclusion'? How far is it possible to measure it? Can sociologists suggest remedies to it? How can we tell how far people are excluded from educational opportunities, different types of housing and different types of jobs? Why is unemployment likely to be different between different groups?

11. How far does the national minimum wage in the U.K. help to reduce poverty? Why is it suggested that it has not always been well targeted? Would other measures such as a negative income tax or working families' tax credit be more helpful?

12. How far is poverty linked to ethnic groups, gender and socio economic class? Are these the only likely sources of poverty? (Hint: Which age groups are most likely to suffer from poverty?

13. How far can quantitative methods help to ensure that sociology can move from perception to reality? What are the limitations of data when looking at fears of crime?

14. What problems might we find in trying to say what peoples' objectives are? Why did Marx think that economic ideas were most important? Does the experience of the 21st century help us to agree or disagree on his conclusions?

15. Why might the study of specialisation of labour be of importance to sociologists? Which of the major sociologists investigated this? Were they realistic about the likelihood of unemployment or extreme boredom? What are the advantages and disadvantages of such a system? (Hint: what are the advantages of higher productivity to consumers? Why might there be role conflicts between people in their consumer role and worker role?)

16. If people move from working class areas to middle class areas even while carrying out the same jobs, would we expect their pattern of social behaviour to be the same? Illustrate your answer with reference to any sociological studies. Why might sociologists be interested in this concept? Would evidence from the 1950's still be relevant today?

17. Why might the development of areas such as Becontree in the U.K. in the 1930's, which was criticised for just being rows of houses be relevant when discussing newer developments such as the Thames Gateway in the early 2000's? Why might there be more resistance to new housing today than in the 1950's. What pressure groups might be involved in trying to persuade the government about the merits of new housing?

18. Some people have suggested that we do not need more new houses in green field areas. What is meant by this and how far, if at all, can sociologists help to predict what would happen if we build on such sites, rather than on brown field sites? What conflicts can arise with building more new houses?

19. High rise flats have been criticised as being unsuitable for families, but in the early 2000's Ken Livingstone then Mayor of London suggested that we need more high-rise buildings. Would sociologists be able to help us understand the arguments for and against such buildings? Does experience from other countries help us to decide on the merits or are there such great differences in culture that other country's problems are not relevant to the U.K.?

20. How far does the movement towards urbanisation mean that we have a move towards an impersonal society? Would the answer given by Marxists and Communitarians be the same? In what ways is the countryside more likely to be a place where people know each other? How far does different styles of housing help or hinder moves towards impersonality?

21. Why might the growing proportion of the elderly population in the U.K. have different social implications compared to other countries such as those in Asia and Africa where the majority of the population is young?

22. Some people have suggested that in order to have the same standard of living, say, with nursing and carers as well as have the same volume of goods per head, that we would either need to work longer, for instance having higher retirement ages, persuade more women to become employed or to have wide scale immigration. What advice if any, could sociologists give on the kind of tensions that might arise with each of these measures?

23. In the early 2000's it had been suggested that only about 50% of the population in the U.K. have permanent 9-5 jobs. If this were true what would be the effects on relationships at work and also relationships within the community? Where do people meet each other at the present time? What would be the effect as well on

young people being able to get loans or mortgages? What would be the effect in the long term on the demand for housing?

24. What is meant by deterministic? Some people have suggested that both Marxist and some puritan Christians are both authoritarian and believe in determinism. How far is this true? If it is true what are the wider implications?

25. Sociologists sometimes use the words 'nurture' and 'nature'? What do these two terms mean and why are they important? How can we alter nurture? Would it be better- as some people thought in the early 20th century -to encourage some people to have more children and some people to have less?

26. How far is it true that religion has played a part in changes in society? Is it true that religion always plays a conservative role? (Hint: Think of what has happened in South Africa and also in Iraq?)

27. What would be the effects if lending of money at high rates of interest were forbidden? (Hint: Think which organisations charge very high rates of interest at the present time; how far are people aware of the true rates of interest being charged?

28. What have been the effects of society on the credit boom on both the poor and the rich? Why might the government be interested in promoting credit unions?

29. How far is it true that due to lack of perfect information, it is very difficult to show whether people are rational or irrational? Which sociologists thought that people would become more rational over time? Have their predictions come true? How could we test this?

30. How far is it true, as Marx thought, that power is mainly concentrated in the same few hands and this is largely due to economic opportunities? How can we test this? How concentrated is economic, legal and political power at the present time?

31. How true is it that there is one general theory explaining why women generally have lower incomes and less power than men? Would all sociologists agree on this?

32. What are the problems of trying to test how income is distributed within the household?

33. What is meant by the term 'merit goods'? How far can sociologists help to predict the demands for education and health? How far will income and class affect

demand for education? How far will age and class affect demand for health? How far can they also help to show what would be the effects of more expenditure in these fields?

34. It is sometimes suggested that the National Health Service in the U.K. is a national sickness service. What does this mean and how far, if at all, can sociologists help us to understand why different ethnic groups, sexes and classes have different patterns of health?

35. How far can people be held responsible for their own health? What would happen if as in the U.S.A, the U.K. had more private insurance rather than government expenditure?

36. 'Higher Education is only provided to people who can show that they don't need it.' What is meant by this and how far is it true? Would it be better to spend more money on nursery education or for people who have not done so well at school? Would sociologists help to give an answer on this? How can we tell by how much people have higher incomes as a result of the university education? What is meant by saying that we want to understand what happens with a measure and without a measure rather than before and after?

37. Why have sociologists sometimes carried out unstructured interviews, particularly where they have been dealing with cults?

38. What is meant by covert methods? Why might sociologists use this in their studies? How far is this influenced by ethics, dangers to the person carrying out the surveys or to the people who are being surveyed?

39. It is sometimes said that observation itself alters people's behaviour, how is this true and what are the implications for sociological research?

40. What is meant by the term positive sociology? Are there any limits at all on positivism? What is meant by saying that there are some matters which cannot easily be put in terms of numbers and that these might be more important than matters which can be put into number terms?

41. What is meant by the term 'value judgement'? How far is it true that we can have a value free social science? (Hint: does it mean that we cannot, for example, say that the holocaust was merely a matter of opinion on whether it was good or bad)?

42. What do the terms 'deductive reasoning' and 'inductive reasoning' mean? Which one is a sociologist more likely to use? What are the disadvantages and advantages of using inductive reasoning? How do we know whether we have a suitable sample of people and how do we know whether we have a sufficient sample?

43. What is meant by the term 'qualitative research'? How far does it overlap with the idea of ranking? Why do sociologists use it and what, if any, are its limitations? Why might we want to use it, say, in looking at quality of life?

44. What is meant by the term 'quantitative research'? Why do sociologists use it and what, if any, are its limitations?

45. Sociologists sometimes suggest that rather than having urban and rural areas in sharp contradiction there is in fact an overlap of urban and rural style of living. What is meant by this and what implications, if at all, does it have on studying sociology?

46. How far are people living in villages in the South East of England or near the Metropolitan areas reliant on rural activities for either their living or for their leisure or shopping? How far, therefore, are they rural rather than urban dwellers?

Chapter Two

Sociology and the Scientific Method

We said in the opening paragraph that sociology is one of the social sciences. What is meant, in this context, by the term "science"?

Positive sociology is claimed to be a "scientific" approach. If we make the assertion that crime is related to deprivation, we are making a statement, which can either be proved or refuted by evidence. Positive sociology itself deals only with what might be called "positive" questions, that is, those that do not rely on value judgements. Some of the early sociologists including Marx would have had very strong views on how society should develop, and so whilst they might have used positive sociology they would also have dealt with normative sociology.

Normative sociology deals with value judgements. The statement, "The government should restrict social security payments even if it leads to higher deprivation" is an example of a value judgement because it is made on the basis of individual beliefs and cannot be scientifically tested.

Positive sociology evaluates by looking at whether the hypotheses successfully predict the results. This has been useful in evaluating empirical evidence, but may have led sociologists to concentrate too much on the areas of sociology that are easily quantifiable. Similarly, "The state should prosecute parents for not sending their children to school even if it means sending them to jail," would be a normative statement. However prosecuting parents for not sending their children to school is an effective deterrent would in principle be a positive statement.

In some cases, even a great deal of the 'evidence' itself may have been subject to bias. Part of the problem is that we mostly rely on secondary data and it is very difficult to determine what bias there may be in the evidence. Also, there may be far too many variables to include them all in the data used as 'evidence'. If we try to compare men's and women's health, for instance, some facts are easy to quantify with a few exceptions -such as people being on a life support machines –we are able to tell whether a person is dead or live. However if we ask someone whether they are well, the answer is very much subject to personal judgement. Even diagnoses of illnesses are subject to fashions, changes in our knowledge and different doctors taking different points of view as it is in mental disorders. One of the points which many of the feminists make is that a lot of sociology has been male-stream sociology in that it has looked at factors from a male viewpoint, rather than looking at such factors as the extent to which women have been subject to male dominance. It has also largely ignored women's work although there have been many studies on work done by men.

Quantitative Research

Sociologists have become increasingly involved in quantitative research, for example, to investigate the relationship between income and crime. Quantitative research has much to be commended, but it should be noted that this research is quite dependent on the quality of data. In particular this is true of areas such as crime. Social workers have often studied sociology due to their interest in social exclusion as a problem. Where a number of different factors come into play at the same time, quantitative research is still possible but the mathematics behind it make it very difficult to be able to interpret data with any degree of accuracy. Statisticians often use a measure of a correlation where +1 or -1 indicates perfect correlation but 0 indicates that there is no correlation. In order to carry out quantitative research, sociologists would need to have an idea of correlation and also how far adequate data has been used. One of the criticisms of sociology has been that in many cases, surveys, which have been carried out in the past often with fairly small number of participants, have been used to try to suggest that this is still a valid argument about modern society. A large survey is not necessarily consistent with accuracy, for example, back in 1936, a very large scale opinion poll of 10 million people by the Digest about the U.S.A Presidential Election gave an inaccurate result mainly because the people being asked questions were telephone owners and at that stage only the rich tended to have telephones.

Information Gathering

If sociologists and others want to obtain information, they may well decide to conduct in depth *interviews*. These are time consuming but may well help to refine hypotheses and to give further information on which to base further hypothesis. One of the best known of in depth interviews in recent years was Professor Barker in her study of the so-called 'Moonies'. The advantage of an in depth interview is that one can really get to know why people do various things, for example Professor Barker in her study of the so called Cults including the 'Moonies' trying to test the assumption frequently made that members of such cults have been brainwashed into accepting certain features of these cults and that they are really not there on their own free choice. In depth interviews will usually mean that people will have to adopt a sympathetic approach in order to get what the interviewees might regard as embarrassing information.

In other cases, sociologists may have to adopt *covert* methods, such as pretending to be a member of a group. This could take place for a number of reasons; the first is that it might be dangerous to appear as an outsider, for example if a researcher wanted to interview members of a teenage gang who are known to be violent to outsiders. The second is that in some cases it may be illegal to belong to a particular organisation such as rebel groups in South Africa during apartheid; freedom fighting groups as it was in most African countries during the colonial era; outlawed sects such as the Mungiki in Kenya; outlawed groups in the former Soviet Union, amongst others.

Thirdly and perhaps of wider validity, is that the very act of observation might -if known- alter the behaviour of the people being observed. Most of us have seen this, say, when people are aware of the presence of a TV crew, they react in an usual manner, either they may be on their best behaviour to try to convince observers they really are good people; or they may behave wildly as they know they are the object of attention. For instance, it is claimed that where there are demonstrations against the police or the state, TV coverage makes matters worse as the demonstrators' wild side is stimulated and they start on destructive activities such as throwing stones. At a more minor level, at times of school inspections both the students and teachers will behave in an unusual manner.

In many other cases, people are quite overt, that is, they are open about their intentions. This may mean that when doing an in depth interview people are much more likely to respond if they are clear on what the interview's purposes are. However, confidentiality is a key issue because people may not necessarily wish to have their views openly known. This could apply, say when interviewing people in their current jobs particularly if they fear they may become redundant or sacked if their views were known. In August 2003 the BBC reported that some doctors were working more than the suggested hours from the Department of Health and that they in turn had been bribed or threatened if they reported this. In this case, the allegation was that the senior health officials would ensure that they either did not get the job for they reported excessive hours or, alternatively, that funding would be cut if the Department of Health found that hospitals or health trusts were not conforming to the current regulations.

Value judgements

Within sociology, a number of value judgements, even if only weak ones, are often found under the guise of positive sociology. The assumption that more goods and services are more desirable than fewer goods and services may be thought to be a positive statement, but it cannot be proved on any positive basis and relies on a value judgement only.

Most people however, would accept this as an indication of what is good apart from demerit goods such as alcohol, cigarettes and drugs. They would probably be willing to see the poor have more goods and services. Whether they are willing to pay for this through the tax or benefit systems or by giving to charity is of course, more open to doubt.

Sociological reasoning

(i) Sociologists sometimes use *deductive reasoning that* is going from the general to the particular. We might test whether higher levels of unemployment lead to greater types of certain crimes. In this case if we believed the assumption when looking at a sample example e.g. problems in a particular city or town then we would see if the underlying cause of a crime wave was the rise of unemployment, say, due to a closure of a large employer in the locality.

(ii) Sociologists more often use *inductive reasoning* that is going from the particular to the general. For example, we might observe a few people changing their life styles having gone from working class to middle class. We might conclude that their behaviour is typical of the population as a whole. From these observations we might formulate a general theory of life styles. This is true of Wilmott and Young's studies which have not only looked at Woodford and the East End of London but also at the household in general. Questions have been asked about how far their surveys have been adequate. For example, as we see elsewhere, Ann Oakley has suggested that the idea that men share more in housework was not adequately tested with their questionnaires.

(iii) To some extent, *introspective reasoning* - asking what one would do in particular circumstances - may be regarded as part of the inductive method. Applied sociology may frequently use this, for instance when dealing with the likely effects of introduction of a new social policy.

Sometimes no data is likely to be available. I had to use a new method to obtain data when considering the behaviour of the single homeless and how it might be related to ethnic groups, to length of time homeless. It may also be related to type of family background e.g. whether divorced etc, to length of time unemployed etc.

Empirical data

In the case of a particular survey the author had to try to look at questions in the first place. A number of hypotheses needed to be tested, including the 2 distinct groups of single homeless – those who had had an immediate problem perhaps due to having had a quarrel which meant that they had to sleep rough overnight but that apart from the State providing shelter overnight there were no long term problems. The second hypothesis was that there are other people with long term problems where shelter was necessary but shelter did not get rid of the problem, it merely alleviated it.

In order to test these hypotheses therefore there were a series of questions asking about the length of time that people had remained homeless. This tended to show very much a bi-polar distribution; a large number of people being homeless for a very short time and at the other end of the scale a very large number of people having been homeless for 5 years or more. There were also questions on where people had come from. As the survey was done in the early 1970s, the majority of the people had came from within the British Isles though a disproportionate number of people had come from the so called Celtic parts, that is, Northern Ireland, Scotland and Wales. This in turn would be either viewed as a racist stereotype, that people from those areas drink too much and therefore have problems or would be consistent with another concept, that in times of high unemployment people who came further would be more likely to face problems of obtaining suitable accommodation. This would obviously require further research in order to validate or invalidate the underlying hypothesis.

There was the hypothesis that excessive alcohol drinking leads to problems, which in turn may lead to homelessness, at the time drugs whilst leading to problems for the single homeless were regarded as less of a problem. Questions on alcohol intake were therefore asked not only to the respondents but also to people who look after those who drink. Care obviously needs to be taken when asking such questions. In this case the reception centre managers were also asked questions as were the respondents. (Questions on alcohol intake may well not be reliable in any case, actuarial departments in Life Insurance Companies used to ask whether people were sober and of temperate habits, and nearly everyone claimed that they were. This does not prove that they were all temperate!)

The assumption was tested whether homeless people came from a particular socio-economic class. This might sound very easy but again problems of bias within data occur. Not everyone knows the occupation of their mother or father and if asked for parents' occupations, the word 'engineer' might either mean a trained engineer or might simply be an unskilled mechanic. Therefore conclusions from this particular survey were not necessarily as reliable as would have been desired.

The further hypothesis was whether people who had been institutionalised were more liable to take alcohol. There is no direct relationship between the two, but in both cases meals and accommodation are provided. One hypothesis that needed to be tested was whether people in such circumstances would be more likely to find difficulties once they came out from the institution since they were not used to making all decisions on budgetary allocations on food, accommodation, among other wants. It is fairly obvious, as the New Right would suggest that some people have become dependent upon others. However, whilst they suggest that this is mainly due to state intervention there are many other forms of dependency. Within the family old people may be conditioned into believing that they are incapable of doing much and will therefore do very little. In other cases it can be seen that men in particular who wish to be lazy can use emotional blackmail on some members of their family to demand more, while they do very little for themselves even when they are quite capable of doing more.

The further hypothesis that needed to be tested was whether homeless people would have lost touch with all relatives. The survey was complicated by the fact that whilst it is possible to interview homeless people in terms of what were then called reception centres (Salvation Army, hostels, etc); it is much more difficult to obtain information from people sleeping rough. In some cases, there are well known places where people sleep rough, in other cases towns or cities may not be interested in the homeless and in some cases may view them as an embarrassment. In this case the information about the total number of homeless people is likely to be an underestimate and not even a consistent underestimate. The local authorities who take responsibilities seriously are more likely to admit to the presence of the homeless people more than others. In spite of the limitations in terms of both the data and questionnaires, one feature, which is obvious, is that the number of homeless men far outnumbers that of homeless women. This is inherently because women realise much more strongly the need for shelter and will remain in the family home to ensure this. On the other hand institutions and society generally may feel guiltier about female homelessness and their vulnerability than about male homelessness. Sociologists may be faced with further hypotheses not merely on what the causes are, but also on what the remedies are.

Social identity

This means the identity which people feel they have because of the way that society or the parts of society in which people live, conditions them to take on certain roles or attitudes. If it is assumed in society that women are passive then it will be difficult for many women not to play this role. Similarly men will be conditioned to take on a macho role. This is sometimes regarded as a self-fulfilling prophecy.

Qualitative Research

In many cases there is no way of using numbers. In such a case the research is usually called qualitative. We cannot say, that we like one person twice as much as someone else. It may make sense to rank people in terms of their influence over us but to say that Mr. X has twice as much influence as Mr. Y makes very little sense. In other cases, we may say we prefer one thing over another but there is no real way of saying that we prefer something twice as much as something else. If we want to know whether conditions would be improved by certain measures, then we probably need to carry out some sort of qualitative research. If we are concerned about deprivation, we would need to find out what people regard as deprivation and what they would like to improve their own lifestyles. There is little point in assuming that they would all prefer different colours painted on their walls as the main aspect of improving their life if they are not at all perturbed by that but are much more concerned about graffiti. One of the criticisms in the past of council housing –in most countries -was that all of them were identical and that in many cases, people would have regarded it as important to have their own choice of certain things like the colour of their doors and so on. Only through quality of research can we see what aspects are important to other people. An authoritarian approach that assumes that certain people know what is best for other people is not likely to produce very good results. This, it might be said, would have been in contrast to early sociologists such as Marx who thought that they would know what is best for individuals and society as a whole.

Qualitative research would help to indicate what influences a person in his/her regard of what is important in his/her lives. For example only individuals know how much they are likely to be influenced by television programmes, schools and parents.

SELF-EXAMINATION QUESTIONS

1. Which of the following statements depends on a value judgement?

   a. The government has placed too much stress on wealth creation at the expense of other objectives.
   b. The virtual abolition of council housing has increased the problems of the poor.
   c. Better education cannot entirely eradicate problems of poverty.
   d. There is a link between educational attainment and income

2. How far can quantitative methods of research help to ensure that sociology can move from perception to reality?

3. Why is it difficult to measure the number of crimes accurately? Why might this make it difficult for us to view social problems accurately? Why would this matter when we are looking for example at problems of domestic violence?

4. Why might sociologists be interested in the concept of risk? Why might it influence the research methods and also the selection of topics they are studying? Why might perceptions of risk be important as well as accurate views of risk?

5. How far can sociologists help us to determine the causes of crime and also the likely remedies of some crimes? In what ways, if at all, can different statistical methods help them?

6. Why might sociologists be interested in the idea of correlation and causality? Why is it often difficult to find out causes of problems?

7. How far is it true that there is one general theory explaining why women generally have lower incomes and less power than men? Would all sociologists agree on this?

8. What is meant by the term 'merit goods'? How far can sociologists help to predict the demands for education and health and how far can they also help to show what would be the effects of more expenditure in these fields?

9. It is sometimes suggested that the National Health Service is a national sickness service whereas it should concentrate on health? What does this mean and how far if at all can sociologists help us to understand why different ethnic groups, sexes and classes have different patterns of health?

10. Can sociologists help in showing the effects of spending more money on higher education rather than on education for deprived groups or possibly giving better family care to poorer families including better accommodation?

11. Why have sociologists sometimes carried out unstructured interviews, particularly where they are dealing with cults?

12. What is meant by covert methods? Why might sociologists use them in their studies?

13. It is sometimes said that observation itself alters people's behaviour, how might this be true and what are the implications for sociological research?

14. What is meant by the term positive sociology? Are there any limits at all on positivism?

15. What is meant by the term value judgement? How far is it true that we can have a value free social science? (Hint: does it mean that we cannot, for example, say that the holocaust was merely a matter of opinion as to whether it was good or bad?)

16. What do the terms deductive reasoning and inductive reasoning mean? Which are sociologists more likely to use and what are the disadvantages and advantages of using inductive reasoning?

17. What is meant by the term qualitative research? How far does it overlap with the idea of ranking? Why do sociologists use it and what if any are its limitations?

18. Sociologists sometimes suggest that rather than having urban and rural areas in sharp contradiction there is in fact an overlap of urban and rural style of living. What is meant by this and what implications if at all does it have on studying sociology?

Chapter Three

Social inequality

Social inequality could be shown by different life expectancies of different groups, whether of class or gender. This is easy to see across gender and data from all over the globe has shown that typically women live longer than men do. In the United Kingdom, according to Social Trends, women have a life expectancy of about five years more. We can also see that life expectancy is different between the different socio-economic classes. There is as one might expect higher life expectancy amongst the richer socio-economic groups rather than amongst the poorer. However, sociologists are not consistent in trying to explain why this should be. In 1997 to 1999, life expectancy in the U.K. for men was 75.0 whereas for women it was 79.7. It is not obvious why presently women should live longer than men do. These statistics contrast with those in 1901 where men could expect to live for around 45 years, while women lived to be around 49.

There are still differences between classes. For professional women, life expectancy was 82.8 years in 1997 –1999, whereas for professional men it was 78.5. The life expectancy for unskilled manual workers was 77.1 for women and 71.1 for men in the same period. There are still more pronounced differences for infant mortality. The mortality rate for babies born inside marriage, whose parents were unskilled manual workers, was 7.2 per 1000 live births, compared with only 3.6 for fathers in the professional class.

Some aspects, for example, easy and affordability of access to better medical care for the richer people would be very easy to demonstrate. It is also easy to show differences in diet, with some sociologists insisting that the poorer classes of society cannot afford good food and are thus in bad health. However, data on the eating habits of the different classes does not necessarily indicate that this is always true.

Smoking and health

Smoking, which is perhaps the main avoidable cause of death, is very much more prevalent amongst the lower socio-economic classes for men but not for women. 29% of all men smoked in 2000 compared with 25% of women in the over 16 age bracket. Whereas the percentage for men has fallen very dramatically it has not fallen so much amongst women. However, there are differences within the different classes, with 39% and 35% of the male and female unskilled manual workers, respectively, smoking, compared to 17% and 14% male and female workers, respectively, in the professional classes.

Alcohol and health

In contrast, alcohol which also contributes to a significant number of deaths is far less class biased and far more gender biased. The average alcohol consumption in 2000 in the U.K. was 17.4 units for men and 7.1 units for women. Men from the professional classes however drank slightly more, that is, 17.9 units compared with 17.1 for unskilled males. Women in the professional class on average consumed 8.6 units compared with 4.3 units consumed by women in the unskilled workforce.

One would need to examine why these differences occur. Is it because of alienation from the work environment, as some Marxists would suggest? Or are there other aspects? If drinking is regarded as being caused mainly by alienation, it clearly does not explain why professional women drink more than unskilled women. A reasonable hypothesis would be that in general we would expect professional people to be less alienated from work than working class people since professional people have more choice of jobs in the first place.

Pollution and health

Pollution might also help to explain differences in both life expectancy and general health. There is evidence that traffic pollution affects poorer people generally more than the richer ones. This is explained by the fact that the location of houses of the poor is usually near to main roads and factories, as opposed to the location of the houses of the rich which are in the affluent areas and the suburbs.

Income and health

There are also differences in health patterns amongst ethnic groups. This might again, be partially explained by diet and living conditions. In some cases it could be due to different life styles. Many sociologists, including Karl Marx, have looked at the differences in income. Generally, men have earned and still earn more than women have, despite the Sex Discrimination Act of 1975 and its subsequent legislation. One would need to examine why this occurs. Is it due to differences in the educational qualifications? Is it due to discrimination? Is it, as Professor Hakim suggests, that in some cases women do not want to get to the top positions in the first place? It may be partly that women do different jobs to men, with more women in the "caring" jobs such as nursing and primary school teaching. Some sociologists have explained this in terms of the differences in the brain, with men having the right hand part of the brain more developed while for women it is the left. In turn this is linked to emotional attributes or intellectuality. There are sociologists who have disputed this.

A great deal of attention has been paid to income, while little attention has been paid to wealth. This is surprising since, in any society, the distribution of wealth is far more skewed than income. Much of this problem arises from the definition of wealth. Does it include assets such as the house in which people are living? Does it include pension rights? In many cases wealth is inherited and if we live in a patriarchal society - as many sociologists including Marx and the feminists would suggest - then this could be part of the explanation.

In a period of rapidly changing house prices, as in the U.K., from 2000 to 2007, we would expect to find two things; first, given that more professional people live in owner occupied houses than unskilled manual workers, this would lead to further inequalities. Secondly, given that the professional classes are likely to have higher priced houses in the first place then this would also lead to greater redistribution of wealth towards the rich rather than the poor. When looking at pensions, occupational pensions are more important for professional classes rather than for the unskilled manual workers, and it is also true that more men than women have access to these.

In most developing countries, a good number of the inhabitants of cities live in unrecognized, informal settlements of cheap basic rentals, with poor social conditions and services. As most of the housing standards were written by colonial authorities, some of these developing countries have had to change the housing codes to allow appropriate housing for people in the low income bracket. The need to revise outdated housing standards exists in dozens of developing countries.

It is obvious, that different socio-economic groups have different rates of owner occupation. For a long while many people from low socio-economic groups had Council housing as their main type of accommodation. This partly changed in the Thatcher Administration (1979-1990) and subsequent Conservative governments. It is more likely now that such people will live in Housing Association houses. But the basic point still remains in spite of large-scale sales of Council houses. In some cases it could be argued that given that the people living in the less saleable Council accommodation, e.g. high-rise blocks, would not either be able to afford them or wish to buy them. This makes income distribution worse. Amongst the upper class property has often gone from the parents to the males rather than the females, so this would partially account for social inequality at the very top. There is less evidence to say whether this is true amongst the middle and working classes. Men generally have more access to occupational pension schemes than women, this is partly the result of part time working patterns, and partly because women have often had less continuity of employment, taking some time out to be with their children, during which time they are not gaining occupational pensions. Since women live longer than men, and also get pensions at age 60 in a country such as the U.K., they are more likely to be old-age pensioners. Women, if on a State pension, would therefore form some of lowest income households. Marxists would suggest that the selling off of council houses would be in line with his prediction that the state would - far from being neutral - be on the side of the capitalist class.

There may also be discrimination in spite of the *Sex Discrimination Act 1975 and Race Relations Act (1976)* and subsequent legislation, which affects the chances for different ethnic groups and in particular for people who are coloured. In some cases ethnic groups, but clearly, travellers, sometimes called gypsies, Romany, tend to have both worse housing conditions and job prospects.

In an effort to bring improvement of housing conditions and results, most developing countries responded to the housing needs of the poor through the formal provision of low cost housing. In the place of thorough policies of slum upgrading or integration, and making use of public land reserves and public subsidies, governments embarked on massive public housing schemes. They targeted, in principle, non-income, low-income and low middle-income groups. But actually they were allocated to the middle classes, government employees and political clienteles. The high cost of this approach was the main reason why the housing needs of the poor have not been met and informal settlements have grown.

Structural theory and social action

Structural theory

Structural theory holds implies that the structures of society are the most important influences upon the individuals in that society. Marx assumed that there were two main classes, i.e. the capitalists and the proletariat. In these cases the individual has relatively little freedom of choice and materialistic considerations dominate how society is formed. Karl Marx predicted that the richer would become richer and the poor would become poorer. In practice, in Western Europe, and in particular in the United Kingdom, the rich may have become richer, but the poor have also become richer in real terms. This means over and above the rate of inflation. This situation is not necessarily reflected in some developing countries such as Kenya. The distribution of the national income is such that 10% of the population controls about 90% of the resources available. People born in poor families are generally seen to stay poor and the gap between the rich and the poor continues to widen.

Social action

Social action, in contrast, is where people make different choices. Weber suggested that there were four ideals. Ideals models would not necessarily be favourable. One of these was what he called **instrumental**, where people weigh up the choices that are open to them and then choose rationally what to do. This is comparable to the ideas of the economists in the perfect competition model. In practice, it seems difficult to reconcile the rational model with so much advertising, which clearly does not try to inform people. In many cases identical products can be sold at widely different prices at different points of sale.

The second of Weber's ideals was **valuing rationally** where the ends are given, for example, with the protestant work ethic, but there are constraints upon the limits. It could be argued that in many cases there will be social constraints upon people's actions. Even if drug trafficking is profitable, many people might object to doing this on ethical grounds, even if is not illegal. Similarly, some people would not wish to be associated with the tobacco industry, even though it is legal and highly profitable.

The third of Weber's categories is **effectual,** whereby decisions are taken on emotional grounds. In modern society, we can find examples where a great deal of advertising appeals on emotional rather than rational grounds. It could be either altruistic - to help other members of the society, including the young and the old; or it could be selfish as in slogans such as 'pamper yourself'.

Charities frequently try to persuade people on emotional grounds to contribute. They mostly use pictures of the young or the elderly but comparatively rarely of people between 20 and 50 years of age, who are not considered to tug at people's heartstrings. Whereas many sociologists preferred the ideas that we should act on rational grounds and that this was linked to progress, post modernists would probably suggest that we need more to life than rationality anyway

The fourth category was that of **tradition**, that is, doing things as they have been done in the past. We can clearly see this in some developing countries where in more remote areas people will carry on their economic and social activities in the ways that have been used previously. In this era of globalisation, this has become less common.

In practice, Weber also allowed for a mixture of social actions.

We might see that older people might wish to continue carrying out activities as they have done before, even if there are, more efficient methods of carrying these out. There can be resistance to changes in technology; with the young more likely to warm up to the use of mobile phones, whereas the older might well be resistant to them.

J. K. Galbraith has suggested that many people in poorer countries are resistant to change, not necessarily because of an inherent dislike of change, but because of avoiding risk taking given their subsistence level of living. We can see that whereas many sociologists thought that progress was both desirable and inevitable other sociologist especially the post modernists would dispute this.

Modernism and post-modernism

Modernism literally means a preference for the modern world. This could apply to arts and culture. Some people might well prefer modern music to classical or traditional music. Some people suggest that in modernism there is less of a gap between the reality and the appearance. Sociologists have suggested that some of the features of modernism are that society as a whole is industrialised, that capitalists exert a great deal of power, and that power, generally is centralised, both within government and within firms.

Postmodernism could be defined as post-capitalism in the ordinary sense. Whilst there have been multinationals in the past, these have now become dominant, as can be seen in the oil industry, which affects not only the market it serves, but it may also be part of the decision process. This might be seen in the bids by American firms, which take part in the reconstruction of Iraq.

Post Modernism can be described as the belief that direction, evolution and progression have ended in social history, and society is based instead upon the decline of absolute truths, and the rise of relativity. It starts with the premise that social history has moved on from that described by the founders.

Some post-modern theories would suggest that the conventional theories of sociology, whether they be Marxism, feminism or functionalism, are no longer useful. They would suggest that social factors, such as class or ethnic group, matter a great deal less than factors over which people are freer to choose. People are able to choose to live with different groups. The town of Brighton - in the U.K., has a large proportion of homosexuals and lesbians, thus they may choose to live in such a town where they feel that the community accepts them, than in other more traditional towns. Similarly, it could be argued that the gaps between the classes are less important than age for many purposes. Younger people may well choose to have separate life styles rather than conform to those of older generations. Critics of post modernism would suggest that whilst richer people do have this choice other poorer people are not in a position to make life styles choices

Some postmodernists have also suggested that the concept of positivism is essentially wrong. It is often difficult to separate the reality and images. It is quite clear that in an era where an average of 21-22 hours a week is spent watching television in some countries, in some cases, people confuse characters with real life. If a fictitious birth takes place in a radio or television programme, then people are known to send presents, especially in the now popular soap operas and serial programmes.

Postmodernists will often point to the existence of mass produced culture, which goes across class or national boundaries. We can see that pop groups such as the Beatles, were well-known far beyond their native Merseyside and the style of music was often copied by other pop groups. The same can be said for other musicians such as Bob Marley, the well known King of Reggae music.

Whereas 19th century sociologists seem to have been influenced by evolutionary arguments and had, what is sometimes called Social Darwinism –that is, the survival of the fittest - and therefore progress was almost inevitable, postmodernists would deny this. They would also suggest that instant communications means that we are aware of what is going on elsewhere, even though images may be more important than the reality. A news item might suggest that the war in Sudan is finally coming to a close, having killed over two million people in the last twenty years. This is less likely to hit the headlines than items about David Beckham's (the football superstar) clothing.

Some postmodernists would also argue that modern firms are less bureaucratic since they have to be able to adapt readily to change. In support of this they might well argue that firms such as IBM, the computer firm, which faced a major crisis in the mid-1990s has learnt to adapt to changes, such as concentrating on consultancy rather than attempting to move very much into the personal computer market.

Some postmodernists would argue that the line between work and leisure has become more blurred over time, with more people carrying out "do it yourself" activities, which could be regarded either as a substitute for employing people in the first place, or in many cases, it could be regarded as a leisure activity. It might also be plain that many people in their 50s or 60s who set up new businesses will often set up what might be called hobby-shops, selling things they like, or setup as craft workers, even if the returns on this are relatively small.

In the U.K. one of the reasons for getting rid of steam engines in the 1960s by British Rail was that people resented the job associated with the driving of steam engines. During that time, most men did not like doing hard dirty work such as driving steam engines compared with the less physical effort of driving diesel trains or electric trains. Many people (including a few women) at weekends working for the voluntary rail societies will do this.

Materialism

This theory suggests that only matter exists and this is all-important. This is in contrast to Descartes, who suggested that the brain was immaterial. Sociologists, including Karl Marx, have suggested that a materialistic approach, which looked at economic factors, is very important. Karl Marx developed his theories of dialectic materialism in the 19th century. More recently Anna Peleert has suggested that by looking at people working in factories we can see how people react.

Idealism

Idealism is the doctrine that ideas, or thought, make up either the whole or an indispensable aspect of any full reality, so that a world of material objects containing no thought either could not exist, or would not be fully "real." Idealism is often contrasted with materialism.

The concept of idealism can be traced to the times of Plato, the well-known Greek philosopher. Plato, in his well known book *The Republic*, looks at the three different classes which he envisages, of gold, silver and bronze. These classes would have different types of education to satisfy the different needs. According to his vision only the gold class really saw reality. It might be interesting to note the tripartite division of education, is similar to that set out under the Butler Education Act 1944.

In contrast, Weber thought that religions, influenced economic forces. Under Weber's point of view both the necessary economic and religious beliefs had to be in place if economic activity was to develop. Weber did not believe that Eastern religions on the whole, encouraged economic activity. It is difficult, however, to reconcile Weber's views with the increasing strength of Japanese post-war economic growth. There might have been other factors, for example the fact that Japan was forced to adopt a low proportion of money being spent on armaments, after the Second World War. This meant that research and development therefore turned to peaceful development, which is perhaps economically more beneficial. However, it could be argued that the recession in Japan in the late 1990s onwards was partly because of a Japanese Puritanism, which involved not wanting to spend too much money and the willingness to save. This might be contrasted with much of the consumerism of the West. It would also be in line with Keynes paradox of thrift, showing that if people try to save too much, paradoxically this could lead to worse economic conditions for all.

How have changes in religious beliefs affected the community as a whole? Weber and others have argued about the protestant work ethic. It is sometimes suggested that, partly because of Luther and partly because of Calvin, in the protestant work ethic all jobs were seen as vocational not just confined to a few religious jobs. Therefore, it was important for people to fulfil their vocation by working hard. In some cases as with Wesley, one of the Methodist leaders of the 18th century, people should earn all they can and give all they can. Wesley himself seemed to live up to this principle. He earned about £3.000 a year from the publication of his very popular hymn books, but lived on a relatively small amount of about £14 a year. Similarly, other Christians in the 19th century sometimes seemed to fulfil the model, perhaps much parodied, of Samuel Smiles of self-help. Titus Salt showed his religious principles forming a model town, Saltaire in the suburbs of Bradford in West Yorkshire. The city is much more hygienic than most of the towns around, which Friedrich Engels rightly saw as 'a horrendous pattern of living for the poor'. Similarly, looking at Rowntree in York, it can be seen that the layout of the factory, the housing around, the garden were all meant to give workers a good standard of life. In Rowntree's case, the product itself, cocoa, was seen as an alternative to drink.

The Rowntree Foundation itself provided sources of funds to many worthwhile projects. In many towns and cities we can see local parks given by industrialists on the basis that if they were blessed by God they also had the duty to provide for other people.

It is also suggested that under the protestant work ethic, one was allowed to work but not to spoil oneself. Certainly, the Quakers, who formed a high proportion of the wealthiest people of the 18th century, had a code of dress, but luxury was not considered correct. This might be seen by some to be in contrast to the 1980s, when it was often suggested that money was all important and how one got was unimportant. Scandals such as those surrounding the bankruptcy of Enron in the early 2000s, the biggest corporate bankruptcy in Western history, suggest that in many cases material needs have become all important.

In other cases the churches, along with other groups protested about Barclays Bank's involvement in South Africa in the 1960s, when many people suggested that it gave a boost to the apartheid regime. Unfortunately, the Dutch Reformed Church itself in South Africa often gave support to the white regime.

In many cases the churches themselves seem to have less power and are more willing to be involved with other groups. In 2003 there were protests by many Christians as well as Muslims, about the legality of the war in Iraq. Some people have suggested that because of the moderation of major religions such as Christianity there has been more interest in cults. Perhaps one of the best examples of this would be that of the Davidians which unfortunately resulted in the loss of many people's lives in April 1993, following a stand off between the Federal Forces in the U.S.A and the members of the sect.

In other cases because some people see a breakdown of the community, they have joined the sects rather than joining the more orthodox religions. It has been suggested that sects such as the Moonies brain-wash members in order to ensure that they are separated from their families.

Whilst Comte suggested that there would be a breakdown of religious beliefs as people became more rational it does not seem to be borne out by the number of people who have half-believed or wholly-believed in astrology, which seems to have no rational basis at all.

Ethnic inequality

To what extent do inequalities cover? Is it only in income and/or wealth? Or does it also extend to working conditions? The Penguin book on Racial Discrimination in England, whilst published in the 1960s, still indicates the type of discrimination which many coloured people continue to experience in spite of legislation. The level of English is more difficult to measure but in some cases the differences could be due to this. It is easier, however, to see the changes that are taking place in the educational process; it seems that at the present time, a disproportionate number of non-white people are entering higher education which could alter differences in the future. Within the ethnic groups, some women will be encouraged to enter the workforce whereas in other cases they will not. This, again, could account for differences in the distribution of income.

Bureaucracy

Weber assumed that bureaucracy meant decisions that were taken on rational grounds on an impersonal system, that is, that it did not favour a person for no good reason. He also assumed that people would be given jobs on the basis of their qualifications or experience. He wrote this, at the time when family businesses were beginning to become less important, and where most family businesses would have family members at the helm irrespective of their suitability for the job. The word 'nepotism' is often used to denote organisations where people are given jobs on the basis of being related or being friends' of the people within the organisation rather than being appointed on merit. Similarly until the 1850's the army had often had appointments made on basis of belonging to a good family. The Crimean War had shown that the British Army in many cases was not well led.

Efficient or inefficient Bureaucracy

The most obvious manner of defining these two terms would be using the economists rather than the sociologists' concepts by looking at the inputs and comparing them with the outputs. The inputs are usually land, labour and capital, while outputs are the production of goods or services. We might notice here that land is not necessarily suitable for all purposes; similarly one unit of labour such as a person per hour is not necessarily identical to a writer being more efficient by employing a typist. Nowadays the same logic would apply to using the word-processor. We can see therefore that whilst Karl Marx tended to regard one hour of labour as similar from one worker to another, most modern social scientists would probably not accept this point of view. Similarly capital can be quite different from one industry to another.

However, using all resources is not of itself a sufficient condition to show that something is efficient. It could be argued that during the Cultural Revolution in China in the 1960s many intellectuals were put to work as agricultural labourers. Even if they were in some cases more efficient than other labourers were, it was almost certainly a waste of talent. For all factors of production we need to look at what the economist would call opportunity cost, that is, the benefits one could have received by taking an alternative action with the same factors of production. Most intellectuals could presumably have done some managerial jobs, which might have been more useful. In other cases they might have been more usefully employed in other sectors such as the education sector.

Problems of defining outputs

Outputs may be easy to define when dealing with volumes of products. In other cases it is more difficult to define and we often use value of production to denote the value of output as it is in gross national product.

However, it could be argued that if many people starved whilst at the same time the rich have more than enough goods and services then this is hardly efficient. Some social scientists argue that we cannot make such inter-personal comparisons. This is using the Pareto concept of efficiency, that is, an economy or organisation is efficient if we can not make one person better off except by making someone else worse off.

Social scientists are often divided about whether more outputs of some goods and services are desirable. In 2004 the European Union announced that it would no longer subsidise the tobacco industry. In the U.K. tobacco is responsible for about 120,000 premature deaths.

Repugnant Output

Most social scientists would also suggest that we need to look at the effects on society as a whole; for example the concentration camps in Nazi Germany. Similarly whilst the Russian Government in the 1930's may have been efficient in some respects, the wholesale slaughter of many of Stalin's opponents as well as people he disliked would hardly be regarded as efficient. The tyranny of Idi Amin in Uganda in the 1970s is also an illustration of this.

In many cases some outputs ignore externalities, for example problems arising from pollution, noise, and accidents, which have no costs to the organisation, but may create problems for the rest of the community. From the point of view of the firm, the cheapest most efficient way of handling waste products, in a narrow sense, is to dump it all in the local rivers and seas. This would keep costs lower for the firm than taking more socially responsible action in dumping its waste products. One of the criticisms that Friedrich Engels made indirectly in the 1840s when looking at the slums of England was precisely this, that a lot of the pollution was ignored because it created no cost for the firms producing it.

The problems of social costs are still important today, and this is why most countries except the U.S.A signed the Kyoto agreement 1997, which tries to stabilize greenhouse gas concentrations in the atmosphere at a level that would prevent dangerous anthropogenic interference with the climate system cut back on harmful emissions of gases etc. Many firms all over the world are guilty of creating and ignoring pollution. In June 2004 a select committee of the House of Commons suggested that the U.K. Government was ignoring the effects of pollution from the rapidly growing air industry, which at the time, was the major cause of the increase in pollution. The

Oil Industry predictably and other industrial firms argued that they could not afford to pay for such measures.

The Stern Report of October 2006 stated that we needed to avoid problems caused by global warming if British industries wanted to produce effectively in the future.

The concept of output is not necessarily helpful, unless we know what is desirable in the eyes of the consumer

One of the problems of the Eastern block before it reverted back from communist rule was that in many cases there was over-emphasis on the number of cars produced, such as the Trabants. This was not based on their effect upon the community as they were considered one of the most inefficient cars if we allow for pollution. The lack of interest in social costs is often held to be one of the problems of capitalist societies, but it can equally be true of a socialist society. The problem here is that the bureaucracy is not inefficient in the narrow sense, but it is failing to take account of what happens to the community around them. The problem is also that it is much easier to specify output than it is to try to measure all the different social costs.

Rationality of consumers

We therefore have a problem in that we normally regard output in terms of the money value of what is produced. This however would assume that consumers are rational, and this is not necessarily the case. In 2004 there were some fuel protests about the cost of fuel in the U.K., following the problems which arose from the Iraq conflict. Most surveys however would show that a typical motorist could save around 18% of their fuel bills if they drove in a more sensible manner.

Non Market Services

There are also services which are not sold in the market such as much of health and education. We therefore need some other measure of output, for example in health we could look at the number of patients treated, though this would still be inadequate. The U.K. has often changed its mind about how to measure productivity in the NHS or in the teaching profession. Clearly any one hospital could have lower death rates if it refused to treat the sickest people. This illustrates part of the problem of looking at death rates for individual hospitals.

Span of Control

However, if we revert to more conventional analyses for a short time, then there are a number of reasons why a bureaucracy might be inefficient. The first is that the span of control might be too great. Whilst some management writers at the latter end of the 19th century and early parts of the 20th century thought that no person could control more than six people, most sociologists now would think that this is too dogmatic and that much depends upon the type of organisation, including bureaucracies, in which it takes place. Obviously, it is much easier to supervise people doing identical duties, for example within a factory where people can easily be watched, than it is to supervise people doing different tasks and when they are spread out geographically over a large area with no quick methods of checking what they are doing. When the Russians in the 1920s and 1930s produced their five year plans for things such as steel, it was relatively easy to check on the total output as well as on the total inputs. Though historians are sometimes divided as to whether or not the Russians achieved all their objectives, there is little doubt that they did make some great strides. It is much more difficult however to try to measure goods and services where there are a great variety of outputs, as in the clothing sector. It is also difficult where there are difficulties in checking on the quality of the product as it is with steel.

Chain of Command

Another reason why bureaucracy may not function efficiently is that the chain of command could well be too long, i.e. the number of layers within an organisation. Many modern management theorists prefer a flat organisation i.e. there are not too many layers between the top people and the bottom people.

In most organisations it is much easier to communicate down the line of command then it is to communicate up the line. The importance of feedback is therefore important. Karl Marx talked about alienation of workers in the capitalist system. Some social scientists would suggest that it is not just in the capitalist system that workers can feel alienated, but also in any organisation where the workers feel ignored by the management.

Weber's Idea's on Bureaucracy

Weber, who was one of the first sociologists to put forward the idea of bureaucracy, thought that the system could break down at times of crisis. For example, the army, which might be thought of as being a bureaucracy, could well have problems, particularly if there is no method of feedback between the lowest layers and the top. Weber wrote his views not long after the Crimean war, in which the charge of the Light Brigade had taken place. This is where the British Calvary went charging into Russian cannons. In many cases the cavalry only had sabres (short swords). The French Quote from the time is (c'est magnifique mais ce n'est pas la geurre) *it is magnificent, but it is not the war*, that is, that the British people stood no chance whatsoever in the circumstances. Whilst this may have been an act of heroism, other people pointed out that part of the problem was that the commander in chief was inefficient and did not know what he was doing. At the time perhaps it could have been argued that this would not have happened to an ordinary bureaucracy, since in a bureaucracy people were appointed to positions according to their talents or merit. The commander in chief had not been appointed on this basis.

It could be argued, however, that in some cases there still exists this problem. Chernobyl problems arose partly because there was insufficient supervision of the nuclear engineers. Here again we have the problem that the output, which included radiation, which affected sheep and farmers in Great Britain, could have been said to be of little interest to that of the Russian authority. The problem is not however confined to "command economies" (the term used by economists to mean a situation where the State makes most of the major decision about the economy's inputs and outputs). Here too in the U.K. we have a definition of what is efficient and inefficient; radiation going across the Irish Sea to the Republic of Ireland may be efficient from the British nuclear industries point of view, but it clearly is not efficient on a wider basis.

Weber assumed that specialisation was desirable as it had been described by Adam Smith in the book *Wealth of Nations* in 1776. Bureaucracy is likely to make the best use of specialisations since the organisation will usually insist on suitably qualified people rather than on nepotism which had often been rife in the civil service and the army in the 19th century. Weber assumed that there would be a set of written rules that would be obeyed by all the people within the firm. He regarded this as important since it meant that people could deal impersonally and not be affected by emotions. He also assumed that recruitment would be based on merit. We might note that this would be in line with reforms in the 1850s in the Civil Service following the Northcote Trevelyan Report 1854. We might also notice that prior to this, people had often been appointed on the basis of their connections and not on their ability to do the jobs. The Northcote Trevelyan Report took quite a long time to implement and was opposed by those who, because of nepotism, gained good jobs without necessarily having much skill.

The idea of professional people or at least suitably qualified people has been accepted by most people. The late Lord Young wrote an interesting book on the rise of meritocracy in 1954 which, however, points out some of the limitations of this approach. It could also be argued that in many cases the idea of qualified people has been taken too narrowly. This was belatedly recognised in the medical profession where trained nurses are now allowed to prescribe some drugs rather than having doctors take up their time in prescribing routine drugs.

Illich on the other hand is scathing about the professionals and suggests that in too many cases professionals serve their own interest rather than that of the people they are supposed to help.

Weber assumed that bureaucracy was generally the best or ideal form of organisation but that in some circumstances e.g. in wartime it might be too slow to react. It could be argued as well, that different types of organisations might require different types of structures; a small marketing organisation might need to have imagination and flair and the same might be said of a small group of writers producing comedy shows. This would be in contrast to the major financial organisations where most customers want a good service arising from an efficient bureaucracy unlike Northern Rock.

Bureaucracy and Red Tape

People often use the word bureaucracy to mean red tape, although this is not the original meaning. The word bureaucracy has come to be used in such a pejorative sense partly because in many cases people feel tied down by rules which become ends to themselves rather than means to an end in efficiently organizing large scale human groups such as government ministries and departments.

Current Examples of the Public Sector and Supervision of the Privatised Industries

This is one of the criticisms of what is happening in the public sector at the present time, or for that matter in industries which have been privatised. For example, rules which talk about time keeping would seem to be sensible as part of an overall pattern for the railways. Ideally we would want to know how many people were likely to be connecting between one service and another, and how much difference it would make to their journey time. For example Clapham Junction is one of the busiest stations in the United Kingdom serving trains from both Waterloo and Victoria. There would be no point in delaying trains at Clapham Junction on their way to London since most passengers would only have to wait a minute or two if their train was delayed. On the other hand some train services are very infrequent and if a train does not connect or if it is the last one they might need over night accommodation. However, if fines means that connections are not made between trains of either different companies or the same company then clearly the rules have become ends, which are not helpful. Similarly in hospitals where output is measured by the number of patients treated, there is the danger that may be unhelpful, for example in cases where people are not treated properly, for example if hip replacements are not carried out efficiently. A person who has 2 hip replacements would seem to indicate that the hospital has been twice as efficient as a hospital which gives one hip replacement in the first place. Clearly this is not sensible.

Some of the most criticised bureaucracies are found in Africa. For instance a farmer in the Central African Republic needs to obtain 38 signatures before he's able to get his bananas on a ship bound for America or Europe, while a businessman in Lagos must go through 21 official procedures in order to legally buy a warehouse. A World Bank Report 2004 accused African governments of perpetuating poverty and restricting business by overwhelming them with a web of regulations

Motivation in Large Organisations

It has been suggested that motivation might be relatively small within a bureaucracy, whether in the private sector but subject to public sector rules, or wholly within the public sector, or in very large organisations in the private sector. The lack of motivation might well be important, since bureaucracy will typically work best where there are no rapidly changing conditions. This means that relying on past precedents or using past data to help make decisions is much more difficult.

Karl Marx himself thought that alienation took place if processes were too much divided and workers did not have any control over their means of production. He mainly referred to firms within the manufacturing industry, but we can apply the same idea elsewhere. For example, if doctors observe that their patients are not getting proper treatment because of lack of time for consultation, then it could be argued that the NHS (National Health Service) becomes inefficient under these circumstances.

The concept of specialisation is nothing new. It was formulated probably in Adam Smith's book *Wealth of Nations* 1776, in which he describes the process of pin making. Presumably he did this partly because most people would be surprised that an occupation such as pin making could be that specialised. Specialisation increases production under most circumstances, but can mean that workers get isolated in not seeing the whole of the production process. For example in the service sector, as in the health service, people may become more specialised but not have an overall view of patients. Similarly, in social services, where people may not get a view of the family as a whole, but may only see individuals within it. Some people would claim, for example, that if one has a specialist dealing solely with children who have special education needs, then there would be insistence on special treatment for children without thinking about the effects of other children who may not have special needs in a class.

Bureaucracy would also imply that recruitment is based upon qualifications. This is one of the points that Weber made originally, and it is one of the reasons why the Northcote Trevelyan Reforms took place in the Civil Service, originally in the 1850s, but some of these reforms were spread over a longer period. It could be argued that this was better than the previous practice of nepotism, where in many cases people obtained commissions in the army or in the Indian Civil Service because of who they knew rather than because of what they knew. The same qualification aspect would have applied to the army, where in many cases commissions were bought and people appointed upon their personal family background rather than whether they were efficient. This was seen in the Crimean war.

One of the features of bureaucracy is that it makes predictable decisions. One would not want decisions to be taken at the whims of the individual bureaucrat. This is one of the reasons why the Civil Service generally makes its decisions upon precedents.

In many cases, for example in the social services, this can be very sensible. One can imagine that there would be a great outcry if families in the same position were given widely varying sums of money when they had much the same problems and the causes were very similar. It could be however that someone who urgently needs a decision made quickly may not get it made on time.

It could be argued that bureaucracies find it more difficult in some respects if there is a globalisation process. This is because changes can take place very rapidly, as in September 1992, partly because of globalisation, interest rates rose in Britain from 10% to 15% during the course of one day. It is difficult in this situation to rely on past decision-making, since there was not past decision-making precedent that could have enabled one to make a rational decision. On the other hand, it can be argued that instant communication makes things much easier within a bureaucracy, since individuals can pass information up the line very quickly through the use of fax or email. Passing such information in the traditional African society was also tedious because of the means of communications used such as drum beats, long distance runners amongst others. In the past, for example in the Civil Service when Britain still had a major empire, it is difficult to see how a decision from a small African country could be passed up the line quickly enough. On the other hand, the concept of quick communications could be overstated, since for example in the 19th century there was a whole number of postal services throughout the day, without the problem of Spam emails, i.e. advertisement emails that can clog up the system, or cause complete computer breakdowns because of viruses.

It could also be argued that in a bureaucracy too much emphasis is paid to concepts that can be quantified quickly and not sufficient emphasis is placed on social skills. This could be one of the criticisms made about the education service. It could be argued that there is overemphasis upon the number of people obtaining GCSEs or A levels, becoming the target for university entrance, and not enough emphasis is placed upon whether people have enough social skills. In many jobs, except those of the backroom technician, social skills are important, and they cannot be judged easily through an examination system.

If we look at a typical firm, we can see that some functions require skills which might fall fairly easily into a bureaucratic pattern. In most cases purchasing requires the use of past data in order to ensure that the best purchases are made. There might be occasions with rapid changes in prices, such as those of oil in 1973, or to a limited extent in 2004, where in many cases it might be sensible to be thinking about hedging, that is, buying supplies in advance of what is necessary to ensure that there is continuity of flows of imports.

There is a need of a bureaucracy to ensure that purchasing by tender is carried out in a sensible manner. Local authorities as well as central government and large firms may all carry out this function. Bribery for large contracts has unfortunately been relatively common, especially with arms' deals, so that a bureaucracy that both insists in standard procedures and checks the background of people bidding would be sensible. Even apart from the sensitivity involved with arms' deals, it would also be sensible to have a logical tendering procedure, for example with major projects such as when the Channel Tunnel was built. In some cases, as with the fiasco over the building of the Millennium Dome in London, where the Dome was way over budget, but also forecasting of demand was completely inaccurate, the bureaucracy concerned was inefficient. A similar case was seen in Kenya in the late 1990s during the construction of several government buildings including the Times Towers, where the company awarded the tender had over quoted and still got the job.

If a firm has a law department, we would expect them to be bureaucratic in the sense of being qualified to carry out their duties; in particular to carry out health and safety procedures in a cost effective manner. At the present time, some people think that the Health and Safety Executive, in the U.K., has insisted on over-tight rules, where the same procedure seem to apply to all railways irrespective of running speed. In some cases trains seem to keep to very slow schedules in order to cater for these requirements. This does not necessarily seem to be helpful, since if the railways are restricted more people might be killed on road accidents, since the road is less safe. In some other functions, for example marketing, it is difficult to see how the basic concept of a bureaucracy can be helpful. Marketing perhaps requires more imagination than other functions within a firm. In the production department it is not just a question of bureaucracy in the sense of having a division of labour, but also seeing whether people can be motivated. Various examples from the Human Relations School, such as the Elton Mayo experiment in the 1930s, have suggested that management taking an interest might be important. Within any organisation, if the rules are not sensible, there may well be a system whereby people obey the rules in one sense, for example, keeping time with the railways, or seeing so many patients, but this is not necessarily good for society as a whole.

One of the problems in modern society is that as we get more mechanisation and automation, the concept of mass production becomes less important to most Western countries. In this case the concept of a bureaucracy, in turn, perhaps becomes less important. In general we can say that it is easier to set up a bureaucracy in terms of secondary sector industries such as manufacturing, and to a lesser extent construction, than it is in many services, where the product is not clearly defined.

Predictions

We could predict that it would be easier to have bureaucracy where there are likely to be few changes, whether in the product or demand or in methods of organising production. In the rope industry one machine was used for about 150 years in Chatham Dockyard and the production methods did not vary. On the other hand in the computer industry where it is sometimes suggested that there is 25% more efficiency each year, then the method of producing computers will not remain the same. Also in the computer industry the demands have changed fairly drastically. For example whereas in the 1960's only the very largest organisations had computers, nowadays even the smallest firms tend to have one and so at the very least the marketing department of a computer company would have to take notice of this.

In many cases firms, before the advent of word-processors, had fairly standard letters that needed to be typed, and a typing pool using whatever typist is available would be helpful in this case. Most standard letters can already be word-processed and the need for word-processing tends to be more in terms of good layout and format which does not lead so neatly to a bureaucratic decision.

Methods of production may also influence, for example 'just-in- time' Production will be more difficult to organise than if we have production which is reasonably constant.

We could also argue that it is much easier to have a bureaucracy where the managers can see very quickly what is happening. This was not true in the 1960's of the railways freight industry where every week there was a list of wagons which had been lost. If the managers can see what is happening they can make decisions quickly, whereas until fairly recently road haulage managers for example would not have known what delays were occurring and so it was best left to the drivers to make decisions about what routes to take.

Similarly it will be easier to make decisions in mass production than in one off production, For example in making suits or dresses to measure, a customer will have his/her own preference and it is often best for him/her to give his/her instructions directly to the dress maker

SELF EXAMINATION QUESTIONS

1. Discuss some of the components that demonstrate (and cause) social inequality.

2. Discuss the theories advanced by various sociologists explaining the causes of social inequality and how they compare to present society.

3. What is bureaucracy? Why do people consider it synonymous with 'red tape? Are they right in thinking so?

4. What is meant by 'inefficient bureaucracy'?

5. What are some of the problems faced in defining outputs? How does this relate to 'consumer rationality'?

6. What is specialization? What are the advantages of specialization in an organization?

7. What is meant by 'social costs'? Why do they occur?

8. How does alienation occur at places of work?

Chapter Four

Stratification

The term stratification itself derives from the word 'strata', which is the term that geologists use to refer to layers of rocks on the earth's surface. In the same way the sociologist will often look at the layers within society and will try to emphasise the implication of the different layers There are several different types of stratification, which the world has known;

Slavery

Slavery means that one person owns another. Slaves can be bought and sold at markets like any other commodity. In the 18th century slaves were sold in much the same way as we would now expect houses or animals to be sold. To ensure that they got a buyer the seller would have to comment on the age, their obedience and a physical description of the slaves is mentioned.

There are however still differences between the different slavery systems. In Greek society, slaves were often well educated and could be craftsmen or administrators using their skill. Slaves were the backbone of Athenian society. In contrast many slaves died in the ships carrying them between Africa and the U.S.A. Some of this was because of the general lack of safety at that time, but in most cases the number of deaths was due to the poor conditions in which they found themselves. The slave system itself often used brutal punishments to try to get higher level of production. Corporal punishment was often used in work places especially in naval ships. In the coal mines punishment was even inflicted on children. In the U.K. slaves were more often used in the plantations. Slavery was abolished in the then British Empire in 1833 following pressure from Evangelicals such as William Wilberforce. It continued until the civil war in the U.S.A. from 1861 -1865 and was one of the causes of that war. It legally ended with the 13th amendment to American the constitution in 1865. Generally the southern states called the Confederation favoured slavery whereas the northern states did not. In the state of Pennsylvania the Quakers had renounced slavery much earlier in 1780.

Though in most African states slavery is uncommon, there are nonetheless cases of child labour and human trafficking to the Arabian countries. For instance Kenya is a source and a transit country for trafficked children. Kenyan children are reportedly trafficked to South Africa, and there are reports of internal trafficking of children into involuntary servitude, including for work as street vendors, day labourers, and as prostitutes. Children are also trafficked from Burundi and Rwanda to coastal areas of Kenya for purposes of sexual exploitation.

The feudal system

Some systems of social stratification are fixed or more usually called a closed society, that is, there is little or no movement between the different classes. The feudal system of stratification is characterized by land ownership.

In ancient Britain, the top of the system was the king who was regarded as the owner of all the land. Below him were the nobles such as dukes and earls. When the Duke of Normandy often called William the Conqueror was crowned king of England after the battle of Hastings in 1066 he was theoretically the chief and only land owner but in practice he gave away much of the land to people he trusted to keep order . He had a fairly dubious right to the throne but at the time the concept of a hereditary monarch had not been firmly established. It is also noticeable that the monarchy which later existed had a system of male primogeniture. This means that eventually the oldest son would become monarch on the death of the previous monarch. If there is no son as in the case of George the Sixth then the oldest daughter would become queen as happened in the case of our present Queen who became Queen Elizabeth the Second on the death of her father in 1952.

At the bottom of the ladder were the freemen who were owners of the land in exchange for carrying out military service. The serfs had a few rights such as being able to graze their animals. There were also other people who had no land at all.

The Germanic kings who were powerful around the end of the first millennium spread the feudal system and so most of Europe had the same or a similar feudal system.

Caste system

The caste system is associated with the Hindu religion, specifically, its belief in rebirth. The caste system is subdivided into a number of different subsidiary castes. The caste system is linked to occupations and these occupations are usually hereditary. Marriages usually take place within the same castes although this is breaking down slightly especially in the urban areas.

Generally the high castes are regarded as being purer in their religious belief than those lower down the caste system. The Brahmin is one of the highest castes; they are usually regarded as holy men and can be devoted to their religious beliefs. There are some people in the lower caste that can perform service to the Brahmin without being thought of as polluting to the Brahmin.

At the lower end of the system are the untouchables now named the davits who it is felt in the rigid application of the caste system will pollute the upper castes by their very presence.

In the caste system found amongst the Borana in north-eastern Kenya, the Watta are consigned to a life of servitude from birth, considered as low caste, unwanted and worthless. Caste is still practised amongst Asians in Kenya, particularly in the socio-economic arena where restrictions on socio-economic mobility remain.

The first Prime Minister of independent India, Mahatma Ghandi tried to alleviate the plight of the davits but did not wholly succeed.

Class

This system is associated mainly with economic differences among groupings of individuals. These differences are not inherited and are not established by legal or religious provisions. Many sociologists have had varying views and theories on this system.

Max Weber very much associated with the concept of life chances as the basis of stratification (differences) in society which is seen to be applicable today. He commented about the ability to go to the arts lying with the middle class and not the working class. Certainly if we look at the price of buying a movie ticket in an East African city such as Kampala in Uganda, we see that in many cases this is above the amounts that the working class might wish or can afford to pay. He also commented on the differences in recovery times from sickness, which according to him were associated very much with class. If we look at the concept of life expectancy from infancy right through all age groups, it is still the case that this varies according to class – a situation which has unfortunately not changed much in the third world.

John Goldthorpe carried out work on the different type of attitudes, which he believed characterised, the working class as opposed to the middle classes. He suggests in his book *"The Affluent Worker in the Class Structure"* that the working class on the whole are much more pessimistic about the ability to change anything and are therefore more likely to act on the belief that success is due to chance rather than to assume that it can be influenced by study or hard work.

Whilst the book was published in 1969 some of the same attitudes might partially help to explain why even allowing for difference in I.Q. level between the classes there are still proportionally far more middle class going to the universities in the U.K. in the early 2000s than the working class. It is also in line with the work by Paul Willis in his book *'Learning to Labour'* on working class students in secondary education.

Trade unions and class

Trade unions are formed on the basis of the industrial sectors of an economy, to mainly promote social, economic, political and other interests of the worker. Trade unions are the bodies used for negotiations to ensure the overall well being of any worker

Some sociologists have differentiated between those who work in either the mainstream or on the fringe activities of the economy. In Kenya many of the workers at building sites fall in the fringe category since the work is often low paid and it has very little job security with a high rate of turnover of staff. Most of the permanent jobs such as architecture, teachers, doctors and lawyers are taken to be mainstream economic activities. In Western countries at specific times such as summer and at Christmas the restaurants and other fast food chains will employ students who do not want permanency anyway. For these and other reasons as well for example the unsocial hours there are unlikely to be high rates of trade union membership whereas at the other end of the working class spectrum workers in the car industry etc will be working in a unionised environment.

In the case of people who drift in and out of jobs there is often a high proportion of people from the ethnic groups. This is not just true of the U.K. It is even truer of former West Germany where the Turkish immigrants sometimes called guest workers made up a large part of the underclass.

Social mobility

Social mobility is the movement of individuals and groupings of individuals between different socio economic positions. Whilst it is often assumed that the U.K. is an example of an upwardly mobile society within the class system and we had phrases such as yuppies (young upward mobile person) in the early and late 1980s, it is far from the truth that we have a very mobile society in terms of class.

Social mobility can be vertical - up or down the socioeconomic scale, lateral – geographical changes, and intergenerational –mobility across generations.

In most societies social mobility is caused by a response to a variety of complex social issues and economic trends. These forces, include, but are not limited to, societal changes due to industrialization, the increased number of women with young children entering the labour force, families with two working parents, a rise in the number of single parents, and the demise of traditional systems of child care and extended family support systems.

The number of people staying on to 18 and hence with qualifications to entry for higher education and to professional qualification has risen considerably .It is still comparatively low amongst the working class and is still much lower than the government would like. The government in particular is trying to tackle what it would see as the problems of the underclass. The Thatcher government from 1979 to 1900 suggest that this was partially because of the problems of dependency. This was put most graphically by Lord Tebbit who memorably said that when his father had been unemployed he had got on his bike. The concept here was that dependency was one of the major causes of the problems of society and that if people wanted to they could solve their own social problems.

Whilst the present government has taken several different forms both of the push and pull variety i.e. to try to make it easier to get employment for lone parent to go to work and in some cases to try to make it tougher to get benefits. The working family tax benefit system can be described as the push variety although it is not confined to lone parent families but is meant to get people to go to work by ensuring that they get a reasonable wage if people do go out to work. The logic of a negative tax on low incomes has been suggested at least since the early 1970s. The advantage of this, it is claimed, is that it would avoid the poverty trap; that in some cases the marginal rate of tax combined with loss of benefits result in people getting very little rather than if they had gone to work or if they had worked longer hours.

The underclass

The term underclass is used to describe the segment of population located at the very bottom of the class system. The underclass arises from people who, amongst other things, have been excluded from full time education for whatever reason. Some of these people include; 'long term' prisoners, the urban poor, the disabled and the slum dwellers.

In pursuing the realization of the Millennium Development Goals, countries such as Kenya and Uganda have instituted free education to reach most of these groups who would otherwise have not accessed education.

Though education (or lack thereof) is the most prevalent indicator of the underclass, other issues also apply including poverty, minority ethnic groups and unemployment.

Women and class

One of the points made by some of the feminist writers as well as by Anthony Giddens in his book, *"Sociology"* is that women have often not been considered in the writings on class. This is sometimes explained by the idea that women's work has always been considered less important to society as compared to that of men; even though no evidence has generally been produced to suggest that this is the case. As the number of sole parents increases and the number of single women increase this is even less likely to be true because women are the sole wage earners in the household. The assumption that so called women's work (looking after the children, cooking, cleaning and general housework) is less important than other duties is a dubious one.

The point about housework has been taken up forcefully by feminist writers notably Ann Oakley.

Giddens notes that the issue of gender inequalities overlaps a great deal with that of class division in men and women. Thus gender inequalities can substantially be explained on the basis of the class system.

Theorizing Patriarchy by Sylvia Walby

Defining patriarchy

Walby points out that originally the term applied to the idea of older men being in charge of both women and younger men. She tends not to be interested in this generational gap for men as a definition of the term, and instead concentrates on the more modern usage of the word which is used to mean domination of women by men.

Alternative theories

Walby points out in her book "Theorizing Patriarchy" that there are four main theories about Patriarchy. The **Marxist** view point is one and it unsurprisingly tends to identify women problems with the capitalist system. He assumes that generally the idea of having unpaid housework is helpful to the capitalist since it means that cheap labour is available, whereas if men had to pay women for housework this would not be the case. She points out elsewhere that this is the traditional argument and also that Marxists tend to assume that women's life is very much tied up with men's.

On the other hand there is the **radical feminism** school of thought, which would argue that it is likely that men tend to dominate in society almost irrespective of the system. She points out that radical feminists tend to assume that women have not had a better life, compared to men and that any victories for women are achieved against the wishes of men.

The third view point is the **Liberals** which tends to suggest a look at individual improvement which has taken place such as the Sexual Offences Act in Kenya. All the same in her view it fails to have an overall picture.

The last one is the **dual system**, which tries to integrate the Marxist and the radical feminism viewpoints.

Criticisms of pure Marxist approach

The Marxist viewpoint ignores to a large extent what has happened outside the modern capitalist system. The Kossovan community is still a dominantly male one, even though for a long while Kosovo was part of the communist-dominated world and subsequently it has hardly become modern capitalist in the conventional sense. We can also see as Marx himself said that there was Patriarchy before modern capitalism anyway.

Marx himself did not seem to have studied religion very much, and so would not have been able to say much about women's place in Muslim society. Many people have assumed that women are often oppressed in Muslim society but this seems to be very different from one country to another.

Part of the problem with looking at the role of women, purely in terms of class is that in many cases many single mothers do not fall into the category of being dependent on the man's income. This may depend upon the level of maintenance and also whether this maintenance actually gets paid. In some cases a single mother may not have the opportunities as the functionalist would argue to look after herself, but would actually be reliant on the man's income. However whilst Walby does not say this it is not clear how many of these women are cohabiting so that they could still be part of the male dominated families. In many societies the number of working women has increased and the tradition of the male breadwinner is no longer so applicable. In some cases in what might be called 'The sunken middle class' as Douglas notes in one of his books on sociology of education, the women might well be earning more than the men anyway.

Problems in formulating a general theory

One of the problems in formulating a general theory is that it is not clear that women are necessarily one group. It is very noticeable among the ethnic groups that there are quite different patterns of work; between the Bangladeshi and the Indian, as well as the so-called black women. It could also be argued that this is also true of ethnic groups which in many cases may have some similar problems but not necessarily a single major cause of the problems.

Walby rightly mentions the fact that women on average earn quite a lot less than men. She does not explain - in spite of her criticism of the functionalist as giving a view which is in many ways similar to that of the perfect competition model beloved of some economists - why if women get less than men, firms aiming for bigger profits do not seek to employ women rather than men.

Perhaps part of the answer lies in the research she did in which she cites that in many cases women and men are not doing the same jobs in the same place. Walby says that in some cases the social interaction between men, means that women do not hear of jobs which are available through the social grapevines. Though she does not mention it, this may have several other effects, including a tendency for the same grapevines to rule out people from the ethnic groups.

We could go further than this to see how far women and men are doing the same work, in which case the legislation such as the *Sex Discrimination Act 1975* and its subsequent amendments should prevent this or whether there are other differences that might help to explain the gap. The act after all covers not only pay, but also promotion and recruitment. She rightly says that even econometric studies have shown that very little of the gap is in terms of what the functionalists have suggested, including economic factors such as difference in qualifications and length of experience. Even at the time Walby was writing her book the differences in qualifications was becoming outdated since at that time girls had overtaken boys in the O levels (the predecessor of the GCSE). It remains to be seen how far changes in women's qualifications affects rates of pay, although if Walby's speculations are valid then there will not be equality if even if - as is happening - women's qualifications are likely at some stage to overtake those of men at most levels.

Developments since the time of the book

Since that time it is clear that with far higher staying on rates for A - level for both girls and boys that girls do better at A levels and there seems to be some evidence that girls now do better at first degree level. It is slightly more difficult to be certain of this since the degrees taken tend to be in very different subjects. The time taken out from work is typically about 5 years for women with children. It seems likely that in view of government measure to encourage women to work particularly single parents that this time has probably been reduced. This would mean that if experience is the reason for part of the differences, then this should have been reduced with more provision for nurseries etc.

We might note that since the time of Walby's book that there have been some advances for women, if we look at the 'Blair's babes', that is the number of women who enter parliament particularly in the Labour Party in 1997. The term 'Blair's babes' is extremely patronising, but has been widely used by the tabloids. Perhaps less noticed was that in 2004, 6 out of the 12 Liberal Democrat Euro MPs were women.

Walby also noticed the differences in employment rate across the regions e.g. it is much higher in North West England than for example in south Wales. Since the time of her book unemployment has become much lower until recently. We still have problems of interpreting the data about unemployment however since many women who might be looking for work may not be unemployed according to the government figures since they will not have paid the national insurance contributions which would enable them to have clams for benefits.

Whilst Walby does not say this we might assume that in a recession that some women might be more likely to work for especially if the job prospects for their partners or husband seem relatively bleak.

Walby notes the difference in employment rates between the different regions which she attributes to the different industries e.g. the North West had a strong textile base which employed women where south Wales had a stronger coal based employment which was traditional and partly because of legislation was thus much less likely to employ women. The Welsh valleys are still some of the poorer parts of the U.K. It is not however clear how far there were also cultural differences e.g. towards women working in the first place with the south Welsh tradition. It seems possible that the different culture will eventually alter attitudes to work by women, especially as the newer jobs tend to be white-collar ones rather than manual jobs.

Bucking tradition, women are quietly and steadily assuming larger leadership roles across much of Africa. Liberia now has Africa's first elected woman president, Ellen Johnson Sirleaf. Mozambique and São Tomé and Príncipe have women prime ministers and South Africa and Zimbabwe have female vice presidents. Tanzania has a female foreign minister and women hold at least 30% of the legislative seats in Burundi, South Africa and Mozambique. In Rwanda, women hold 48% of the country's legislative seats. In addition a woman heads the Supreme Court and half of the country's judges are women, as are half of its college graduates. Similarly, female dropout rates - once high in Rwanda - have plunged after the country's female minister of education began sending social workers to the home of girls who quit school. The workers now try to find schools closer to home for girls who had to walk too far, for instance, or impress on parents that educating girls is as crucial as educating boys.

We might want to know how wages differ between men and women. In some cases, this could be due to union's pressure where the trade unions are powerful enough. Walby makes the point that male trade unions might be able to exert pressure. It is not however clear why women also could not exert pressure. In other cases as with clerical work it could be due to the different locations. Social Trends shows men are more likely to have access to cars than women or even to travel further to work where wages are higher. Hours of work partly account for the differences in gross pay, with men generally being able to put in more hours and overtime at work than women.

Walby ignores the points made by Professor Hakim that perhaps women are not always pursuing the same objectives as men any way.

Criticism of Braverman

Braverman talks about deskilling of labour and Walby seeks to know why, therefore, such classes as the clerical class have come into this category without mentioning the gender element given the fact that women form a large part of these lower clerical groups. It is not however clear whether Braverman's hypothesis is correct in the first place since it could be argued that in many cases new skills have to be learnt, for example, there is no longer scope for big accounts offices in which many women were employed at the lower levels because of the invention of the computer - and its related skills for usage - which has led to this.

Wages could also differ where there are monopolies or oligopolies that is, either a single or a few buyers of labour respectively. This could apply to the armed forces where governments are the only sources of recruitment or to nursing where governments are amongst the few categories of buyers for this labour market.

This could explain why in most cases, the armed forces seem to have done comparatively well whereas the teachers have seen their pay fall compared to average earnings

Violence against women

Walby also talks about violence. She claims, unlike most sociology writers who see violence as an exception and thus the men who commit these crimes are seen as aberration, violence is much more the norm. As she rightly said it is not always obvious how much violence has decreased and whether, for example, an increase in reported crimes are more due to better reporting leading to this apparent decrease. Some people such as Pizzey who formed the first women's refuge at Chiswick in London have suggested that wife beating occurs partly as a cycle of violence.

She makes the points that violence is spread much more evenly across the socio-economic spectrum than most people would probably have thought. She suggests that this is because a lot of violence is not reported. To illustrate this she quotes Russell as showing that in his survey in the U.S.A, marital rape was consistent across the social spectrum. However the figures she quotes are from the U.S.A and it is not all clear that these would necessarily apply globally. An article in the Guardian in autumn 2004 (based partly on research by Professor Walby) did however show that violence against women still ran at about 2 deaths per week in 2004 in the U.K. This was some 30 years after the publicity given to violence when Erin Pizzey highlighted the need for women refuges. One commentator suggested that the government seemed more interested in fox hunting and cruelty against foxes than cruelty against women. It could be argued, though, that abuse against animals may well lead to abuse against people i.e. cruelty is indivisible. Whilst Walby seems to quote from an alleged Victorian law that the term 'rule of thumb' was the size of the cane that a man could use against a woman it is not clear that such legislation would affect current attitudes. What is perhaps more disturbing was the assumption that women consented to any sex with their husband and it was not until 1991, that is, after Walby's book that there was an offence of marital rape. The argument that few men who committed rape were psychologically disturbed judging by the low rate of referrals to psychiatric help seems to place more reliance on judges' ability at psychology and psychiatry than might have seemed plausible.

Generally in African countries the concept of 'marital rape' is not accepted by the male members of society. A proposal to criminalize marital rape in Malawi in 2001 sparked a fierce debate in the country. In Kenya, the Sexual Offences Bill was watered down when several male MPs refused to pass the Bill if such concepts of marital rape were left in. Most women therefore rarely report being raped in their marriage bed.

Figures on domestic violence are for fairly obvious reasons difficult to determine with accuracy although they are equally likely to be underestimates rather than over estimates.

Walby correctly makes the point that in most cases, violence against women is not from strangers but from people known to the woman. This has not been helped by the undue prominence given to the few cases of abduction, while the media has generally not acknowledged the extent of domestic violence, except in few cases such as those involving prominent sportsmen and other celebrities. In U.K., the police since the release of her book seem to have taken some steps in ensuring women that they have more of a chance of being heard and treated sympathetically.

The State

Walby shows that even the trade unions have relatively few women in high places. She also suggests that it is difficult for women to get elected in political positions. For instance in the U.K., the House of Commons has not been women friendly; there is a shooting gallery but until recently no crèche. In the African context, women have for a long time not been expected or encouraged to take up political leadership positions, because traditionally, their sole responsibility was only limited to taking care of the home. She also points out that Marxist feminists have very little to say about the role of women generally.

Employment

By the year 2008 the U.K. had 70% of women in employment compared with 79% of men. This figure was higher than the EU average at the time, where only 55% of women were employed. Women are far more likely to work part time since in 2008, one half the women were part time where only one in six men were part time employed in the U.K. Total employment for both men and women was around 13.6 million.

In 2002 the number of women unemployed was around 700,000 where it was just under a million for men. For both men and women the unemployment rate was much higher amongst the young, 22% of 16-17 men and 18.3% of women. The number of women unemployed was however lower for all age groups amongst women.

20 years ago, the African women's shares in African labour forces ranged from 17 per cent, in Mali, to 49 per cent in Mozambique and Tanzania. They have always been

active in agriculture, trade, and other economic pursuits, but a majority of them are in the informal labour force. Though their numbers in the labour force have increased in recent years, they are still lower than those of men in employment.

Culture

Until recently, sociologists, often seemed to suggest that children learnt behaviour which was appropriate for their sex; Walby suggests that this is not necessarily helpful. Many examples on this theory are usually given such as giving girls dolls houses, while boys get toy trains. However, this assumes that people are passive and do not react against this. Presumably although Walby does not develop this, girls who are very keen to play football for example will probably eventually get their wishes granted. The assumption that children are always defenceless and never get their own way seems to fly in the way of most observations. Some women presumably would want to be more interested in sport especially if their favourite sportsperson were to continually win. As Walby points out, the socialisation theory doesn't indicate where the ideas come from in the first place. It is not obvious in whose interest such socialisation takes place. What would happen if girls were given toy train sets and men were given dolls houses, would their behaviour be different at a later stage? People often talk about different styles of dress for men and women, but if we look at the museum of children's dress, we sometimes find that what we would regard as female dress has been worn by men.

Some women such as Chodorow suggest that women get used to nurturing and this is the reason why women become oppressed. Chodorow's remedies are criticised by Walby by saying that men should also take part in parenting. However, this does not necessarily seem reasonable since child rearing would seem to be more important than menial work in many factories or the routine jobs within the house such as ironing. The point that Walby makes about the low value given to mothering is perfectly reasonable.

Walby also comments about what she calls the private sphere and public sphere. For instance, she notes that following Florence Nightingale work in the Crimean war, nursing was a function, which could be carried out by women. She does not however seem to notice the determination, which Nightingale showed in getting the nursing function recognised in the first place. At that time, the lack of medical treatment often killed more people than the wars did directly. Walby suggests that women generally could not move out of the women's private sphere which were generally all female communities and had little or no mixing of genders. She also notes the importance of social workers such as Octavia Hill, 1838 -1912.

She does suggest that there is still a great deal of difference between the subjects which women study compared to men. It is not clear why this happens or where the different preferences by men and women come from: is it because careers advisors are suggesting only certain jobs for girls or boys or is it that the parents themselves have decided on the careers which they want for their sons or their daughters?

Walby also suggests that some forms of liberalisation have not helped, such as pornography.

She also points out that some jobs have been helped by changes in technology, the moves towards desktop publishing amongst others. The two world wars have also made a difference, in that, jobs which were thought suitable for women, would not have helped in these two periods.

SELF EXAMINATION QUESTIONS

1. What is stratification? Which are the various types of stratification?

2. What is meant by the term 'social mobility'? What are some of the barriers to class mobility?

3. Which are some of the groups of people that constitute the 'underclass' in society?

4. What is patriarchy? What are the diverging theories of patriarchy that have been advanced to-date by various sociologists?

5. Why is it difficult to formulate a general theory explaining patriarchy?

6. What are the reasons why wages might differ between men and women?

7. Figures on domestic violence are difficult to determine with accuracy. Why is this so?

8. How far is it true that men and women learn their behaviour and functions that are appropriate to their sex when they are young? How does this determine the kind of jobs they take?

Chapter Five

Race

The term race is generally used by people of all walks of life but most sociologists prefer to use the term 'ethnic origin'. This is partly because there is only one race; the human race as judged by DNA sampling. In a DNA sample, one cannot tell whether a person is white or black. It is also partly because the term has often been associated with ideas of racial superiority, from the institutionalized racism, especially in colonial times, to recent times where the effects of neo-Nazism are still felt. Racism has not been confined to problems of one era or area. Some more controversial social scientists have suggested that there are significant differences in IQ level between black and white. However this is highly dubious and it is difficult to test the hypothesis since in the U.S.A experiments have shown that, for instance, on oral tests, a Black person's IQ will differ depending on whether the tests are administered by a white or a black person.

Even if it were to be proved that one race had a higher IQ than another what would we do with information since there would always be a large proportion of the "Inferior race" which had higher IQs than many of the superior race?

Ethnic groups

To define the term 'ethnic group' is often considered a complex task. It could mean a group of people who can be identified by either themselves or others, as belonging to a particular race or group. There is sometimes confusion with Jewish people, as to whether it means those who belong to the Jewish faith, or those who historically/genetically belong to the Jewish race. Hitler in the Second World War would have obviously defined it in terms of the race irrespective of their faith.

An ethnic group or ethnicity can in other cases be defined as a population of human beings whose members identify with each other, either on the basis of a presumed common genealogy or ancestry or recognition by others as a distinct group, or by common cultural, linguistic, religious, or physical traits.[

Travellers

Travellers are in some instances referred to as 'gypsies'. The term 'Gypsies' is in many cases used as a term of abuse. As their name suggests, Gypsies were initially believed to have come from Egypt. The Gypsies' true ancestors, however, were a group of people who left India during the very early centuries (between AD 800 and 950). The gypsies are a race of nomads and some commentators who are opposed to their way of life, and suggest that whilst they have sympathy for the pure Roma, (one of the best known gypsy group, sometimes called Romanies), they do not have much sympathy, for travellers, partly because of the alleged character of untidiness due to their nomadic way of life. There may be differences in culture between gypsies and other people; for example the role of the man as the head of the household is much more emphasised with many gypsy families than it would be the case with other people. The Roma have often been persecuted in other countries particularly in Eastern Europe and this is one of the reasons why they have wanted to emigrate to the United Kingdom. The gypsies were often victims of the holocaust.

Parental background when looking at race

It is not clear, when we talk about ethnic groups, whether we include people whose parents may have come from a different country. Michael Howard, the previous Conservative leader in the U.K., has been described in the press as Jewish, and his parents came here in the 1930s to escape from persecution elsewhere. Some of his relatives were sent to the gas chambers. In February 2005 just before the general election that year one of the headlines in the Daily Mail was the concept that Howard's grandfather who came from Rumania may have been an illegal immigrant. The concept of Michael Howard being Jewish came under more press scrutiny just before the 2005 General Election when the Labour party issued a poster showing him and another member of the shadow cabinet as flying pigs, an action that allegedly caused offence since pigs are regarded as an unclean animal by religious Jews. Similarly, Michael Portillo's -a Conservative Minister- parents emigrated to the U.K. during the Spanish Civil War, in the 1930s to escape from the brutality of Franco, the Spanish dictator.

Comparisons of 1930s and present day

If we look at Europe and the newspaper comments at the time of the 1930s, we will see that the comments about Jews escaping from the Nazi regime and how the Jews were going to spoil the British culture are very similar indeed to the comments that we can still find in many of the tabloids at the present time. The difference is that nowadays there are less press comments about Jews and more about immigrants generally. This is particularly true of asylum seekers. The term itself is often used as one of abuse whereas the term 'refugees' is less prone to this interpretation. An article in the Guardian has compared the comments about Jews then and Muslims now.

Number of people in Ethnic groups

The number of people in the United Kingdom who describe themselves as belonging to a minority or ethnic group was about 4.5 million in 2001-2002, which was about 8% of the population, with the proportions varying rapidly between different areas. Leicester and the East Midlands have one of the highest proportions whilst the north east of England has fairly low proportions. Minority ethnic groups tend to be younger generally than the white population. For example, 19% of the white population were under 16 whereas those describing themselves as of mixed origin 55% were under 16 (source Social Trends). This is important for instance when looking at crime statistics because if the young are the ones who predominantly commit crimes - which is usually the case- then even if there are no differences between ethnic groups and the rest of the population, that is, if we have a standardised population, we would expect to find a higher proportion of ethnic and mixed groups committing more crimes than the white merely because of the age distribution.

Boys between 10-17 are three times more likely to be guilty of crimes than girls and the peak age for committing crimes is 17. The total number of crimes by young people was 100000 in 2008 which was 30,000 lower than the year before

Race and crime

In the U.K., the Caribbean population is over represented in the prison system; sociologists however are divided about why this might be so. It could be partly related to income and class, or it could be as well that the police are more likely to investigate crimes if they feel they are committed by black people. This highlights once again the problems of looking at evidence in sociology. The World Trade Centre disaster on September 11th 2001, added to fears that the Muslims might be targeted. The media in some cases seem to have picked very much on a small group of Muslims who do not seem to want to live a peaceful existence in the U.K. In 2005 it was suggested when there were proposals for a law against racial hatred, that the British National Party was targeting the Muslim population since there were no laws against this yet there were laws against racism. There certainly seemed to be more racism in Northern Ireland after September 11th 2001. Ironically some Sikh people were also attacked partly due to the fact that they wear turbans due to their faith, and the racists assumed that they were Muslims.

Increasingly the Indian community seemed to be trying to enter the professions; this could be seen as a way of overcoming prejudices, or even in some cases as over compensating for perceived or actual racism. In other cases, it might be suggested that the Indian population could be more ambitious than some other ethnic groups.

The Metropolitan police have been accused of being institutionally racist as there are relatively few black people in the police force.

Ethnic group/Race and Size of families

There are differences in size of families between different ethnic groups. Sometimes this is because of such factors as differences in religious opinion and family planning. For example in the Kosovan tradition (Kosovo is at the moment administered partly on behalf of the United Nations and has many residents who claim that they are of Albanian origin but about 10 per cent of the population are Serbian), almost certainly the refugees will have come from the Albanian majority, it would be usual for women to be married as not being married and not having a family would be a disgrace.

According to an article in Social Trends birth rates are highest among minority ethnic groups. The data collected by the Office for National Statistics (ONS) between 1992-1994 and 1997-1999 showed that the number of people from minority ethnic groups grew by 15% compared to 1% for white people.

In its latest quarterly Population Trends report the ONS estimated the number of people from minority ethnic groups in Britain had hit four million - 7% of the population - for the first time. The report said that the age-sex profiles and the proportions of each ethnic group born in the U.K. are greatly influenced by the timing of the various waves of immigration into the country as migrants are mainly young adults

Population growth
Black (Mixed): 49%
Black (African): 37%
Bangladeshi: 30%
Pakistani: 13%
Chinese: 5%
Indian: 4%
White: 1%
Black (Caribbean): 0%
Source: ONS

Those groups that had been in the U.K. for the longest time, tended to have the least growth in their numbers.

Black people of Caribbean origin - who came to the U.K. in large numbers in the 1950s and 1960s - registered no growth at all.

But among black Africans whose immigration to the U.K. peaked in the 1980s and 1990s the growth was 37.

That trend was also reflected among the Asian population with the numbers of people of Bangladeshi origin - whose immigration to the U.K. peaked in the 1980s - up by a third.

However the longer established Indian community grew by just 4%.

Southern bias

The figures also revealed that on average Britain's ethnic minorities have a much younger age profile. The average age for the white population surveyed in the 1997-1999 period was 37 years or less but only 26 years for ethnic minorities. The report concluded: "Their young age structure and the consequential large number of births and relatively small number of deaths helps to explain the disproportionate contribution of minority ethnic groups to population growth in the 1990s.

Significantly the ethnic group with the youngest age profile were those who described themselves as "mixed" with 58% being aged 14 years or under. Overall their numbers increased by 49% in the periods surveyed - the second largest growth among black groups. The report also revealed that most of Britain's ethnic minorities live in England with just 3% living in Scotland, Ireland or Wales. Fewest of all live in Scotland where just 1.7% of people said they belonged to a minority ethnic group.

It also showed that most non-white people are concentrated in the urban areas, particularly in southern England. Nearly half live in London comprising more than a quarter of all residents.

Patterns of Immigration

Although the word 'immigrant' is frequently used in a hostile fashion it should be noted that there has been differences between the ethnic groups which themselves have followed different trends. For example the so called new Commonwealth countries such as India, Jamaica and Nigeria following the British nationality act then refugees of the Asian descent following the 60s and 70s from countries such as Kenya, Malawi and Uganda. The push factor is obvious when we look at refugees of Indian descent being expelled from Uganda in 1972 under the brutal Idi Amin regime (1971 -1979).

Contrary to most people's opinions, there was a net loss of people from the United Kingdom during the 1970s whereas by the year 2000 to 2001, according to Social Trends, there was a net increase in migration of 126,000. Again the total number of asylum seekers remained relatively steadily since 1999 although in August 2003 there was a suggestion there was a fall in applications.

In January 2005 Michael Howard - the then leader of the Conservative Party - said that if his party was elected that they would impose a maximum limit on the number of immigrants who could come in each year and also that there would be a limit on the number of asylum seekers who could come in. The United Nations and the main Refugee bodies as well as the EU said that it would not conform to international obligations.

In June 2004 it was suggested that one in twelve people living in the United Kingdom had been born abroad. These would not necessarily all be immigrants, it could be as in the case of M.C Cowdrey - a former England cricket captain who was born in India - whose parents were British people living abroad. Not all immigrants would be coloured, although most of the prejudice until recently seems to have been directed at coloured people. However perhaps because of the media in the last few years there has been more hostility towards those from Eastern Europe. This increased with the entrance of 10 new countries to the E.U. in 2004 and by another two in 2007.

Most surveys suggest that the populace is very badly informed about the number of people immigrants and in many cases the media manages to confuse people on the difference between asylum seekers and immigrants. It seemed ironic that on the sixtieth anniversary of the liberation of Auschwitz in 2005, there should have been the idea of the limits placed on the total number of refugees who could come into the country. Auschwitz and Belsen were two of the most notorious concentration camps where large numbers of people were exterminated in the gas chambers in the Second World War.

Reasons for discrimination

Some sociologists have suggested that it is partly a legacy from the time of the British Empire, since the British generally assumed that people with coloured skin often belonged to different religions, and people belonging to different religions were generally inferior. Whilst immigrants arrived from so called black Africa at the time of the loss of the empire during the 1950's it is not clear that there is very much of a connection.

Rudyard Kipling a well known English writer perhaps illustrated this attitude best, with his phrase "lesser breeds outside the law" from the poem '*Recessional*'. However; it seems unlikely that many of the young people at the present time would be aware of what the British Empire was. It also seems unlikely that even if they did have an idea of the British Empire that they would have had these views from their studies. Whilst immigrants arrived from black Africa at the time of the loss of the empire during the 1950's it is not clear whether there is very much of a connection between peoples' racist views and the loss of the British Empire. In some respects, we can regard this as part of a class system which has largely come to an end or we can regard it as an extreme form of racial discrimination since the slaves were generally thought of as belonging to inferior races. Adam Hochschild in his book *"Bury the Chains"* shows the sheer extent of slavery and also how a very small pressure group managed to end it. The pressure group included William Wilberforce, 1759 -1833, who for a long while was the only M.P. fighting for the abolitionist causes. The extent of slavery and bondage is amazing. Adam Hochschild reckons that about three quarters of the population of the world were in some form of bondage. During the period of the slave trade over two million people were shipped to the Caribbean area alone.

The abolitionists also included John Newton, 1725 -1807, a former slave trader who like many converts to a cause reacted strongly against his former ideas and fought extremely hard in the abolitionist cause. He is perhaps best remembered however for the tune *"Amazing Grace"*. One of the methods the abolitionists used to get the slave trade abolished was boycotting sugar. Adam Hochschild estimates that at the height of the boycott, sugar sales fell by a third. This was extremely important because of the size of the sugar trade.

Racial image

The image of people from other countries has not perhaps been helped by the proliferation of war films which show American and British troops but seldom show, for example, Indian soldiers even though the Indians lost about as many armed forces as the U.S.A. It might be noted that at the time India comprised what is now India as well as Pakistan as well as Bangladesh. If both U.K. and U.S.A citizens were more aware of this, some of the problems of racism might be alleviated.

In some other cases it may be a throwback to the time when Britain had a huge empire, and partly in order to justify imperialism, people had suggested that the British were superior in some way, particularly to those of other colours, such as black people or Asians. 2000 years of civilisation was contrasted to what was thought to be relatively recent civilisation amongst black people in Africa. It could also be thought of as a variant of social Darwinism, that is ,that countries that were more economically developed were also the most civilised. Critics would probably reply that in practice there is not necessarily much of a link between economic development and civilisation, as the problems of Nazi Germany in the 1930s or the brutal regime of Stalin in Russia would have shown.

In other cases, racism might be yet another form of the problems of the extremely authoritarian people whose own views are so rigid that they cannot cope with people who are different in any way. We can see examples of this in the playground, where children with spectacles, different hair, dress differently from the rest of the class or have any other glaring difference from the rest of the children, will be made fun of or will be subject to insult. Most racists are expected to have an authoritarian personality.

Surveys have shown that men are more likely to admit to being prejudiced than women. There is also a relationship between age and prejudice, with the older people more likely to admit to being prejudiced. Perhaps it is slightly more surprising that the unemployed have often been more hostile to ethnic groups. This however could be explained by the belief – by the unemployed - that the "immigrants have taken our jobs". Surveys have often shown that the number of immigrants in the U.K. is vastly overestimated, with many residents assuming that it is about 20 million whereas the true figure is about 5 million. It is thus not surprising that some people feel that they have been overrun.

Integration

There have been suggestions that people need to be integrated into British society, but it is not quite clear what is meant by British society. Does it mean that they should play the same sports as the British? Eat the food eaten by the British? Could it mean shared values? If so, what are the shared values? We could look at the citizen syllabus to see if this might be helpful not only to newcomers but also to the young people. In Australia people (including the immigrants) have to vote in General Elections and are strongly encouraged to vote in local elections so that they feel part of society.

The late Lord Jenkins (1920 -2003) supported the idea of integration and in 1966 a Race Relations Board was set up to intervene if race discrimination could be proved. However, in 1968 there were laws to control entry into the U.K. and this could be seen as an example of discrimination. Enoch Powell (1912 -1998) once a Conservative front bench spokesman, said, "Like the Romans, I seem to see the River Tiber flowing with much blood." Opinion polls at the time seem to show that the vast majority of the population were sympathetic to his views. He was removed from his shadow position by the then Conservative leader the late Sir Edward Heath because of these words.

Assimilation of ethnic groups

Some people have suggested that ethnic groups need to assimilate. But it is not quite clear what this means. Do they mean that these people in the different ethnic groups should speak in the same way as the local working class? Or, should they adapt to the middle class culture? Others would tend to suggest people need to glorify in their differences. Perhaps, part of the tension is between those who speak English and those who don't. David Blunkett the former Home Secretary suggested that immigrants should speak English at home. It is clear that for white-collar jobs in most cases the ability to speak and write English is helpful. It is not however clear whether being bilingual will help or be a barrier to being able to achieve this. Being bilingual might help to learn another third language. On the other hand it could be argued for many people that having less practice in the English language could push down the performance in the subject.

There are often differences within the ethnic group families in terms of linguistic ability. In cases where the women do not go out to work, the men will often have a better command of English than the women. In addition, where the women go to work, they are more likely to pick up the language as they are more sociable creatures than men. There may also be a generation gap, with the younger generation having more ability to pick up the English language than their parents do. One possibility to overcome this problem would be to allow the parents of school children to attend the same classes as the children if they wished so that they would both improve their English and also have a clearer idea of British education.

Race sport and national identity

Race can often be used as a method of identification but it is not always clear which race people would say that they came from. Lord Tebbitt (a former Conservative Minister in the U.K.) suggested on one occasion that one should see whom people supported in cricket tests. His assumption was that people living in Britain should support England. This would apply even if people came from the West Indies or from India. The whole concept seemed to be odd since relatively few people in the U.K. are interested in cricket if we judge by attendances at matches at county level compared to those supporting local or professional football teams. It also seems sexist since it is quite likely that the majority of English women would not be interested in cricket.

If, however, we apply the same logic to other sports we will find many different ideas; for example in European football or the World Cup many people will support England, Wales, Scotland or Northern Ireland. On the other hand when the Republic of Ireland was the only side from the British Isles left in a football tournament most people seemed to support them. The people of Berwick - an English border town- which plays in the Scottish league are alleged to have problems of knowing who to support when Scotland play England.

At football club level in Uganda more people support Arsenal or Manchester United and will watch them on television, than if the local sides were to play. Globalisation means that people may no longer identify with local team or even with teams in their own country

In February 2005, for the first time ever, a Premier League side, Arsenal (the Premier League is the top division in English football), which has a French manager (Arsene Wenger), fielded a squad without a single British player in it. Increasingly football clubs have had players from a variety of nationalities and also increasingly non-English managers such as the Swedish manager Sven Eriksson.

However the number of black managers of football clubs is very small. In late 2004 Spanish supporters were very racist towards all of the Black English players in a friendly international between England and Spain. It was, for many people, horrifying to hear jungle chants every time a black player was near the ball.

In the Olympics on the other hand Britain has a team which includes people from all the different countries. However most of the notable athletes are from African countries such as Kenya and Ethiopia, who are well known for their runners. Some countries- such as Qatar - have been known, in the recent past, to 'poach' runners from these countries.

In Rugby, Ireland, consists of players from both sides of the border, i.e., Northern Ireland and the Republic of Ireland.

In golf there are occasions when in the Ryder Cup Europe has a team as a whole competing against the United States of America and presumably most British people would identify with the European team.

Identification with the Nation State

We tend to take it for granted nowadays that the nation state is important, and that most people will associate themselves with a particular nation. The nation state itself tended to date from the 16th century. The philosopher John Locke (1632 -1704) who was in favour of religious tolerance in the late 17th century did not extend this to Roman Catholics since he assumed that they owed allegiance to a foreign power, that is the Pope in Rome.

However, in the U.K. some surveys have shown that people will associate with a smaller part of the U.K. rather than the whole U.K. In the North of England some people may associate themselves with Yorkshire. The Welsh and Scots associate themselves with Wales and Scotland, respectively rather than the U.K. A few people associate themselves with being European and this is also true of the other 26 countries within the European Union. In some cases as with shown in the 1930's some people of German origin identified with the wider Germany even though at the time they were living in either Austria or Czechoslovakia. In the U.K. the boundaries are fairly well defined except in the case of Northern Ireland where at the time of partition in 1922 the boundaries were set in the hope that they would always give a Protestant majority. In some other countries as for example with the Basques in Spain, there is a wish by some of them to form a separate country. In other cases as with the Kurds in the Middle East they formed a separate group in many ways as in Iraq but do not have a national home.

Race and fostering

There has been a shortage of black foster parents, and some Social Services have tried to match up foster parents with the same ethnic group of child. The current fashion is that children should have people from the same ethnic background, since they should learn about their culture. It is not quite clear why this would always be helpful since in some cases the children themselves would not identify in the same way - as the Social Services - how they should be classified. Surveys have shown that people who have been in care often have stronger prospects of going to jail than other members of society, so even allowing for the problems of distinguishing between causality and correlation it would seem helpful to have - as a main aim - keeping them out of care if at all possible.

It has often been assumed that mixed race children lack self esteem but there seems little validity in this belief. There have been a number of people of mixed race who are proud of both sides of their family and are not happy to be labelled for example as either white or black.

Link between religion and ethnic groups

There is a link between religion and ethnic groups. Whilst there are white English Muslims, the majority of Muslims will be of other ethnic groups. In the U.K., there have been suggestions that Muslims should have their own schools, in the same way as the Church of England, or Roman Catholic schools, although other people have suggested that this would be divisive.

In early 2005 there was controversy about how far Muslim schools would enable people to be able to cope with British society as a whole. The Muslim population has often had a more puritan attitude than the rest of the population, so there can be problems arising from this

Anti Racism Bodies

The anti Nazi league was formed in the late 1970's. The idea of the league was to have a single body which would fight against racism and during the 1970's they managed to organise large scale carnivals to demonstrate against racism. Whilst many people attended these, there seems to have been no lasting impact. Some local authorities notably the former Greater London Council (GLC) were very strongly against racism and tried to use newspapers advertisements and other forms of communication to stress the need to be anti racist. There was also an anti apartheid movement which was set up to oppose the apartheid system in South Africa. It tried to use different methods including getting boycotts by Barclays Bank employees because of the bank's investments in South Africa.

Racist Parties

During the 1970's the National Front fought many local and Parliamentary elections although without success at the Parliamentary level. The British National Party is now the main racist party which gained quite a large number of votes in the European elections in 2004 and 2009 gaining two seats in the European parliament and also in the General Election 2005 without gaining a seat. The leaders will deny that the party is racist although a B.B.C documentary showed the extent of violence within the party.

Sociologists have used experiments to test the extent of discrimination where actors applied for jobs and it was found that in most cases white actors were preferred to black actors. This method is highlighted in the Penguin book on Racial Discrimination in

England 1968. The book is old but the method of approach is a good one and it seems likely that many of its conclusions are still valid. It is not at all clear whether laws which are meant to lead to equal opportunities however have had any effect on this.

There seems to have been differences for example between the discrimination between different types of jobs with less discrimination against women than with men.

Eugenics

Partly because of the domination of much of the world by the Europeans, there was an interest - particularly in the early 20th century - in a pseudo science called eugenics. This seemed to show that there were differences in brain sizes between different races using odd experiments. Frances Galton is often associated with this concept. He was a relative of Charles Darwin and well known in the field of statistics .The science however was not just about race but tended to lead to a belief about who should be allowed to breed and who shouldn't. Some famous names have been associated with eugenics such as Sir Winston Churchill. In some respects Eugenics seems to have been very similar to the ideas of social Darwinism. In 2004 one of the leading doctors, suggested that people whose children were likely to have criminal tendencies should not have children. There is very little evidence that brain size is very much to do with intelligence anyway.

The Nazis carried on with similar ideas with some of their scientists trying to prove that the Nordic races were superior, say, to the Jews. Joseph Mengele is well known as a Nazi who carried out experiments on identical twins before finally sending them to the gas chambers. The Nazis had very many similar ideas about a whole variety of different races and this showed with their treatment of prisoners in both ordinary prisoner of war camps as well as in the concentration camps. One of the concerns is not that a few people were racist, but that in contrast to many people's ideas, there was little opposition by the majority to the horrors of threats and deaths to the Jewish community. The phrase "for evil to prevail it is only necessary for good people to do nothing" seems to be appropriate. It is very noticeable that whereas the majority of the Dutch Jews were killed by the Germans, this did not apply in Denmark. The Danish took the view that all the Jews were also Danish and therefore the police did not cooperate with the German authorities and only about 150 Danish Jews were killed. These ideas about race were however not confined to Germany and in the 1920's laws were passed in the U.S.A to prevent people of allegedly inferior races that is, from Eastern and Southern Europe, from being able to immigrate so easily to the U.S.A. The Greeks described outsiders as barbarians and Jews were expelled from England in 1290 and there had been a massacre of Jews in York in 1190. It was not until 1655 that they formally returned to England during the period of the commonwealth. Dislike of Jews can be seen in Shakespeare's play Shylock.

The Nazis had to modify their ideas on race when Japan fought on their side in the Second World War, and the Japanese were denoted as honorary Aryans. The Japanese at that time also regarded other races as inferior. What the Nazi's experience does show is that it is easy to convince people that racism is justified. The use of scapegoats is very common, especially with authoritarian people as blaming other people rather than ourselves (for problems) is very convenient.

Root causes of racism

Little attention seems to have been paid as to why racism exists. It may be partly that people have always worried about other people who seem to be different. This would be particularly true of very authoritarian people.

Professor Zygmunt Bauman

He has made a thorough study on the reasons why the Holocaust could take place. He suggests that people see other ways of life as threatening the existing population. This might be in line with Mrs Thatcher's phrase of British culture being swamped by immigrants. In extreme cases, extermination would be the final answer to the problems. He also suggests that the phrase "I was only following orders" can be a problem of extreme bureaucracy where people do not question orders from above.

New Racism

Some sociologists have talked about the New Racism. Martin Barker, in 1981 had a book published on this issue. The new racism according to them is based on the idea that different cultures will have different characters. This does not necessarily have to be because of biological reasons. The assumption, however, is still that some groups - notably the Aryans - are superior.

Racism and violence

Racism has been a problem for many years. Hostile attitudes towards other races had perhaps its best known effect in the Second World War with Nazi Germany when about 6,000,000 Jews were killed in concentration camps along with homosexuals and gypsies etc. It is not however just an old problem. More recently in the Balkans in the 1990s the concept of ethnic cleansing has come into modern conversation. This means that everyone not of the right race has to be either killed or at least removed from the area.

In most cases racism may be present but is unlikely to lead to such extreme violence.

Part of the problem is that it is difficult to find someone who will describe themselves as a racist. In some cases racism is difficult to distinguish from nostalgia. Such people will hark back to the good old days, and this will apply to the idea that there were no people of other races living in the area at that time. In some cases, as with the inner city areas, there are problems which are associated with the current ethnic groups even though the problems pre-date the entry of most of them.

Race and ethnic educational performance

It is a mistake however to think that all ethnic groups are the same, or even that gender does not matter. Girls from the Caribbean group have consistently done much better than the boys in education. We will see that there are strong differences between the ethnic groups. This would not be in line with the racist ideas of inferiority, nor on the other hand can racism explain the differences unless we assume that racists very much distinguish between some of the ethnic groups and the others.

When looking at ethnic groups we can look at different ideas; different ethnic groups will have different size families. Evidence from other countries seem to suggest that in many cases the second or third generation will have a family size which is nearer to that of the country in which they are living. Larger families might be expected to have slight differences in education or performance from smaller families, since they are likely to have less income per head.

There are differences also of the percentage of one-parent families; this could sometimes be due to religious influences. In the 19th century it is alleged that some Christian groups suggested to the West Indians that black people should not marry.

There are also differences in education between the different ethnic groups, and the Sikh group which is mainly originally from India has often done better than many other people of different ethnic groups. It is not clear quite why this might be so, although it could be argued that a puritan culture which encourages hard work is more likely to be successful in educational performance.

There are also differences in both patterns of employment and unemployment with the different ethnic groups. Self-employment has been much more common amongst people of Indian extraction; this can have two possible causes. It could be seen as a method of over-coming racial discrimination or it could be because the extended family system is more common and self-employment gives the family the opportunity to use informal method of credit and an opportunity for the whole family to take part.

Rastafarians and black racism

Rastafarians have been more influential in the U.S.A, than in other countries. Their beliefs are based on the works of Marcus Garvey 1887-1940. He believed that the whites and blacks could not get on together and they needed a separate home land in Africa. Some of the followers assume that Haile Selassie (Emperor of Ethiopia from 1930-1975) would organise the transport of black people to Ethiopia and so they would no longer be subject to Western imperialism.

Does lack of English knowledge worsen racism?

If we look at the opportunities for people of different races, problems seem to be more acute where a different language is spoken at home. This can cause more problems for women who are more likely to be at home, and therefore not exposed to English as the language, whereas the men going out to work, will usually have to speak some English. In some cases in the public sector where people require information for example, about medical treatment, taxation or benefits there is adequate language provision but in other cases just a dictionary has been provided. The National Health Service as well as Social Services have increasingly tried to make sure that leaflets are available in relevant languages.

Attitudes toward asylum seekers

The debate about where asylum seekers should go and whether they should be allowed into the country in the first place was a problem from 2003. The media were very hostile to asylum seekers. It is not clear whether the readers of the newspapers really understood much about the asylum seekers. In many cases it would seem that hostility towards accommodation for asylum seekers would be linked with racism although the organisers of such protest would often seem to suggest they were not. The extreme right wing parties such as the British National Party would often seek to suggest linkage between asylum seekers and crime.

Racism and legislation

The first main law against racism in the U.K. was the Race Relations Act of 1976. This applied to employment including recruitment as well as promotion and training. There are a few exceptions, such as acting, where someone of a particular colour or racial group might be required.

The Race Relations Act was amended in 2000 but positive discrimination is still not allowed. This means that even if some ethnic groups are under represented they cannot be given first place over other ethnic groups.

Police and ethnic groups

In spite of this, differences still seem to occur, and the McPherson Report talked about institutional racism within the Metropolitan Police Force in London. This followed the murder of a black teenager - Stephen Lawrence - which did not seem to have been taken too seriously during the when investigation. It may be that if we look at the number of black police officers, we see that they are underrepresented in terms of total number for example in London. There have been a few high profile black policemen but in general they are not represented in the higher ranks. One exception was the present Chief Constable of Kent, Bob Ayling who was appointed in 2003. He was the first Black person to hold such a rank.

Race as Scapegoat

Hitler, as with some other Germans blamed the Jews for the fact that the Germans had lost the First World War. During the depression following the Great Crash of 1929 when unemployment started to rise, both in the U.S.A and across of most of Western Europe people were looking a) to solve the problems, b) in many cases to find a scapegoat for the problems. During high unemployment periods, often called recessions, it becomes generally easier to blame other groups for the problems of society. In some cases the stereotype would be as in Nazi Germany, that the Jews controlled the main firms and industries, and that they were therefore responsible for the ills of unemployment. In the case of the Nazi they themselves burned down the German Parliament called the Reichstag in 1933. They then blamed the Jews for this and many people chose to believe this.

Scapegoat and Unemployment

In other cases scapegoating is the other way around; that at the time when unemployment was very high in the U.K. that most of the 3 million unemployed were scroungers and many of these were from the different ethnic groups. As we mention elsewhere it is often easy to find selective evidence we can find some people from the ethnic groups who are not making an effort to find a job and then using inductive methods to assume that this is true of the whole population.

At the other end of the spectrum, people have sometimes argued that if it was not for immigration, the native white English people would have been able to get jobs. One does not have to believe in Say's law; that an increase in population will increase both demand and supply, to realise that more people will create more demand. For some time some economists particularly from the Chicago school seemed to believe that a free market economy would create full employment and this would be the case unless there were artificial obstacles. Over the years the British population has increased considerably, without necessarily an overall increase in unemployment for example during the period 1945 – 1960.

Immigrants and the inner city

There has usually been a pattern across Western Europe and other countries that the inner city has tended to decline, whilst the suburbs have become the areas in which to live. Sociologists have often referred to "push and pull" factors to explain this. In the 19th century there were often immigrants from Eastern Europe particularly when the Russians had periods in which they blamed the Jews for problems. There were outbreaks of violence particularly in 1859, 1871 and 1905. These led to waves of emigration where some people emigrated to the U.K.

Immigrants and poor housing

In the 20th century black and Asian people were often used as the scapegoats for problems which have historically occurred in the inner city, for example, less attention has been paid to the houses in these areas, and they have often therefore deteriorated. This has sometimes led to lower relative house prices, compared to the rest of the areas around them. There has also been a higher crime rate. This is nothing new as can be seen from the time of Jack the Ripper case in the 19th century when the crime rate in the Whitechapel area in the East End of London was very high.

Sometimes, there has been a higher crime rate amongst black or Asian people, but one would need to look at the data to see whether this was due to the age structure of the ethnic minorities before jumping to further conclusions

Some people have suggested that higher unemployment rates amongst people of different ethnic groups would prove either of two things: **a)** that it must be because of racism; **b)** it clearly shows that people from different ethnic groups are more likely to be scroungers. Once again, we would need some statistical evidence. One would need to know how far higher unemployment was linked to the types of jobs that people had previously been employed in; in most recessions, the percentage of people unemployed who were previously in unskilled manual work would be much higher than for people in the professional classes. Therefore, if people of Pakistani origin have a higher unemployment rate, one would need to look at this figure first before jumping to conclusions.

More details of this can be found in *Minority Ethnic Groups and Crime: Findings from the Offending, Crime and Justice Survey 2003*. This survey was carried out by interviewing people and may not necessarily tally with police figures.

Ethnic groups are not necessarily the same as racial groups; and even within racial groups, some may not feel that they share an identity. Indian Muslims may well feel more allegiance to being a Muslim than to being Indian. There may also be other subcultures within what would normally be regarded as one ethnic group. India is such a large country that the Bengali population might well regard itself as slightly different from people with other Indian origins, such as the Punjabis.

Emigration and immigration

Whilst sociologists have often looked at immigration to the U.K., less attention has been paid to emigration from the U.K. In the 1950's many British people took advantage of a £10 fare to Australia to emigrate. In most cases they had to have sponsors in Australia to guarantee their conduct. This is important since many ordinary people have heard the argument about overcrowded Britain yet for a long while the reality was that more people were going from Britain than coming into the country. The new arrivals generally occupied proportionately less land since they tended to go to the urban area and had smaller houses than the average member of the population.

The move to Australia was because in the aftermath of the Second World War Australia seemed to be an attractive place to go, with more egalitarian tendencies and more opportunities for the working class. Jobs were available particularly for skilled workers and greater amounts of space for housing meant that people could find this attractive especially if they had lived in overcrowded areas.

In Britain until recently most immigrants came from the New Commonwealth partly because of language ties, and partly because as in the 1950's they were encouraged to do so to fill gaps in the Labour market. The New Commonwealth was those countries in both Asia and in Africa as well as the Caribbean where the inhabitants were non-white. Enoch Powell a Conservative Minister when Minister of Health encouraged nurses to come from the West Indies. It seems ironic that Enoch Powell who had been a professor in Australia had not noticed that the white Australians had been immigrants who had not behaved well toward the native population .Even now there are a high proportion of nurses and other NHS staff who have a different ethnic background. As we noticed in the section on employment, people from ethnic groups are very much concentrated into certain occupations.

Racism within Britain

Whilst problems of race are often assumed to be people from outside of the U.K. coming into the U.K., it could be argued that there is racism within the U.K. itself. The Welsh have often felt particularly in the rural areas that the English have brought second homes at the expense of the Welsh since the increased demand leads to higher house prices that local people, particularly those in the agricultural sector, cannot afford. There have also been tensions between those who want to extend the use of the Welsh language and those who do not. In Wales most road signs are bilingual as are railway station names; not all people approve of this especially in those parts of Wales where Welsh is not much spoken. Some more extreme Welsh Nationalists have been able to whip up hatred against the English although this seems to have died down.

Race and Employment

One of the problems for ethnic groups is that in some cases qualifications from one country are not recognised in another country. For example people who served in the army in the Second World War and immediately afterwards could often only get unskilled work in the transport industry in spite of their experience.

Ethnic groups; concentration in certain occupations

Ethnic groups tend to be heavily concentrated in some areas of work; they are more likely to be found in transport rather than in communication or in public administration education and health. This may be partly due to the pull factor, for example, in the 1950's people from the West Indies were strongly encouraged to come to Britain to fill the shortages in the NHS.

However, some of the public sector - notably the army - has a very low proportion of ethnic groups. This and the relatively low number in the police force does mean that few black people are seen in positions of authority. There are also differences in the number of people who are self-employed perhaps contrary to the usual impression it is the Pakistani and Bangladeshi group who are most strongly likely to be self-employed with the Indian population only slightly more likely to be self-employed than the white population. The Chinese with about 19% self-employed in 2001-2002 were also the group with the second highest percentage. This may reflect the types of jobs in which they are in such as restaurant trade for the Chinese. In contrast the black population seems to be under-represented. The groups most likely to have a degree were Chinese (31%), Indian (25%), and white Irish (24%), compared with 17% of white British people. However, a relatively high proportion of Chinese people had no qualifications (20%), compared with 15% of white British people.

In 2005 55% of whites gained 5 GCSEs (grade C or above) or more whereas for Chinese the % was 81 but for African it was only 48.3% and for Caribbean 41.7% (Source: Social Trends).

In 2002 only one chief constable out of 53 was from an ethnic group and only 369 sergeants were from ethnic groups compared with 18,674 altogether

Self-employment could possibly be seen as protection against prejudice on the part of other people or could be seen as part of the extended family system. It seems likely that this is much more common in the Indian Sub-continent ethnic groups even amongst middle class families whereas it is comparatively unusual amongst the white middle class. The extended family structure may mean that it is easier both to find finance for a small business and also to staff it than for some ethnic groups.

Far more black people are in prison, possibly due to a variety of factors, such as, the difference in age structure, the discrimination of the legal system or possibly due to different families' structures or income.

The Race Relations Amendment Act 2000 tried to strengthen the law, but did not allow for positive discrimination. There is always the problem that people regard all ethnic groups as the same, even though the differences between the groups may be as varied as between the white population and the rest.

In 2001 – 2002 people from the minority groups had higher unemployment rates than those in the white group. The unemployment rate was high for the 16-24 age group, but again there were differences with 37% of young Bangladeshi people whereas it was 11% for young white people.

Immigrants at the present time

In 2005 before the General Election of that year, there were calls by the Conservative party to set an agreed limit on the amount of immigration on an annual basis whereas in the 1970s there had been a net outflow of people; more people emigrated than we received immigrants, this position has changed so that by 1997 the year when the present government took power there was a net inflow of 46,800. In 2008 It was estimated that average net immigration was 160,000 during the preceding decade.

There were three main groups of immigrants. There are asylum seekers who numbered under 45 000 per year in 2004 which was down in previous years. Obviously this figure has its origins in the amount of conflict in other countries for example, the conflict in former Yugoslavia means that the U.K. had Kosovan refugees for the first time during the 1990s when previously this would have not been an obvious place for them to come to. This number has been reduced partly because of government restriction on numbers. The massacre of around 8000 Muslims at Srebeniza Bosnia 1995 meant that many Muslims feared for their lives. Overall, the main number of new people is from workers and the majority of these are not the unskilled workers which we might expect, but the professional and managerial kind. In some cases as with the health service and the teaching profession the government has made an effort to bring these people into the U.K. to fill in the gap which exists. The alternative would seem to be to pay people in those jobs more or use non monetary methods to keep them in the jobs such as reducing the workload for teachers.

A large number of foreign workers are from the EU with over ½ million in 2003. This would be difficult to alter since one of the main features of the EU is that there should be free movement of labour and this would be a logical extension of free trade. The late Milton Friedman who is often associated with right wing economic views generally supported the concept of free movement of labour to move to all areas whenever they wish to.

There have been arguments about how far the U.K. needs more economic migrants in the first place. Farm labourers often do the work that the native population does not want to do. In this case the migration may be seasonal since students from Eastern

Europe may well be able to get extra cash, which will be low by British standards, but which will be high by Eastern European standards and therefore the British farmers gain the labour that they want. The U.K., as with most western European nations has had a low birth rate which will make it difficult to maintain numbers of people in the NHS career's jobs in the future unless something happens to alter this trend.

Population Highlights (Source: Social Trends)

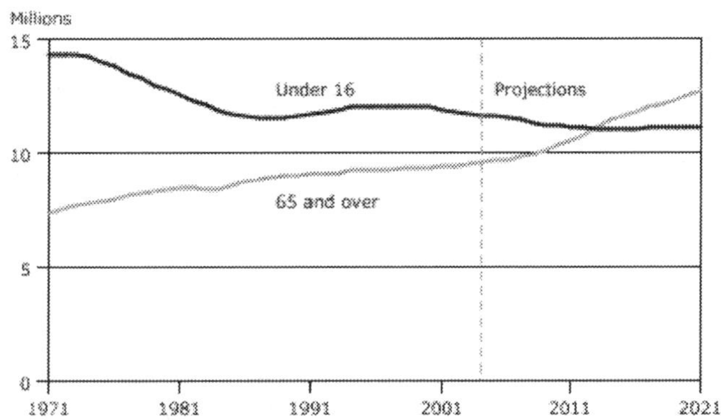

Under 16s and people aged 65 and over, U.K.

There are more people living in the United Kingdom than there have ever been – 59.6 million people in 2003.

Information on population estimates: The United Kingdom has an ageing population. Between 1971 and 2003 the number of people aged 65 and over rose by 28 per cent while the number of under 16s fell by 18 per cent.

Information on the ageing population: The Mixed ethnic group has the youngest age structure of all the main ethnic groups in Great Britain – 50 per cent were aged under 16 in 2001. There were 696,000 live births in the United Kingdom in 2003 – the largest single year change since 1979 and the highest number since 1999.

Information on fertility: In 2003, Wales gained 15,000 people from net migration within the United Kingdom and Scotland gained 13,000 people. England experienced a net loss of 28,000 people.

In 2003 an estimated 151,000 more people arrived to live in the United Kingdom for at least a year, than left to live elsewhere.

Below the rank of consultants, the National Health Service would find it very difficult to maintain reasonable quality of service if it was not from people from the ethnic groups.

The Chinese are found more frequently in the highest social economic groups, for example, those earning more than about £600 a week, and the unemployment rate for the Chinese is relatively low The Indian population has a relatively high proportion of people going into the Universities.

There may be unintentional racism if local authorities or more frequently housing associations nowadays insist that they would give priority to people with family connections in the area or to people who have lived in the area for a while, then it would be more difficult for the ethnic groups in many cases to get priority.

One of the reasons why many people from the so-called New Commonwealth came to the U.K., immediately after the Second World War, was that they had been involved either directly in the armed forces or indirectly through other war work, especially those from the Caribbean.

They often filled posts which the population seemed reluctant to fill, especially as full time employment; for example many West Indians gained work on the buses and other transport undertakings.

Racists

One of the aspects of racists is that they are likely to be authoritarian and are often very pre-occupied with power and status. In many cases they will see coloured people carrying out more menial jobs thus reinforcing their prejudice that black people are incapable of carrying out higher level tasks. In many cases they will also be very prone to bullying people who are below them in status. Given that ethnic groups are often over represented in the lower ranks, this will make it easier for them to be racist. Authoritarians will often be hostile to what Theodor Adorno calls the 'out groupers.' This will be easy to do with coloured people since it is easy to detect such characteristics.

Marx himself talked about false consciousness, where people are influenced in the way that they are taught and will act upon these premises rather than on reality.

SELF EXAMINATION QUESTIONS

1. Differentiate between 'race' and 'ethnicity'.

2. What do certain sociologists say is the relationship between different races and the size of their families? What about the relationship between race and sense of national identity?

3. What is 'eugenics'? Why was there an increased interest in eugenics in the early 20th century?

4. Some sociologists have suggested that discrimination is partly a legacy from the time of the British Empire. How far is this true? What other reasons could there be for discrimination?

5. There have been suggestions to have ethnic groups integrated and assimilated in to the British society. What are some of the challenges that face these processes, and why?

6. What do some sociologists consider to be the relationship between ethnicity and crime/violence in society?

7. A puritan culture which encourages hard work is likely to be successful in educational performance and general success in life. How far is this true and how do different ethnic groups compare in this aspect?

8. What is the difference between 'emigration' and 'immigration'? What is more prevalent in Britain, and why?

9. Employment qualifications differ from one country to another. How does this affect the employment levels and rates of concentration in certain occupations for ethnic groups that have emigrated from their countries of origin?

Chapter Six

Urbanism

Growing importance of the urban area

In the United Kingdom - until the 18th century - most people lived in the rural areas. There were some exceptions notably London as the major commercial centre and a few other major cities such as Bristol and Norwich although these were very small in comparison to London. London had a population of 200,000, as early as the 1600s and had long been the biggest city in the U.K. By far the majority of people would however have worked in what is usually called primary industries. Primary industries include agriculture, forestry and fishing as well as extraction industries such as coal mining and more recently oil from the North Sea. Because of the limitations of the road system which meant that journeys were very slow and also therefore expensive, the majority of produce, unless very valuable, would only be transported locally.

Changes in the 19th Century

The 19th century was the age of urbanism. In 1801 it was estimated that only 1/5 of the population in the U.K. lived in towns or cities, by 1901 the proportion was 4/5. Friedrich Engels (1820 –1895) who worked closely with Karl Marx vividly described the problems of the slums with poor sanitation, drainage and unpaved streets. At the time of his writing, land use planning was almost unknown and so ventilation and sanitation from working houses was poor. He also commented about the physical segregation of the poor and the rich where the working class were generally living close to their place of work often in factories or mills with the middle class living slightly further away. Houses were often overcrowded and cellars often used as dwellings. Whilst some sociologists have disputed the degree of segregation, what is easily identified is the difference in living standards between the poor and the rich. A government report in 1842 on *"The sanitary conditions of the labouring population of Great Britain"* highlighted the difference in mortality rates between Manchester and rural England as well as between the classes. It should be noted that this report was published just before Engels and Marx wrote the Communist Manifesto.

The rural areas are slightly glamorised in John Constable (1776 –1837) pictures which show a slightly idyllic countryside, but there were also many disadvantages of rural living. John Constable is often described as the first of the modern landscape artists and his pictures being commonly reproduced, many of us will have their impressions of this period from pictures rather than from more detailed analysis. Local populations in the rural areas were very susceptible to either gluts leading to low prices or famine. If you have studied economics you will be aware of the cobweb theorem explaining the interaction between high prices one year following shortages and the likely reactions the next year. Changes in the price of wheat also had very strong effects on the lives of the urban poor since they would spend a high proportion of their money on basic foodstuffs.

Durkheim, who deals with the idea of division of work, suggests that this in turn led to concentration of workers in a particular area. Wirth suggests that as time goes on people move away from local kinship groups and secondary groups become more important. Is it less importance of families that leads to more impersonal towns or is it that as people move to towns there is less importance for kinship groups?

Poverty in rural and urban areas

Though many social commentators including Karl Marx observed the realities of poverty in the towns, it should be realised that it is an over simplification to think that the countryside was necessarily preferable. Perhaps the clearest example of this is the famine in Ireland in the 1840s, which was a predominantly rural country apart from Belfast and Dublin. Ireland then was one country and not separated into Northern Ireland and the Republic of Ireland as it was then part of Great Britain. From Ireland perhaps one million people either emigrated or died in the 1840's which was one of the many reasons which lead to the repeal of the Corn Laws which kept up the price of food. The Irish emigration was both to the U.S.A and to become navigators, usually abbreviated as *navvies*, in the United Kingdom. Thus the migration was by no means confined to the United Kingdom.

It is estimated that during the 19th century perhaps 25% of the Swedish population emigrated mainly to the United States of America. The repeal of the Corn Laws in the 1840s showed that there were tensions between the manufacturers and the farming community. The manufacturers wanted cheap food for their workers, sometimes for altruistic reasons and sometimes - as the Marxists would suggest - so that wages could be lower while the farmers wanted high prices to be maintained. The ruling class were therefore not necessarily united. It also highlighted differences within the Tory party with Sir Robert Peel as leader acceding to the repeal whilst the more reactionary Tories such as the Duke of Wellington thought that the pressure from the Irish should not have led to the repeal. There were also pressures from Cobden and

Bright who are often regarded as the leaders of the anti Corn Law league who were doing this for altruistic reasons.

Transport and its effects

Few people had any form of transport apart from walking as the carriages were confined to the relatively few rich people. The quality of the highways even in towns was poor. This led to the invention of the sedan chair. A sedan chair meant that a person was carried in a type of closed carriage carried by two men. The main need for the urban area apart from the few major cities such as London was to act as a market town where mainly local produce would be sold. The pattern of these towns can be seen in many of the older towns in the United Kingdom; usually they would be linear partly because of the inadequacy of the road system, and with the shopping centre being about 1-2 kilometres from the residential area as most people would not wish to walk longer. There is also often a market square where richer people might have been able to obtain basic goods and luxuries. Markets on the whole would be selling a very limited range of goods, such as wheat, meat, fruit and vegetables. Until the coming of the faster sailing ships and steel ships and also the railways, most produce would have been very local. This is a contrast to the present day supermarkets where fruit and vegetables are available all through the year. Apart from poor food, outbreaks of cholera and other diseases were quite common, partly because of lack of drainage systems and also because of lack of pure water.

The industrial revolution and urbanisation

At the time when Marx was writing, the growth of the large towns was well on its way and steel processes had lead to large-scale firms. The 19th century was often said to be the age of urbanism in the West and certainly this is true of the United Kingdom. We can still see the influences of the industrial revolution near the Ironbridge Museum in Shropshire and see how Abraham Darby "The Quaker Ironmaster" had been partly responsible for the plants at Coalbrookdale. Most of the industries at that time and for a long while after were located near water such as rivers or canals. This was partly because rivers gave the water used in the processing of steel and partly because the sea and river provided the cheapest and most efficient form of transport compared with a highway system which was usually slow and could not transport heavy loads at that time.

The influence of this location has had an effect even where the location has changed of the original industry. This is because most people would not have wished to live near the noisy and very visually intrusive steel mills especially the rich people. The poorer people often flocked to the towns for both pull and push reasons. The agricultural revolution meant that few poorer people had their own land. This was partly because of the enclosure movement, which meant that a lot of what had previously been common land was enclosed. Also crop rotation meant that more produce could be obtained on the same patch of land. It also meant that fewer jobs were necessary since the same production could be gained with fewer people. This is the push factor. At the same time there was a growth of factory employment in the town pulling most people into the towns. The advantages of factory employment were that work was available throughout the year, which was not the case for the agricultural sector. In the early stages of industry, families were often employed as a whole, rather than as individuals although this changed later.

In many cases with deindustrialisation in the latter part of the 20th century the Docklands areas and warehouses tended to be derelict which made the cities seem unpleasant. This meant that there was a vicious circle where the richer people moved out while poorer people stayed towards the centre now usually called the inner city areas where previously the term slums was more frequently used. We could suggest that there was a pull factor for the poorer people to live in the inner cities since they would work in shifts and public transport would often not be available for example to ensure they got to their shifts at 6 a.m. It was also extremely unlikely that they would have their own form of transport. Where locations hadn't changed the pattern was still similar. For example in the 1990s on the Isle of Sheppey, the poorer people lived near Sheerness Steel whilst richer people lived a couple of kilometres away at Minster on Sea or sometimes on the mainland. The suburbs on the other hand exerted a pull factor for the growing middle class since it offered more pleasant surroundings.

The industrial revolution and life expectancy

The industrial revolution had an effect in turn on life expectancy since with higher real incomes eventually people have longer lives in spite of the appalling pollution. It altered both the location of the industry and also led to the opening up of the coal mining industry. In turn the coal mining industry often had a multiplier effect attracting other industries to come near to it.

The range of goods for the average poor person in the early 19th century would be very limited mainly involving the staple diet of bread, eggs, flour, bread, milk, cheese, potatoes, a limited amount of meat and possibly other vegetables. Water supply as well as the range of fruit and vegetables was also limited in towns. There was no real method of keeping perishable products for most poor people although the largest richest houses might have had an icehouse to keep some things fresh. We might note this in contrast to modern supermarkets where it has been estimated that a fairly typical medium sized supermarket will stock 40,000 items or more.

Town or city leaders and the urban environment

In the 19th century, where local politicians perhaps had greater power, one could see the influence of the city leaders. Joseph Chamberlain in Birmingham created wide streets and a Civic Centre, amongst other things, which was in keeping with Birmingham's claim to be the second city in England (Manchester and Liverpool might well dispute this claim). The railways were often re-routed in the countryside because of the influence of landowners; in the towns however, poorer houses were often destroyed to make way for the railways or at a later stage for newer roads. In other countries, noticeably in France, slums in the 19th century were destroyed in order to have, as the French leaders would see it, a suitable, grandiose town worthy of being the capital of France (Paris). We can see a similar pattern at the present time as the Chinese prepared for the Olympic Games in Beijing in 2008; they were drastically altering cities such as Beijing and other large cities, partly in order to give a good impression of the Chinese economy. In fairness it should be added that, as far as one can judge it, the Chinese economy is expanding quite rapidly even with the credit crunch.

Towns and open spaces

The Victorians, perhaps belatedly, recognised the need for open spaces as well as parks. Partly for this reason, Epping Forest (which is to the East of London) and which had been encroached on considerably by urban development was recognised as a recreational area for Londoners and was kept as an open space.

The Victorians also built public parks as well as keeping the Royal Parks, which already existed and were there for use by Londoners. In other major towns some parks were also built. Similarly, in the post-war years, in Britain, the 1947 Town and Country Planning Act created a green belt of about 15 to 20 km. from the centre of London. The problem of the capitalist system is that many residents want to be the ones who are nearer to the countryside, and it becomes what the economists would call a zero sum game; that one person can only gain at the expense of somebody else. It would also lead to leapfrogging as people who were previously on the edge of the country now find houses beyond them and in turn will want to move on.

The economists often use the phrase 'public goods' to denote goods and services which are used up by greater use. These are usually things such as defence, but also include parks and open spaces. Clearly, a business, which is out to make profit, would not usually create parks or open spaces. There have been some exceptions as with some of the Nash buildings near the Regents Park area and squares in central London, whereby buildings were built with a square in the middle, perhaps only available for use to the residents of those fifty to sixty houses. Clearly, in order to have parks or open spaces one would need either the public sector or a large-scale landlord to be involved. The London Docklands Development Corporation, with its power to get rid of derelict buildings, compulsory purchase, as well as being involved in the transport network, has an advantage over most small private landlords who can do little about derelict buildings even if they affect the price. Whilst it might be thought that parks and open spaces are generally for the benefit of the poorer sections of the community, ironically, at the other end of the economic scale, the rich have sometimes separate private estates which can be blocked off by gates. This is partly to give the rich a feeling of security, although it might be noted that in general, robberies occur more amongst the poorer sections of the community.

Growth of the canal system

The coming of the canal system, which was developed during the 18th century, meant that transport prices fell considerably. Canal speeds were slow; in most cases an average of 4 kilometres per hour could be obtained. This was partly because horse drawn barges were slow and partly because of the need for locks so that gradients could be overcome. The staircase of locks near Bingley in Yorkshire look very picturesque and is one of the wonders of the industrial revolution. It would have made life very difficult for the poor people who often used to live with their families on the so called narrow boats. These were usually about 2 metres wide to get through the narrow locks (seven feet wide just over 2 metres) and up to about 20 metres long. The canals did open up the possibility of being able to ship goods such as coal from one place to another. Certainly it is difficult to imagine centres such as Birmingham which has very little in the way of rivers being developed without the canal system. The Manchester Ship Canal was the last major U.K. canal built in 1894 and was extremely useful opening up the prospect of imports from the U.S.A particularly cotton as well as exports. Unlike most canals it can accommodate large ships of up to 40,000 tons deadweight. The Manchester ship canal had much greater dimensions and was from Liverpool to Manchester. In contrast most canals had seven foot wide locks which led to the development of the long boat or the narrow boats as they are called. Other canals often called the broad canals such as the Grand Union canal had 14-foot wide locks which meant larger ships could be accommodated Even with the seven-foot locks, however, the amount that could be carried was much greater than the amount that could be pulled by one horse on the roads.

Growth of the West Coast Ports

Trade with the Americas was important even after the American war of independence (1775 -1783). The West Coast ports such as Liverpool also became predominant apart from London. Both Bristol and Liverpool are unfortunately notorious for taking part in the slave trade. Whilst older geography books sometimes suggested that Lancashire grew because it was nearest to the U.S.A, and the wet climate this is perhaps a necessary but not sufficient reason since other places such as Bristol and Devon would have the same advantage. Similarly Cornwall was perhaps the original industrial area in the U.K. Cornwall had tin mines and until recently had clay. The predominance of trade with the U.S.A meant that for a long while cities such as Liverpool, Manchester and Glasgow tended to become even bigger as they could offer great scope for employment. In the post second world war period, the pattern of trade with Europe and the EU meant that the East Coast ports became more important in the latter half of the 20th century. This has led to the development of ports such as Felixstowe and also more recently Thamesport which is now the third busiest container port in the U.K.

Development of the railways

The railways are not a 19th century discovery. Railways had long been used for the transport of coal using horse drawn traffic or sometimes ropes with a stationary engine. The first steam engine "Catch as Catch Can" was shown in 1804. The 19th century saw the development of steam power with Stevenson's Rocket being perhaps the most famous but not the most important steam locomotive being used in the 1820s trials. The development of the railways in the countries such as the United Kingdom was so comprehensive that it has been estimated that only two villages, with the population of over 3,000 were more than 5 km from the nearest railway station. It is difficult to be sure of the motivation for this development but nearly all towns and villages wanted to be connected to the main network.

Effect of the railways

The railways meant that cities were not reliant on their immediate hinterland for such items as fresh dairy produce. London could now obtain dairy produce from as far away as Gloucestershire around (100 miles) 160 km away. The railways often dominated the urban setting. It has been estimated that in York about 30 % of the land space were used for the railways including the station and sidings. We might compare this with modern cities such as in the U.S.A where it has been estimated that in Los Angeles for example about 2/3 of the total inner area is used for vehicles mainly for roads and parking.

York was the home of George Hudson, (1800 -1871) the so-called railway king and at one stage MP. He announced many railway plans some fraudulently and this lead to the railway mania in the 1830s and 1840s when it seemed every one with any money assumed that they could make a fortune out of investment in railways. Cynics might well think that things do not change by comparing this with the rapid price rise in share prices in the 1920s before the Great Depression or the increase in share prices in the 1990s with the dotcom boom. Within parliament there were many railway directors who were likely to pursue the general interest of the railways.

Railways and Monopoly

The coming of the railway destroyed local monopoly and also opened up areas to greater competition for products especially coal. Whilst a lot of industries were located near the coal fields other industries which did not use vast amounts of coal could be located elsewhere. Paradoxically however it could be argued that together with later transport revolutions such as containerisation in the 1960s onwards they also increased the chances of large-scale monopoly capitalism. The Victorians were obsessed with competition on the railways so that by 1914 there were about 120 different railway companies. The fears of monopoly meant that there were restraints on the amount that railway could charge their customers including passengers and there was an upper limit of the penny a mile act. This was the old penny worth just over 0.4 p in the current currency.

Railways and pollution

Railways were noisy and polluting which is why the rich in the City of London kept the railways out. The stations such as Fenchurch Street, Liverpool Street, Kings Cross, St Pancras, Euston, Paddington and Victoria and Waterloo (and in the past Broad Street) are all either on the fringes of the City of London or just outside it. This still leads, paradoxically, to problems today where one of the obstacles to the encouragement of rail transport for journeys not terminating in London, is getting across the London area. The proposal for Cross Rail including Paddington to Liverpool Street being part of a through network has now been accepted.

In the poorer areas most people were tenants anyway and therefore regarded as of lesser importance so that whole swathes of housing could be demolished to make way for the new railway lines.

Influence of the radial pattern of railways

The railways have a linear pattern and with London then as now being the main city, it is comparatively easy to travel in the direction of London and out again but more difficult to make journeys in other directions. Places of work then tended to be along the railways as before they had been along canals or rivers. The railways extended the distance from which people could travel to and from work. The usual assumption is that people will not normally travel much more than about an hour each way although in the London area this is often exceeded. This also tends to be true of the large conurbations in other countries.

The social impact of the railways is also important. William Wordsworth the famous poet had feared that at the countryside, the working class would be able to mix with more middle class people which would not have been, in his view, a good thing. The original railways in the U.K. had three classes; first, second and third. It was assumed that gentlemen would not demean themselves by saving fares and going in the cheaper classes.

Cars and towns

The Buchanan Report in 1963 shows both the cost and benefits of cars in Towns. The late Colin Buchanan suggested that cars should be grade separated at junctions to avoid collisions and reduce pollution. Grade separated means that cars and vehicles should cross at different levels. Unfortunately the amount of money which would have been necessary to implement his suggestions was never found.

Traffic in towns

One of the many problems in modern towns is pollution which in turn is very much dependant upon the volume of traffic. Some effort was made to reduce pollution with the Clean Air Act in the United Kingdom in 1954. The smog (a mixture of smoke and fog) was very noticeable in most areas particularly around November when the coal fires in most houses would have likely been very busy as with the factories using coal. In December 1952 it was estimated that about 2,000 Londoners had died from the peasouper. This was the name given to the thick smog which was caused by water condensing on particles of smoke from domestic coal fires smoke from factory chimneys as well as railway locomotives

Road pricing

Ken Livingstone the former elected Mayor of London was brave or perhaps foolish enough in March 2003 to have a road pricing system which tries to reduce the pollution from cars. There is considerable evidence to show that the poor suffer more than the rich do from car pollution whilst at the same time being less responsible. The volume of the traffic in central London seems to have been reduced by about 20 - 30% according to evidence presented by mid 2003. Again we notice the tensions between different groups. The John Lewis partnership which owns Waitrose supermarkets amongst other shops welcomed the fall in pollution but did point out that many shops which relied on outsiders for a great deal of their trade had lost a considerable part of their business. In many Northern European cities, Governments of different political complexions have been willing to spend more on public transport and using public transport has less of a stigma, particularly, bus travel in most of the Northern European Countries. In the U.K. travel by bus has often been looked down upon.

Public transport and urbanization

The provision of or absence of public transport would also affect the ways in which towns grow. Public transport particularly with the tram or rail system is often radial. In the U.K. the Southern Railway, as it was then called, to the South of the Thames, was electrified providing a clean and a fairly frequent system so that many people in the 1930's were persuaded to live in the newer suburban areas . This included ones such as Chessington since they could obtain housing relatively cheaply alongside fairly convenient access to the city. The Railway companies themselves acted as property developers noticeably the Metropolitan Railway to the North of London which extended at one stage right into Aylesbury - about 80km from London.

The former poet laureate John Betjeman (1906 -1984) has written poems about what he called Metroland. The Docklands light railway system is likely to lead to some changes in the urban area particularly with the Olympic Games taking place in London in 2012. It is hoped that the games can form a basis of regeneration of much of this poorer part of London. If we had site valuation tax as many politicians from different parts of the party spectrum would like, then this might help to finance many of the major projects now. As Dave Wetzel said in a talk to the Transport Economist Group in January 2007, land prices and therefore prices of houses and offices have gone up where there have been significant improvements to the transport system.

Attitudes towards public transport

Different countries have had different attitudes toward public transport. The French governments of whatever political complexion seem to have been quite happy to provide suburbs with suburban train services. The Réseau Express Régional (RER) in Paris provides a very rapid form of transport across the town centre, whereas in Britain the railways usually stop at the outskirts of the city.

Perhaps Steve Norris, the Conservative candidate for Mayor of London in 2000, summed up the British attitude towards public transport by suggesting that people did not like travelling by train or other forms of public transport. This was because they had to mix with other ordinary people who might not be considered suitable.

Noise and towns

Noise is easier to measure than pollution usually using decibels, which is a logarithmic basis of measure, that is a noise level of 130 decibels is much more than 8 % louder than a noise level of 120. It is fairly easy to see that people in houses abutting roads will suffer more from road noise than people with long front gardens. The externalities of the transport system especially from the roads will usually fall more and more heavily upon the poor rather than the rich. It also affects the current housing mix so that most of the new housing developments will be for the middle class rather than the poor. The newer housing developments have far more houses situated in cul de sacs than the traditional grid patterns of roads in the older areas.

Unemployment and pattern of transport

In the 1980's unemployment rose to very high levels, around 3,000,000 in the U.K. partly because of less importance being paid to this as a policy objective. Unemployment rates in particular rose very considerably in the main conurbations. We thus had a different pattern of urban dwelling with the wealthier people being able to move out from the inner city areas and to a limited extent poorer people - often immigrants - taking their place. Lower real incomes for many people led in turn to reductions in transport demands in the peak hours.

Effect of transport on different classes

Professor John Hibbs, in an article in the Chartered Institute of Transport and Logistics journal, makes the point that in some cases, town planners have not helped poorer people. Buses have been kept out of the city centres with pedestrianisation, whereas car owners can park very near the town centre in multi-storey car parks. The Rail Development Society, now called Rail Future, has made much the same point. The railway stations have often been separated from town centres by newer roads, which make them much less attractive for people with heavy shopping, young children and old people.

Entertainment facilities and towns

One of the other roles of larger cities has to be to provide entertainment facilities. This is very true of London with its multitude of theatres and cinemas in the central area. How far this is important to local people as compared to tourists is fairly difficult to say.With the growth of home entertainment such as computers, televisions and DVD, it is not too obvious what the future will hold. However, there has been some revival of the cinemas which are usually provided in the large centres through an increasing number of people watching the cinema. In recent years the multiplex cinema is itself often being placed away from the city centre. This again poses problems for those who are less likely to have cars and also for the poorest of the public.

Sports and towns

If we look at some of the other activities of households we can see that monies spent on passive sports like watching football will be affected by the location; by far the majority of the major football clubs in the United Kingdom are in the conurbations. One can think of Arsenal, Tottenham and Chelsea within the London area, Manchester

United and Manchester City within the Manchester area, Liverpool and Everton in Merseyside. However, whilst in the 1940 and 1950's the majority of people would have walked or perhaps taken the tube (the name most Londoners would give to the London underground) in London to the sports grounds, this is no longer quite so important and many people will not travel such short distances. If on the other hand more people watch sport on television and watching football is the main objective of leisure life, it does not matter too much where they live as many people watch sports on televisions including in the local pubs. Thus the location is hardly important now. Some sports such as darts and snooker seem to have had their audience extended to a newer generation and location is also immaterial.

Drainage and Sewage facilities

One of the features of London was that some of the older rivers, such as the River Fleet - which gave its name to Fleet Street - have rapidly become polluted and unsuitable therefore they are not good for anything unless to be used as a sewer. In contrast, the New River in London has become a very fashionable area to live in the late 20th and early 21st century. It is in effect a canal built to bring water supplies to London from Chadwell and Arnwell in Hertfordshire, which was built by the New River Company following the idea of a Sir Hugh Myddleton who became the first governor of the company and the project was finished in 1619. We might notice that many of the problems, which Engels mentioned in the 19th century of lack of pure water, still apply in many third world countries today. Some sociologists would suggest that in third world countries there is a greater need for basic water and sewerage systems and for less emphasis to be placed upon prestige items.

Theory of Urbanism

Hurd G suggests in the book *"Human Society; Introduction to Sociology"* that there are three stages of urbanism. The first was up till the 18th century when few towns had populations of more than 100,000, the second was that of industrialisation and the third is that of metropolitanisation when various factors come together and are centralised in one area which has cultural political and economic wealth. We could perhaps summarise this as saying that the first stage is when most towns as in the U.K. fulfilled the market town role except perhaps London. The first underground line in London used the term Metropolitan in 1863. London still has the majority of the nation's large theatres, the major art galleries such as the Tate, the Tate Modern and the National Gallery, the major museums such as the Science and the Natural History Museum located around the Kensington area and because of previous monarchs' connections the Royal Parks in London including Green Park.

Political power has been concentrated at Westminster although it remains to be seen how far devolution will affect the role of Edinburgh with the Scottish Parliament having some powers and Cardiff being the home of the Welsh Assembly which has lesser powers.

Industrial and agricultural revolutions

The other influence in the United Kingdom was the industrial revolution partially caused by the development of steam power. There is interaction between the industrial and agricultural revolution. The result of land enclosures, the abolition in many cases of common land meant that there were fewer jobs available to people in the country side. Land enclosures meant that fields became much larger rather then being scattered in several places. This raised productivity but meant that fewer workers were needed on the land. However it is important to realise that agriculture in the early 1840s was still very important with the 1841 census showing that 1,434,000 men were employed in agriculture and only 525, 000 in textiles and 218,000 in mining. The old pattern for the richer working class who perhaps would have had few animals and would have had some limited amount of land as well as being able to carry out processes such as hand made weaving and spinning had soon almost vanished. It is perhaps ironic that in the late 20th and early 21st centuries there has been some reaction against this. Usually in the more middle class areas we see that there are craft shops and craft centres where people can buy hand made goods. The development of the coal mines mainly in the Northern parts of England, Scotland as well as South Wales and some isolated coal fields in Somerset and later Kent meant that people from poor areas flocked to these areas. Whilst conditions were often appalling and child labour was very common the conditions were presumably better than people would have obtained at home otherwise they would not have moved in the first place.

Some idea of the conditions can be obtained when we look at folk museums such as Beamish in the North East which is itself based on an old coal mine. The extent of overcrowding of houses and sanitation led eventually to Chadwick's Reform in the 1840's. It was not until 1833 that there were first restrictions on child labour. Prior to this children had often been employed at very young ages to work in coalmines and factories.

Mortality rates

Mortality rates were often appalling. It has been estimated that in 1820, the average life expectancy for a working class man in Manchester was around 20 years whereas for an Anglican Vicar it would have been about 40 years. This is however slightly misleading presumably the Vicar would have at least obtained the age of 20 in order to become a vicar in the first place. There were during the 19th century, a few enlightened business men who tried to build reasonable centres for their workers. If we look at the grid layout of Saltaire in the Bradford Suburbs we will find a town, which still seems quite pleasant and has been designated as a heritage centre. We might be amused about the hierarchy of housing so that whilst sanitation was good, there is a clear cut distinction between the house for poor men, operatives and others. Similarly, Cadburys built by a Quaker in what is now the Birmingham suburbs to the south of the city would have provided a pleasant contrast to the majority of city dwellings. In the North West of England, Port Sunlight is again an example of enlightened entrepreneurship. Port Sunlight is a garden village which was founded in 1888 by William Lever (later Lord Leverhulme) to give accommodation and good facilities to the factory workers who were making soap including the famous Sunlight brand.

Reduction in mortality rates

Mortality rates have fallen considerably which is one of the reasons for the rapid growth in total population of the U.K. in the 19th century. This could only have been accommodated in urban areas given the limitations of the transport system.

They have also fallen because of better land use planning, sanitation amongst other factors. We can contrast this with much of the third world where lack of clean water for drinking and cooking is still a major cause of death.

Importance of urban growth as condition for economic growth

For the conditions of economic growth it would have been reasonable to assume that there was little choice about urbanisation if economic development was wanted. The failure of the *laisser faire* regime, which was common for industry in the 19th century, was to ignore collective needs such as adequate sanitation and need for land use planning. 'Laissez faire' meaning *leave alone* was an economic system which assumed that industry could flourish as well as the nation if there was minimum interference. We can still find the same debates going on. In October 2004 a proposal to reform the gambling laws might have been welcomed by some local authorities as a way of bringing in jobs and comparative prosperity to some towns but was opposed by many others since the incidence of gambling addicts, conservatively estimated at about 300,000 people in the U.K, was thought by many to outweigh any benefits. There were similar arguments in January 2007 when it was announced that Manchester had been given the right to have the first super casino in the United Kingdom. The government hoped the super casino will help to regenerate the City of Manchester still further but has now abandoned the plan.

Present pattern of urban and rural life

Generally people made a distinction between the pleasant lives of the rural dweller compared to the impersonality of town life. It is difficult to find out directly whether people would have preferred rural or urban location although one indication would be that of looking at the elderly whom are not usually tied to a particular work place and are presumed to choose where to live. Using observation methods commonly used in sociology, it would suggest that people without ties such as the elderly would ideally choose are coastal locations noticeably along the unkindly called Costa Geriatrica like Eastbourne and other towns along the South Coast. In other cases particularly in Cornwall there are large numbers of elderly people who have migrated from elsewhere. The term geriatric is unfair since many old people can and do live full lives. The elderly may not however be typical of the population as a whole since their patterns for spending and on entertainment may well be different from that of other generations.

Patterns of spending

If we look at the patterns of the spending of a single adult on state pensions we find that in 2001/2 about £20 of their expenditure was on food and alcoholic drinks. This is clearly not affected by living in the urban or rural areas. Recreation or culture would have take up £11.40 of £101. However this is much more likely to be affected by urban areas where entertainment will be available. Housing costs count for another £19. This will vary tremendously by region. If we look at expenditure of all households we find that recreation and culture accounts for almost £ 77 billion out of a total of £631 billion and will be affected by the location.

Necessity of urban life

When considering whether urbanisation is desirable or undesirable in a country such as the U.K. one would ideally need to ask people. Many people would look at the new towns which were born immediately after the war originally to provide self contained units so that people could work and live in the same areas rather than commuting. The new towns themselves could be sub-divided into two categories for those such as Basildon in Essex, Stevenage in Hertfordshire and Crawley in Sussex which were meant to provide for the London overspill and relieve the diseconomies of the scale of London. In practice however, this has not always occurred and a town such as Basildon has in many cases become a major area for commuting to London. The other categories of new towns such as Wellington in Shropshire or Washington in the North East of England were there to act as a focal point for development of areas, which were thought to be deprived. Whilst many people would decry the new towns and say they often looked rather bleak, if one was to ask mothers with young children they might well say they are more pleasant since it is possible to cross roads in comparative safety and pavements are wide enough. We might compare this with some of the older towns which may look pleasant but have very narrow pavements and with considerable volumes of traffic making unpleasant noise and visible pollution.

When looking at urbanisation and the rural areas one would need to consider what could be done and what has been done. There are many criticisms of the high rise blocks which were built in the 1960's. Part of the problems of the high rise blocks is not that they are necessarily unsuitable for everyone but clearly if the lift system were inadequate with a tendency to break down then living with young child in such a place would be unpleasant. In the early 2000's there has been some reversal of thinking. Ken Livingstone (former Mayor of London) has been an enthusiast of high rise towers particularly near Paddington Station in London where space could be found relatively easily.

Some towns seem very pleasant in their own right judging by the number of people who wish to visit them such as Bath and York. This is partly a matter of time. In the late 19th Century Charles Booth 1840 -1916 carried out one of the first surveys of poverty which showed the extent of the crowding of the narrow streets and other factors. He also, in perhaps a wry comment at the time, complained that it was relatively easy to find money for Soup Kitchens that is, to provide soup to give to the poor but less easy to obtain money to look into the causes of poverty. In that respect nothing much seems to have changed. Poverty including homelessness is more visible on the U.K. streets than for much of the post war era. There was controversy in 2003 when Westminster council wanted to end many of the soup runs since they claimed that this meant people lived on the streets rather than going to suitable accommodation. Critics thought that Westminster found the idea of the homeless an embarrassment.

The original function of towns as market areas seems to have been partly superseded in the United Kingdom by the out of town shopping centres such as Lakeside and Bluewater in Essex and Kent respectively and the Gateshead Metro Centre in the north east of England. Therefore when we look at the pleasantness or unpleasantness from a social perspective, particularly whether poorer people are more likely to be non-car owners to gain access, much will depend on the planning assumptions. The 30% of households in the U.K. that do not have cars often seem to be overlooked with new developments. Care however has to be taken with this figure as it does not represent 30% of the total population since non car owning households are usually smaller than average. On the other hand the fact that 70 % of households have cars does not necessarily mean that people within those households necessarily have access to the car all the time.

Ebenezer Howard (1850 -1928) had the idea of garden cities with a vision that towns could be pleasant rather than unpleasant. He is often regarded as the originator of the garden city concepts. His influence can be seen in developments such as Welwyn Garden City.

Pollution and location

Within towns themselves, because of the nature of the prevailing wind pattern in the United Kingdom, the East is usually poorer than the West since the East bore the brunt of the pollution whilst the West did not. This pattern can clearly be shown in the voting patterns between the Conservative and Labour parties; the Labour party holds far more seats in the East of most major Towns and Cities whilst the Conservatives holds more in the West.

Pollution was often worse in the lower lying areas and where sanitation was inadequate. Thus the upper classes were literally the upper classes as they lived at the top of hills. This influence is still there in the London area.

We have mentioned that the problems of pollution are more difficult to measure because of synergy that is, it is not always obvious how one chemical will react with another. People, partly for altruistic reasons, have become more aware of pollution thanks partly to lobbying organisations such as Friends of the Earth and Greenpeace. This could also be a Nimbyish (not in my backyard)attitude noticeably in people opposing newer transport developments such as the possible expansion of runways at Heathrow or the building of a new airport such as that proposed in 2003 at Cliffe on the North Kent Marshes. The proposal for Cliffe was later dropped because of the costs and time of building a new airport rather than for environmental reasons.

Changes in docklands areas

Most cities in the U.K. with the noticeable exception of Birmingham had some major source of water for transport purposes. In many cases because of the decline of the inland waterways in the U.K. but not necessarily the rest of Europe, the use of rivers for commercial traffic has gone but leisure traffic has tended to boom. From the mid 1980's, many areas such as the Docklands in East London have reversed the pattern of being in the poor area of London. In many cases, particularly the height of the property boom in the early 1990's, the Docklands was very fashionable. London is not the only area where former wharves have been transformed. In the early 2000's Leeds became the fashionable area for young people to congregate.

Towns and universities

It is also arguable that urbanisation is necessary for the development of large scale universities. The university population is a large part of the social population and this will give incomes to people providing food text books and so on. This is shown in cases such as Durham pop 42,000 in 2001 and Aberystwyth pop about 12,000 in 2001 but with about 9,500 students in 2009which are smaller towns. Even in bigger towns such as Loughborough, with a population of about 55,000 in 2001, in Leicestershire the university is the major employer in the town. Universities therefore give what the economist would call 'the multiplier effect' for the towns.

More rural areas such as Cornwall have been strongly in favour of having university education there as it would partly alleviate the problem of winter unemployment and partly to ensure that residents of Cornwall who are students do not have to travel such long ways to the closest University because otherwise the students from Cornwall would have to travel such long ways particularly if they live near Penzance to the nearest University which is likely to be Exeter or Plymouth. At the present time fears are expressed that with the expansion of higher education, many universities want to encroach on to green belt land in order to match the increase in student numbers.

It can be argued that even at the secondary stage of education, one needs a fairly large population to support schools if they are to offer more choice of curriculum. There is also a tendency, until fairly recently, to close most village schools particularly those that have small catchment areas.

Changes in rural amenities leading to changes in towns

According to the push approach people argue that it was more difficult for people without cars or motorbikes to have access to reasonable facilities. With the patterns of local shops in villages closing and reduction in Post Offices, it meant that the rural areas became the preserve of the middle class rather than the working class. The remaining agricultural labourers therefore found it increasingly difficult to obtain accommodation at a reasonable price as they were priced out of the housing market. They also had to walk or take taxis - since rural bus services had become more infrequent -when they wanted to use local facilities. The rural branch railway lines had in many cases closed with the Beeching report, "*The Reshaping of British railways*", published in 1962. The number of people working as agricultural labourers, forestry workers has declined rapidly with mechanisation and larger farms.

The culture of a country and legislation

One of the features of pleasantness or unpleasantness of life in the cities will depend partially upon the culture and legislation. In Sweden even in a large city such as Gothenburg with about 500,000 population or Stockholm with a population of about 1 million, litter is conspicuous by its absence. This is unfortunately not the case in the U.K.

The size of the town with the same population will obviously depend upon the density of the same population. In most parts of Europe the provision of flats and even council flats is quite common even for professional people. If you visit council houses or flats in cities such as Gothenburg you will get a social mixture of people, whereas in the U.K. the housing association or in council houses, there will be few - if any - professional people.

Influence of land use planning on society

In Sweden, the council houses are built so that the layout of the square or rectangular blocks of the flats all have in effect a large communal back garden. The advantage of this is that people from any one flat can readily see where their children are playing and that outsiders can only be admitted by going through a particular gate.

This model seemed to work quite well in a sense that there seemed to be no social problems and the perhaps over hyped fear about abductions seemed not to prevail in the Swedish areas.

Effect of increase in property prices

The rapid increases in property prices in the early 2000's meant that there was not so much as a class divide as there is an age divide. People in their 40's and 50's who had already bought houses perhaps in their 20's are able to move up the property ladder. Also people who bought houses where the prices increased have what is usually called equity; this is the difference between the amount of mortgage owed and the price of the house. This means that in an era of low interest rates such as those prevailing in the year 2006 they were able to borrow very cheaply compared with non-property owners using the house as the security on which to borrow. In 2009 the problem is being able to find someone who will lend money.

Urbanisation and the changes in the power structure in society

The effects of urbanisation have sometimes been said to be the change of power from the agricultural aristocracy to the urban rich in the 19th century. This is not necessarily true. If we look at the richest people in the U.K. in terms of wealth, they include people with large amount of properties such as the Duke of Westminster. However if we look generally at the richest people in the late 19th century in the U.K. we will find that industrialists will have featured more as well as people from the commercial fields.

In the U.K. there were both religious and political differences which were accentuated with the rural/urban split. Generally in the 19th Century Conservatives were seen as the political party supporting the farming community whereas the Liberal party was the party of free trade. There was therefore a division between the older Anglican community and the Non-conformist groups partly because of their exclusion from the establishment tended to favour the Liberal Party. There are still traces of these attitudes even in the early 2000's although the religious differences have largely been ignored.

Segregation of rich and poor

The segregation, which took place in 19th century Britain, may have been overstated. The majority of poorer workers had to live near their places of occupation noticeably the mills, whilst the richer people lived at a further distance and came in by carriage. This pattern still prevails in the U.K. with the richer people apart from in the London area tended to commuting by car, whereas the poorer people commute by bus or increasingly by rail. In the London area subsidies are mainly given inadvertently to the rich.

Positional goods

Some economists such as Fred Hirsch have talked about positional goods. This particularly applies to the goods that one person owns and therefore another cannot. It is quite possible in a modern society for the majority of people to afford an 1100cc car but clearly not everyone can have a house with fine views of the seaside. Even where the seaside is not the objective, in many cases people have tried to live with views overlooking the countryside. In the absence of land use planning there is clearly a leapfrogging aspect whereby, as people from the inner areas as people get richer they will in turn want their easy access to the country side, thus the town will get bigger and bigger.

This is perhaps more noticeable in Australia or U.S.A where land is more readily available and the size of towns such as Los Angeles will become absolutely enormous.

Wilmott and Young's survey

There has been considerable discussion since Peter Wilmott and Michael Young's survey in 1957 entitled *'Family and Kinship in East London.'* They suggested that whereas people traditionally in East London had close relationships and extended family so that they knew people in the local pubs and corner shops, this was less true of newer areas such as Woodford in Essex where people were less likely to live near their relatives. If we look at television programmes such as Eastenders or Coronation Street we still see this pattern as people in the inner city areas know each other very well in contrast to the suburban areas, which are often portrayed as being anonymous.

Influence of different occupations on urban life

Perhaps often ignored is the type of industry in which people were working. People working in the docks at Tilbury, partly because of the shift system, would have been a very large part of the total community and would have wanted to have been near their place of work because of not wishing to walk large distances when public transport was not available. They therefore would have common grounds for conversation. It is possibly also one of the many reasons why worldwide the docks, coalmining and for other reasons the car industry have a higher prevalence of strikes than amongst most other industries. The social relationships formed in the docks seem to have been long lasting and partly because of trade unions pressure jobs were often obtained within the docks industry from one generation to another.

Coalmining reflected a similar pattern whereby most people would have lived within easy access of the mines. This is true of South Wales but even within East Kent mines for example Snowdown the same living patterns emerge. The shipbuilding areas too have suffered. In 1913 Britain supplied about ½ of the worlds ships. Nowadays it is a relatively minor industry although there are some possibilities in the scope of providing employment in the luxury yacht industry.

Future pattern of urban life

What is more difficult to ascertain is the future pattern of the urban areas. As manufacturing in the U.K. and many Western European Countries becomes less important the service industries have become more important. Some unkind commentators have suggested that Britain is turning into a mini Disneyland with odd areas being turned over to be a reflection of the past. It is very noticeable that the Tourist Industry is subject to shocks to the system for example if American visitors get scared off for one reason or another then problems occur. American tourists in particular will tend only to know some towns noticeably London and Oxford and Cambridge but not visit other areas which are perhaps more pleasant. Even major commercial centres such as those in the Docklands have recognised the importance of tourism for example with St Katherine's Dock, and a small museum in Woolwich. The need for large factories has tended to diminish and so major places of employment such as the steel industry reduced considerably.

There are also newer patterns for living whereby people may well go to offices a couple of days a week and then work elsewhere at other times.

Influence of working from home

Both the CBI and the TUC in the early 1990's suggested about 6 million people would work from home by the turn of the century. This would mean presumably, that they would have a choice of urban or rural living. It would be subject to their visiting the office or factory on some occasions during the week if for no other reason than for face to face contact with other colleagues. Though there seems to be more people working from home, the figures have not been as high as these estimates.

However, these figures in the reports seemed to ignore the problems of working from home such as, the lack of social mix. There is also the question of status. People who work from home complain in some cases that people do not regard working from home as serious and they will therefore have more interruptions than if they worked in an office or factory.

In spite of fictional programmes such as the Archers on the radio, which has been broadcast for over 50 years, relatively few people work in agriculture nowadays. The figure is less than 2% of the total population and only in a few areas such as in mid-Wales. Brecon and Radnor are agricultural workers of great numerical significance. It remains however to be seen if such trends will continue. Some commentators noticeably Prince Charles suggested we need more organic foods. Michael Meacher a former Minister for the Environment tended to take up this call. Organic production without the use of pesticides tends to be more labour intensive than large scale agriculture.

Some commentators have suggested that it is a myth to think of areas as urban, suburban or rural but really to think of a mixture of areas ranging from the completely rural to the completely urban. We might think of areas such as Brecon and Radnor in mid-Wales where the sheep outnumber the people, to be a purely rural area. There are few other jobs available apart from the agricultural industry; it is noticeable in these areas that car ownership is extremely high with over 90% of households owning a car. This contrasts with say the London area where the car ownership figure is around 50%. At the other extreme we might wish to take many of the inner areas of London as being completely urban. For example, whilst Islington is often portrayed in the media as being the area for the rich people including Tony Blair, the former Prime Minister, the reality is that there are few open spaces near the Angel, Islington.

Communitarianism

Some political factions noticeably the more right wing Christians in the U.S.A, often called Communitarianism suggested that the current lower moral standards are due to greater mobility, since if people knew each they would impose standards on their peer groups

They believe in locally based institutions for example schools and voluntary groups being strengthened. They also believe that communities should be able to help by looking after each other. Almost paradoxically, the Liberal Democrats of this country would come to similar ideas but almost certainly from different premises. Liberal Democrats would claim that both the Labour and Conservative party have been far too centralist and that as far as possible decisions should be moved down to the local communities, the lower level the better except where there are reasons to the contrary.

The hint in late 2003 from the Labour government that local authorities influence over education would be reduced or possibly removed would not be welcomed since Liberal Democrats would feel that local councils were in a better position to know the needs of individual areas than Ministers or civil servants at Whitehall.

Immigration and urbanisation

The inner city often has a high level of recent immigrants. In the 18th century the Huguenots (French Protestants who fled from Roman Catholic persecutions); Jewish people fleeing from Russian oppression in the late 19th early 20th century, tended to move in to East London. There have been similar waves virtually ever since; for example in the early 1970s Asians fleeing from Uganda's late dictator Idi Amin who made the Asians the scapegoat for Ugandan problems. In many cases, there are also social problems, but this does not necessarily prove that immigrants are responsible for the problems, such as overcrowding of houses as being an inherent problem of the inner city. People on lower incomes may well move into multi-occupied houses, since the rent will be comparatively cheap.

We can say that in many cases current asylum seekers are moving in response to what sociologists would call the push factor that is; there are reasons to try to move out of their present condition. There are problems with immigration and reaction to it as with any other type of population movement.

There are often differences in culture and the extreme right wing noticeably the British National Party, has drawn upon this. They have often been able to as perhaps with other authoritarians to assume that there are normal families who are almost certainly white, where there is great stability and good marriage. Further, they assume that newer liberal influences are to blame in interfering with this. As we have already said, the patterns of urban life are often similar irrespective of the time or racial mix.

The concept of 'insiders' and 'outsiders' is a common one. C. S. Lewis the well known theologian and children's writer, comments about insiders and outsiders in one of his books. Anyone who has read stories about the Second World War will realise there were tensions between the people who were evacuated from the major cities because of fears of bombing and the people with whom they were evacuated. At that stage the myths were reasonably similar; the country folk feared that urban dwellers were sophisticated and likely to commit many crimes in areas which had not much had crime before.

Wales and the tensions between incomers and existing residents

In recent years Plaid Cymru (the Welsh Nationalist party) has concentrated on the hostility of many of the local Welsh people particularly in the poorer rural areas - to the richer English people who are able to buy property which the local community can not afford. The same problems also exist in other areas such as Cornwall. There is some anecdotal evidence that, paradoxically, the Irish who were often the poor relations in the 19th century have sometimes been able to buy up property in the Liverpool area where many of them have some roots.

Influence of divorce on urban settlement

It should be noted that whilst the population of the U.K. is not changing very rapidly, the number of people requiring houses or flats is rising more rapidly due to increasing numbers of divorced couples who often require two houses rather than one. The divorce rates are currently running at about 40% for the U.K. and by 2001 were 157 000 according to Social Trends 2003. In contrast the number of first marriages has fallen from a peak of 390 000 in 1970 so that it was less than half this number (180,000) in 2000. The divorce rate has now fallen perhaps because of the credit crunch. However, the concept that the 19th Century had very stable long marriages is not borne out by the length of marriages. Generally they were short, because life expectancy itself was very short for the majority of people.

Was there ever a stable moral society?

The concept that in the past everyone was community minded does not seem true, given the number of brothels which were prevalent in Victorian England suggesting that the faithfulness in marriage in England was not necessarily there. One does not have to be a Republican to realise the concept of stability within marriage with it being very much the exception within the history of the Royal Family. The Royal Family has of course some of the best known history within the U.K. for obvious reasons, as does the aristocracy. We, have less knowledge of ordinary people so that we can only guess as to how far they led similar lifestyles.

The concept of community is perhaps an odd one anyway. In some cases the differences seem less between races than between age. The young people will often have almost a different language for most of their undertakings compared to older people. In the past 50 years, young people have often adopted a particular type of music whether it be rock in the 1950's or rap in the 2000's as a way of excluding themselves from other generations. The 'normal' family of husband, wife and 2.4 children is far from being the reality. Mrs Thatcher while Prime Minister said that there is no such thing as society.

Ethnic groups and the towns

It seems likely that people of Indian origin own proportionately more multiple occupancy houses. Without further research it is not possible to ascertain whether the multiple occupants are related in some way or that multiple occupancy is just a method of people of the same race relying on a few richer people to get them over their problems. This in a way would seem to be a repetition of the first building societies, which were temporary organisations whereby people would club together to give each person a chance to buy property. Council housing had criteria whereby people were often given property according to the length of time they had been in an area. Unsurprisingly, people who had been recent immigrants were more likely to be discriminated against compared to the white population.

The dispute about asylum seekers in 2003 did suggest that racism was fairly inherent in the U.K. It seems rather ironic that 'The Sun' which has an Australian owner (Rupert Murdoch) with American citizenship married to a Chinese lady should be attempting to tell the native population who should come into the country.

Problems of the inner city

Sociologists have been interested in the problems of the inner city, for example in Brixton in South London and Toxteth in Liverpool where there were riots in July 1981. Whilst there is no doubt about the tensions, sociologists will not necessarily be able to put their finger on the precise causes. In some cases there were examples of racial tension, with the media not helping by continuing to call people 'migrants', 'asylum seekers' and so on. In other cases, particularly in the 1980s, unemployment was very high, rising to over three million people, with the rates even higher in the inner city areas. Apart from anything else, this meant that young people - with time in their hands – were easily attracted to mischief and crime and it is easier to attract disaffected youth to riot than young people in jobs with reasonable prospect of promotion are. Marx talked about alienation of workers whilst at work. We might suggest that lack of reasonable prospects of an interesting job with reasonable security might lead to even more problems.

Nimbyism

The concept of Nimbyism has come rapidly into the English language. Nimby stands for "*not in my backyard*"; to mean that people want facilities such as roads and airports but not where they are. The phrase was first used by Nicolas Ridley a former Conservative cabinet Minster

One of the problems when looking at the class context is to see how far Nimbyism is due to inherent decision making and how far it is due to the influence of different pressure groups. It is sometimes argued that the middle class will be much more willing to distribute leaflets and be much more aware of what is happening in local government. The working class in turn may have better reading ability than newcomers from non Commonwealth Countries where the native language is not English. It is also seems plausible that people who own property would wish to fight harder than tenants who will lose less or gain less from other developments.

Some of the comments about Asylum Seekers would seem amusing if they were not serious. The comments for example about asylum seekers living in what would have been Naval Barracks complaining about the influence of single young men would have seemed rather odd given that there is no great likelihood that the single young men whom had been in the Royal Navy would have acted very differently to any other group. The navy is not well known for its celibacy!

Typical urban patterns

If we look at patterns within towns, they seem to be relatively constant though their causes may be different. The sizes of the areas described will also change as town and cities expand. Generally we find there is a *central business district* where prices are very high for property. This property will usually be used by the commercial sector sometimes for offices and sometimes for shops. In London, the shopping centre around Regent Street, often called the West End, is quite distinct from the City of London around the Bank of England which is usually referred to as the city. In other cities, such as Birmingham, the two are much less separate. Outside this there is usually an *inner city area* which is usually characterised by immigration whether it is the Russian Jews in the late 19th century and early 20th century who would often speak a different language, that is, Yiddish. From the 1950's, the cultures of the immigrants may have changed to have first included West Indians and later in the early 2000's to include refugees from Kosovo. Outside this inner city area there is the *suburbs* where the property is often better maintained and there is more owner occupation. Within the U.K., the size of the town has been often limited by the size of the Green Belt which was imposed in the late 1940's following the Town and Country Planning Act 1947 to prevent cities becoming too large. The Green Belt was typically about 20 –30 km outside the centre in London.

Proposals for more housing in the South East

In the early 2000's we see tensions building as the government proposes far more houses in the South East where some commentators have suggested it is not really needed as there is already overcrowding. Other people have suggested that there is a need to be able to house not just traditionally lower paid people but also teachers and teaching assistants without which society cannot easily function.

Marx predicted great tensions between the different classes. However the tensions may also be racial although class and ethnic groups are not necessarily very clearly apart. In Bradford there seems to be a clear division between the Indian population who have tended to come from more affluent urban areas of India and who have relatively liberal views compared to the more fundamentalist Muslim Pakistani population who have often come from the rural areas. To treat the two groups as identical is not necessarily correct. Neither is it helpful if one is considering educational needs amongst other needs.

Financial Institutions and Loans

It is not always clear how far financial institutions such as building societies that at one stage refused to lend money to certain red line areas, helped to keep people particularly those within ethnic groups - off the property ladder. Since the majority of people can only buy houses on a mortgage or some other form of loan, if there is no possibility of getting this then it is likely that the area will decline. This is sometimes known as expectations blight when house prices are falling in a specific area when they are not falling elsewhere. This is in contrast to planning blight, where a housing area is expected to be used at a later stage for roads and railways, then, no one is likely to be willing to buy it.

One of the noticeable features about urban environment is that of pressure groups which mobilise people on what they see as a threat. In the case of the Newbury by-pass in the mid 1990's, a large number of ordinary people campaigned against the road. The protesters would have included the obvious green pressure groups such as the Friends of the Earth, Greenpeace as well as local environmental groups and the Nimbys.

Perhaps ironically one of the features, which was not remarked on, was that Newbury had appeared in the Buchanan Report official title 'Traffic in Towns' and that at the time more people used cycles 15 % than used cars but the needs of cyclists were ignored.

Big cities and employment

Sociologists have sometimes described part of the industrial era as one of Fordism. In 1913 Henry Ford invented the moving assembly line. This reduced the time needed to assemble the car from 12 ½ hours to 93 minutes. Whilst the work was boring many of the labourers would have been pleased that their work pay had increased from 2 $ to 5 $ per day. In western countries such as the U.K. nowadays many of the firms occupying large amounts of space and labour have gone. These include the large steel works in the Ebbw Vale area near Newport, South Wales area which was over 4 miles long and was closed in 2002 having been there since the 1960s. The car factory in Dagenham, which has been there since before the Second World War in Essex, has also been closed, as has Longbridge in the West Midlands partly because of globalisation.

Dagenham was in a place, which was there because there was plenty of open space and in effect a new town was built in more pleasant former countryside than in the more densely populated part of old London.

If we look at much of Britain's declining manufacturing industry new units in the industrial estates which look very much alike in most towns or even rural areas have become the important employers.

The Docklands in East London has long since shed its workload and places such as Tilbury, the port on the River Thames about 20 km from London which employed about 20,000 workers at its peak has been reduced to under 1,000 workers. While large firms have become even more important it is less likely that they need large numbers of people in any one location.

Footloose firms and effect on large towns

In the 1960s it was estimated by Luttrell that about 2/3 of firms were footloose and this figure seems to be even higher today. The city centre commercial district has also changed. In September 2003, Reuters - who are well known for the press coverage - moved out of Fleet Street so that the last remaining link with the newspaper industry disappeared. Many of the commercial firms have moved out from the City of London like the Royal Sun Alliance moved out to Horsham in Sussex many years ago.

Towns no longer have their specialist roles for example the coal industry that reached its peak in about 1913, but which was still a substantial industry in the 1980s is no longer important. Even South Wales which was renowned for its coal mines no longer has any deep pits.

The development of footloose industries

In the United Kingdom there has been a movement away from the centres of towns and away from London itself. The Location of Office Bureau encouraged firms to move away from the London area. This they did by showing firms what the rents were in London compared with elsewhere and explaining the amenities. This was perhaps a reaction to a survey conducted by Luttrell, which showed that many firms were ignorant of the costs of locating in one area rather than in another, although many firms were in fact footloose. Often firms have grown up in an area but there are no longer pressing reasons for them to stay. Sometimes, however, there are other reasons, since the fortunes of one firm can depend upon other firms. Even in the City of London, because so much of the shipping industry was located about the Tower Hill area, the college, originally called the City of London College, later grew into the London Metropolitan University, and offered shipping courses. In the North of England some colleges would put on textile courses, which were not likely to be available in similar towns of similar size. The tendency nowadays is to have far less manufacturing industries in the U.K., and much more light industry, which can be located anywhere.

Changes in shopping patterns and influence on towns

The nature of shopping has changed so that we have Lakeside in Essex and Bluewater in Kent and to a lesser extent the metro centre near Gateshead being developed as major shopping areas without any people living there. It could be argued that the distinction between classes is slightly changing, since for instance it is difficult to get to Bluewater by public transport whereas it is easy by car. The distinction between car owning and non-car owning seems in many ways more crucial than socio economic class.

The shopping centres do however require large populations to survive within a reasonable travelling time. This could be well over 30- 40 miles as people will travel a long way with the car to shop at such centres. They also require staff and again it will be easier for people with a car to work in such centres. The social costs of increased congestion on the already overcrowded M25 have largely been ignored although the government has announced that it views with disfavour the creation of any new out of town centres of such a size.

Optimum size for tourism

Towns such as York, Canterbury, Bath and Oxford and Cambridge are already well known as tourist centres. London whilst being thought of as a commercial centre is also the biggest tourist attraction. With the exception of London it is perhaps not coincidental that the other major tourist centres have populations of about 100,000 to mean that they are big enough to have a large centre of interest whilst not being too big for people to be able to wander around without being overwhelmed by the size. Large cities such as Liverpool with its revamped Docklands, the Albert Docks area, have also become tourist centres.

The advantage of tourism from the British point of view is that it gives a large export market when manufacturing seems to be in almost permanent decline. The poor linguistic ability of many British people does not help to develop the tourism industry as much as it might be desired from a commercial viewpoint.

It is however susceptible to shocks to the system; the foot and mouth crisis in the early 2000s meant that many visitors especially those from the U.S.A stayed away even though in London the direct effect of foot and mouth would be negligible. The Twin Towers tragedy on September 11th 2001 will have had a number of effects on the tourism industry. It is likely that fewer U.S.A people will have travelled abroad. The longer security checks will also possibly deter some people from using air travel for tourist purposes. The Olympics in 2012 are expected to attract large numbers of visitors to East London and elsewhere in the U.K. and because of this there has been great emphasis on improving public transport services. This was generally thought to be one of the likely obstacles to London being the venue in the first place.

Urbanisation in other countries

Urbanisation is not confined to the Western countries. In many cases manufacturers have switched production to the Third World countries, especially in what were in the 1990s called the tiger economies of South East Asia. Many of these had very high growth rates at that time. At the present time the economic growth rate in Mainland China still is very high. Whereas manufactures were often carried out in Japan, this in turn became too expensive, and therefore China, Taiwan, Malaysia, became more important. In 2009, India became more important for service jobs as it had gained such jobs as call centre jobs. It may also be gaining other positions in December 2003 there were reports of legal executive work being done in India rather than in the U.K.

In many cases towns and cities in the Third World have grown immensely, and often there are shantytowns that have grown in an unplanned way and have little if anything in the way of sewage, drainage, or any other public facilities.

Sociologists such as Ferdinand Tonnies 1855 –1936 a German sociologist who founded the German sociological association devised the words Gemeinschaft and Gesellschaft to describe two "ideal" patterns of life.

In the first - Gemeinschaft - we have a society in which relationships are spontaneous. The organisations are small scale. The culture is homogenous and people know each other well. In the second -Gesellschaft - we have impersonal relationships as in a bureaucracy. Organisations are bigger. Some people would argue that this is similar to part of the distinction between rural and urban life.

Rural life and the community

As we have said elsewhere there is an assumption about the desirability of rural life compared to urban life. Some people have used the word community and it is fairly easy to see this if one lives in a small country village that may only have one primary school. Going further than this, back in the 1940s, when the school leaving age was raised from 14 to 15, schools catered for the entire 5-14 age range. The brighter pupils will if they passed the 11+ in some cases go on to Grammar Schools. In this case, not only pupils will have known each other for a long period, but also the parents. Children would have often seen each other whilst walking to school. Community would mean that there was an interest in common. John Major, the former Conservative Prime Minister, in a slightly derided speech, talked about his vision of former Middle England where people knew each other. The identification could well be the local cricket club playing on the village green. Indeed there is a television series Heartbeat now depicting life in the 1950s-60s, and they would probably show this as one of its features. There would also be clubs such as the Women's Institute going to church that would help to knit the community together. People going to different churches such as the Church of England, or Methodists or Baptist may have had relatively little to do with each other. People often in the village used the word church to mean the Church of England whilst the word chapel meant the nonconformist churches such as the Baptist, Methodist or the former Congregationalist (now part of the United Reformed Church). Community also meant that people had multiple roles, in a small village school the teacher might also be the parent of one or more of the pupils, so that people would know them in these two roles or sometimes even more. This would help to develop close relationships.

Association

In contrast, sociologists have sometimes used the word 'association', which has the opposite meaning, that is, it is impersonal. If we take the current large supermarkets, which until recently had been located near the high street or in the high street, we can see that the shop assistants are far less likely to know any individual customer compared with the small village shop. However, this is a slight oversimplification, since up to the 1950s even in the urban areas, many small shopkeepers would have known their customers very well, and would have offered them informal credit facilities long before the days of credit cards.

Association would also imply that people had fewer interests in common. This is more likely to be true in large cities where people are less inclined to belong to organisations anyway, but even if they do, the numbers involved mean that they belong perhaps to one association and not really know anyone from their own street or neighbourhood. Large numbers of people do belong to some organisations such as the National Trust which had over 3 million members in the year 2009 and the Royal Society for the Protection of Birds (RSPB) had just over 1 million members in 2002 according to Social Trends. Whilst these are worthwhile organisations they do not generally lead to people getting to know each other better. Social Trends claims that there are links between organisational membership and social trust; people who join organisations are generally more trusting of others than those who do not. This can also be found in city centre churches, which, since the population has moved away to the suburbs, means that the city church does not cater for people so much in the city or town centre as it does to people living in the more affluent suburbs. This would be true of some of the Birmingham central churches. It would be even truer of the churches of the City of London, which are often really only utilised during the week days rather than the weekends, since the total resident City of London population is probably less than 5,000.

It also implies that people only know each other in one role, compared to what we said earlier. People working in many of the Civil Service departments in Central London may travel very long distances to get there, often because of the location of the termini. People from Kent or Sussex will find it easier to get to Whitehall than people coming from the North of London. Some other people may well come from considerable distant places, so they will have fewer opportunities to meet except at work. When we look at the data in Social Trends 2003, it measures neighbourliness by age and by frequency of speaking to neighbours. Only 17 % of people in the 16 –29 age group claim to speak to their neighbours everyday whereas the figure is 43 % for those aged 70 or more. Most of the over 60s will not be working full time so will have more time to talk. A society in which the average person watches television for 171 minutes per day in 2000 according to Social Trends, is hardly likely to be one in which great interest in other people is taking place.

There have been suggestions on why people will move away from the bigger cities. Certainly in the 1980s many of the big cities saw a decline in population such as those in inner London Merseyside, Greater Manchester.

For the individual, houses were often pleasanter out of the central area and considerably cheaper. People particularly in inner city areas suffered from high crime rates. Pollution and noise are less than in the big cities particularly nearer the centres as opposed to the inner cities where a great deal of pollution is caused by passing traffic. Many firms were more willing to move to green field sites rather than brown field sites which meant that they could have the size and shape of property that they wanted.

However there are some signs that some of the decline caused by the IRA bomb in June 1996 which caused much of the destruction of the city centre in Manchester has been reversed with the rebuilding of the centre of Manchester.

Government policy and urbanism

How different roles affect urbanisation

In modern urban settings we can perhaps look at other roles as well as that of producer-worker. People may also have a role as house owners or even tenants, which will affect their views of modern developments. They may also have a role as consumers. If we look at London at the present time, house prices have been rising very rapidly from 2001 to 2008, but they had also risen generally over the decade compared with the rate of inflation. This means that it has become difficult to attract workers, whether they work in the post office or newly trained teachers, since if house prices are very high, these people are unlikely to find suitable accommodation. Rented accommodation is both very scarce and expensive. Rent Acts, according to some people, may have made the situation worse by preventing people from moving from accommodation that may be unsuitable in many ways, because they would then lose the protection of the Rent Act. . Since 2008 house prices have fallen rapidly. People such as Ken Livingstone, the former Mayor of London would like, not unreasonably, to make sure that vital services, whether postal or education are carried out effectively. There is relatively little room in London itself, since it is generally built upon, and hardly anyone would suggest that the parks and open spaces should be built upon. One solution, therefore, would be in effect to extend the London barriers. The government in 2003 announced that it wished to see large numbers of houses built along the Thames Gateway.

Thames Gateway

People living near the Thames Gateway whether in Essex or Kent, will, if they are house owners, tend to resent newcomers coming into the area. On the other hand they may in their worker's role welcome the idea of new jobs coming in and as consumers they may wish to have new shopping centres or enlarged shopping facilities near them.

Similarly, we can see that even with an improvement to the transport network, people will have different views. The former Mayor of London has suggested that there should be a tramway system in West London, slightly on the lines of the existing tram link in the Croydon to Beckenham area. Many householders and shopkeepers living along the route have objected, on the basis that householders would find it more difficult perhaps to park, and shopkeepers see that it is allegedly not in their interest if people cannot park near their shops.

Role tensions

The tensions, therefore, arise partly between people in their different roles, and in particular, in the London area between different age groups. We might also notice, in line with sociological theory that in other towns there is still this conflict between the established inhabitants and the desire for new houses. This could arise amongst either younger people wishing to have houses for the first time or other people moving into the area perhaps for employment purposes.

Non manual workers buy some of the relatively expensive houses. The workers conform to the Goldthorpe suggestions in the late 1950s, that these people have houses as their main priority and that their social life revolves mainly around their home rather than being involved in voluntary organisations. The people's interest in these newer houses will only be in terms of how they can get to and from work and/or shops, and also the perception of the quality of the local schools. It also seems probable that they would be less likely to vote than people perhaps living in the established areas, who know the local councillors and MP.

Current typical pattern of a town

The typical pattern of a town has long been, a Central Business District (CBD), which has had more and more commercial property; an inner city that has usually been characterised by relatively poor older housing, and in many cases multi-household accommodation; and the suburbs which have been the preserve generally of the more affluent. The present pattern is perhaps slightly subtler than this. The inner city areas have often spread so that what were previously fashionable areas have in turn become part of the inner city.

Following the Brixton and Toxteth riots, the government has taken action in order to have better results. In the late 1970s and early 1980s there were inner city partnerships to develop the inner city as a whole. There has also been so-called gentrification. This has particularly occurred in the part of Islington around The Angel just to the North of the City of London. This is partly because there is a demonstration effect, if people think that house prices are going to rise in one area, then, other people will see this and will try also to purchase property near there. It is also partly because The Angel is very near the City of London, so that people do not have to spend very much money on commuting or on other transport since many entertainment facilities are on their doorstep. It does not necessarily mean that public facilities are good, since people may well be able to send their children to schools in other areas. There was considerable controversy when Tony Blair, the then Prime Minister, sent one of his children to Brompton Oratory School rather than one of the local ones.

SELF EXAMINATION QUESTIONS

1. What were the main influences on urbanism in the 19th century? (Hint: How much of an influence were the changes in transport, agriculture and industry?) Which of them were push factors and which of them were pull factors? Why do sociologists distinguish between these two factors?

2. Why has the east side of most urban areas been poorer in the U.K.? (Hint in which direction does the wind mainly blow?) Why might this have been very important if there was a considerable amount of pollution? Why does it matter if we are studying urban areas? Are there any links between this and the ethnic mix of the population? Will there be differences between the newcomers and the established population? Why might this lead to tensions? Is this just a historic factor or are the influences still there?

3. Why did factory workers live near their place of work until fairly recently? How far will different shift patterns have made this more important? Why did the factory owners live at a greater distance? Why did the owners often live towards the top of the hills, whereas the rest of the population lived down the hill? How far could we test the idea that workers and owners lived at a much greater distance apart than before the industrial revolution? What would be the effects of such a separation on society? Why might there still be differences between where the working class live and the managerial class? (Hint: think of house prices as well as public transport)

4. How far did the changes in agriculture affect the population in terms of encouraging people to move to the towns? What were the main changes, and how did they affect the growth of towns? (Hint: What happened to the increase in production of farms?) How far did changes in transport affect where farms could reasonably send perishable products such as milk? Do changes in technology especially in transport still have an affect on both the urban and rural populations?

5. What were the effects of changes in industrial production i.e., moving from a home base to a factory base? Some people have suggested that with changes in technology we might be moving back to a period where far more people could live and work at home. What would be the disadvantages of working at home according to some sociologists? What would be the effect of this on urbanism?

6. Why are there many different roles which people have at the present time? What are the main roles and do they coincide with the ideas put forward by the classical sociologists? How far will this influence their views on urban development? Does this affect the government's attitudes when thinking about new major developments?

7. How far do Goldthorpe's suggestions in the late 1950's apply to the present day? How far have changes in factory jobs as well as types of employment and job security meant that we need to be careful about applying his theories?

8. Are there any lessons in which newly industrialised countries can learn from the mistakes of the western countries? (Hint: How far can the newly industrialised countries avoid the problem of pollution and also of major congestion caused by cars? Would it be possible to avoid the problems of the slum areas and the problems of the inner cities?) Many people have commented about the rapid economic growth for example in China. Would it be possible for China to avoid the mistakes? Does having a communist system make it more or less likely that these mistakes can be avoided?

9. What is meant by the term 'zero sum game'? Why might it be relevant when looking at expansion of the urban environment? (Hint: What happens if there is no town planning and everyone tries to move nearer to the country-side?)

10. How far would it be possible to have the same population as in a country such as the U.K., if we did not have major towns? How far does the influence of globalisation affect the way in which goods are sent from one country to another, even when the products seem virtually identical?

11. In the 19th century there were some moves towards garden cities, such as those devised by Ebenezer Howard. Would it be possible to re-introduce the idea of garden cities? Do most British people want to have the same amount of green space as in other cultures? If there are differences between British and other countries how far can sociology help to explain this?

12. In some newer estates in both the U.K. and more so in the U.S.A, there are gates that separate the residents of these upper class areas from the rest of the population. Why might sociologists be interested in such developments? What would happen if these areas had an entirely separate system of local government to the rest of the population?

13. Some sociologists have suggested that we might be moving to the end of the great cities as being a necessary evil during the period of the industrial revolution. What more evidence would we need before accepting this idea? Do changes in home entertainment have any effect on where people might want to live, and if so why?

14. Do the changes from heavy industry to light industry alter the way in which planners should be separating places of work from residential areas? Do we need, any longer, to segregate light industrial firms from residential areas? How far will this help or hinder the fight against pollution?

Chapter Seven

Population Growth

Influences on population growth

Population growth has mainly been associated with the increase in urban population. Towns are often regarded as second best places for citizens to live. The urban areas are often regarded as second best because there is more noise and pollution. In many cases, people who have a choice regard the countryside as more visually attractive, although some people might be attracted to the metropolitan areas where there are more facilities for entertainment amongst others.

Death rates have fallen considerably in recent times due to myriad reasons. Most of these reasons are associated with the advances in medicine and surgery, but this is by no means the entire story. One of the best-known reasons for improvement in health, particularly in the 19th century, is the understanding of germs. Pasteur, who gave his name to pasteurised milk, realised the importance of germs. The same is true of Lister. The use of anaesthetics for operations would have avoided the problems of shock. Operations prior to their use often resulted in death through gangrene etc. In many cases in wars more people died as much of bad treatment as they did directly of wounds inflicted by the enemy. Florence Nightingale (1820 -1910) the British Nurse is well known for her work in the Crimean war in the period 1853 -1856. She was often appalled by the lack of hygiene and basic discipline within the army medical personnel. Her influence was however not just confined to that war, but spread throughout the nursing profession. The issue of cleanliness in hospitals is still prevalent with more awareness of the effects of MRSA (methicillin resistant Staphylococcus aureus). There have been claims that even in the 21st century there are problems of lack of cleanliness within the hospital environment.

Another important element was that of the use of drinking water, which needed to be pure. There was a lack of fresh water in many countries, including in some cases, problems of water pollution caused by firms in Asia. An Oxfam report in 2003 suggested that in Bangladesh by having water going down to about 13 metres rather than 20 metres, the new wells had managed to save lives in a very cost effective manner.

We can see that pure water is one of the most important features for almost any country. One of the problems in the aftermath of the war in Iraq was the lack of pure water supplies available to hospitals. It was even more prevalent in North Korea after a train disaster in 2004 where the absence of facilities in hospitals was highlighted. This was presumably one of the reasons why there was not only a high death rate following the accident but also why the life expectancy of the nation was affected.

Egalitarianism

Egalitarianism is perhaps more important for life expectancy than merely for Gross National Product. It has been estimated that since the collapse of the Soviet Union in 1989, expectancy for men has fallen by about 7 to 8 years. This is partly because of the high increase of poverty at the lower end of the income distribution. If we subdivide the population into quintiles we will see that in most cases the death rate in the lowest quintile, by income, has a much higher death rate than people in the highest quintile.

Death rates are still higher amongst the working class rather than the middle class, though for all classes mortality rates have fallen.

Income and diet

As people got richer, they could afford a better diet. We now get concerned about additives in food, but in 19th Century Britain adulteration of food was by no means unknown. Chalk would be added to flour to give it more bulk and make it cheaper, although less healthy. The Chief Medical Officer for the British government Sir Liam Simpson in 2003 would like to see people eating a healthier diet, including five portions of fruit and vegetable per day. Some people have suggested that Britain was perhaps healthier in terms of diet during the war years, where nutritionists and others were perhaps more readily listened to than in later years. Diet is still of course a matter of controversy as was suggested by people being concerned about the Atkins' diet in 2003. During the war years few people could overeat unless they were very rich, for food was rationed.

In Africa, the first heart attack was recorded in 1967. As recently as 20 years ago, most general physicians would only see abut two to three heart patients in a given year. Today, though, a deadly cocktail of lifestyle diseases, characteristic of the people in high income brackets, is quietly taking the lead as the number one killer. In Kenya, young people between 30 and 40 years are falling victim to such lifestyle diseases as heart diseases, hypertension and diabetes due to lack of exercise and poor diets.

Obesity is another of the lifestyle diseases which is mainly associated with the children and adolescents of parents in higher income brackets. In Kenya, with increasing urbanization, many children are found at home watching TV or playing games on the home computer as they partake of junk food. These youngsters are growing up as 'couch potatoes' and continually become unhealthy which leads to eventually leads to the dangers of obesity.

Death rates for children and mothers

Childbirth for women was a risky process with great number of women dying at the time. This was not helped by some clergymen and others who claimed that the use of anaesthetics at childbirth was against God's wishes. The selective use of the Bible is of course nothing new, anymore than people from other quasi religions, including Marxism, choosing the bits that they want rather than looking at Marx's overall concepts.

In many third world countries, the risky age is from 0 to 5 years. In Kenya the infant mortality in this age bracket stands at 115 per 1,000. This kind of risk was only noticed in the U.K. in the Victorian times. It is easy to see this by visiting any Victorian graveyard in the U.K, where a large number of graves are that of children who died before the age of five.

When examining information about infant mortality, some of the features which sociologists might be interested in, is the absence of clean water and also the importance of breast-feeding as causes of high infant mortality. There were criticisms of some of the baby food manufacturing companies, which seem to suggest that people should use baby food in preference to breast-feeding. Part of the problem is not so much that the formulated food does not have all the necessary contents, but to obtain clean water into which to prepare the food in the first place. Over the last several years, the importance of breast-feeding has been recognized as one of the most valuable medical contributors to infant health.

We mentioned earlier the risks for mothers and children. Death of mothers due to childbirth has presently become relatively rare. However, in the Western countries, there is concern about the increasing number of caesarean births, with the assumption that more people choose to deliver through caesarean to avoid pain. The main concern is that childbirth through caesarean section may lead to higher risks for the mothers.

Government and birth rates

In 2004, the Australian Prime Minister suggested that more children needed to be born in this country. The birth rate may be affected partly by people's expectations. For example, if people expect to have someone to look after them in their old age they may be inclined to have more children.

As prospects for children improved in the U.K., there was less need for people to have large families in the first place. Another important aspect was that one needed fewer children to provide for old age. This in turn interacted with the birth rate, since once the welfare state came, partly as a result of the Liberal governments in 1906-14, as well as the Labour governments from 1945-51 there was less need to have children who it was hoped could provide for the elderly parents if the need arose. Lower deaths amongst children also meant that the need to have large families partly for this reason did not usually arise.

Death rates amongst the elderly in the U.K.

It seemed as though old age was provided for by the state in any case. In 2003, there was controversy about wages paid to pensioners at the Labour Party Conference. There have also been scares about pensions paid by pension companies with the rapid decline in stock exchange prices.

Poorer pensioners are more likely to die from hypothermia even in a richer country such as the U.K. than richer pensioners. There is a fuel payment paid to all people over 60, which has not kept pace with the inflationary pressure of fuel prices. A better and more efficient system might be to ensure that houses are better insulated since it is likely that older people will live in older and worse insulated houses.

Kenya's National Hospital Insurance Fund

National Hospital Insurance Fund is a state parastatal that was established in 1966 as a department under the Ministry of Health. The original Act of Parliament that set up this Fund in 1966 has over the years been reviewed to accommodate the changing healthcare needs of the Kenyan population, employment and restructuring in the health sector. As at 2005, the fund covered only about 20-30 per cent of the population and was more skewed in favour of the formal sector, leaving out the population categories in the informal sector.

In terms of accessibility, NHIF has offices in less than half of the current 72 of Kenya's administrative districts, and about 400 accredited health care providers (for in-patient services), which are unevenly distributed. Access to NHIF services in the rural and, in particular, remote areas has been minimal due mainly to poor infrastructure and long distances to the Fund's offices. Thus, the initial intention of NHIF reaching out to all, by making the scheme accessible to as many Kenyans as possible, has not been attained.

The Fund offers an affordable package, given the nature of services provided. Monthly premiums (ranging from Ksh 30 to Ksh 320) are low, as compared to those of the conventional insurance schemes, which are actuarially determined. However, even with the low contribution levels, many Kenyans have not been able to join NHIF, mainly due to the high poverty levels. In relation to the benefits offered, NHIF has no provision for exclusions. As such, all medical conditions are covered, including maternity cases. There is also no limit as to the number of a beneficiary's dependants.

The NHIF Act No. 9 of 1998 provided for both in- and out-patient cover. But up to now, only in-patient benefits are offered.

Demerit goods and death rates

The economist often uses the words demerit goods to mean goods such as alcohol, drugs and, tobacco, which are not thought by the government and medics to be good for people. Sociologists, as with most of the other social sciences, are often divided about what can be done. Few people would suggest an outright ban on alcohol as in the prohibition era in the United States in the 1920s; or the attempt by the minister for health in Kenya to ban smoking in public in 2005. In both cases, banning seemed to be ineffective. In the latter case, the ban was revoked on a technicality on legislation of the country as Kenya's Constitution (and all Kenyan Laws) has no provision on such an act by the government or any other individual/organization.

In most cases these demerit goods are subjected to legislation that is meant to discourage people from tasking it. This legislation may take several forms such as making the goods' production, distribution and imbibing, illegal. In other cases, the goods attract high duty rates, which make them expensive to attain.

During the First World War the Western governments had taken some interest in restricting the amount of alcohol, not so much to save lives, but because it interfered with arms production. In traditional African societies, local brews were taken socially, at feasts, and by a particular age group.

Birth rates

There is no argument that birth rates have fallen, but there are arguments as to why this is so. Women generally marry later than they did. They also tend to have children later than they did. What is a matter of dispute is whether or not this occurs because there is a conflict between career and marriage, or whether it is because women prefer to have some freedom before taking the nurturer role. The so-called –*dinky* family, "dual-income no kids yet", has become perhaps more fashionable than in the past, the world over. It is also unlike, say the Kosovo culture in Eastern Europe, where it is a matter of pride that one should be married and that necessarily one should have children.

Immigration

People tend to move from a low-income country to a high-income country. Movement to such countries depends on such factors as the relative cost of living as well as availability of jobs and perhaps perceptions. The perception is quite fundamental since few people have perfect information about their own country, let alone information about other countries.

There has been an increasing number of African immigrants living in Western countries such as the United States in recent times. The significant increase can be said to follow three important developments. The first is an increase in the number of African students and professionals who stayed in the U.S. as a result of political and economic difficulties at home beginning in the 1970s. The Immigration Reform and Control Act of 1986 made it easier for this highly educated group to obtain permanent status and remain in the country. The second wave began in the mid-1980s with the arrival of large numbers of political refugees, particularly from the Horn of Africa, who were fleeing repressive regimes and violent conflict in the region. The third wave came in the early 1990s with the introduction of the Diversity Visa program by the Immigration and Naturalization Services. What distinguishes 20th and 21st century immigration from Africa to America from that of earlier centuries is that it is not the result of forced sequestration from Africa but is rather due to a voluntary decision by the Africans themselves.

In the U.K., immigration has often been much debated with perhaps more heat than light. In the 1960s Enoch Powell, a Conservative Minister of Health often regarded as being a racist, ironically encouraged nurses and other medical people to come from the Caribbean to serve in the United Kingdom. In the early 2000s, doctors and teachers have also been encouraged to fill the gaps. There has been some controversy about this, especially when doctors have been obtained from South Africa, which has enough internal problems of its own without Britain in effect poaching people who have been trained at the South African government's expense. One of the problems with trying to predict numbers of immigrants is that it depends partly upon unpredictable political events. For example, Idi Amin tried to get rid of many of the people of Asian descent who lived in Uganda in the early 1970s. In the early 2000s people of Kurdish origin fled from Iraq because of the brutality of Saddam Hussein's regime. People also fled from Afghanistan, both before and after the fall of the Taliban regime.

Internal Migration

Internal migration occurs mainly for work-related reasons, that is, in search of better jobs and higher salaries. On the other hand though, older people may move from their areas of residence to other places which they feel have a better retirement climate like seaside resorts or rural areas rather than staying in the town where they have worked.

The increases in internal migration and the rate of urban growth associated with economic and political transitions in countries of Asia, Africa, Latin America and the Pacific, have made migration a salient feature of life in developing countries. Ethiopia has been identified as one of the countries in Africa with a relatively high level of internal migration and population redistribution. Studies done in that country in relation to this issue have shown that internal migration occurs following prolonged civil war, famine and forced resettlement by government. Studies have, amongst other factors, shown that the resort to migration and/or resettlement as individual and government policy response to periodic unfavourable conditions in places of origin is not the key to improved living conditions in the country.

For government planning purposes, overall population projections including internal migration are important. This is mainly seen when planning for social infrastructure such as schools and hospitals.

Population of individual areas

Inner City Living and Slum Dwelling

Central business districts and inner cities have traditionally been the melting pots of races, classes, and nationalities. Historically inner cities have also seen workers, farmers, traders and immigrants moving through. Some stayed and others traded. These areas became the heartbeat of business, trade, residence and pleasure.

The reason for the attraction is easy to understand. The structure of most cities is radial in nature where road, rail and other modes of transport move through or to the city centres, resulting in a sustained concentration of business services, retail and consumer opportunities, public and social amenities and government services. Accommodation in proximity to this plethora of services, opportunities and amenities became sought after. As population densities grew, these sectors proliferated.

Over time the more affluent people move to the more spacious suburbs. Businesses, in pursuit of cheaper office space, rates incentives and less crowded areas also started to move. The decline of inner cities arose from a combination of factors: residential governance faltered as large swathes of property was abandoned, taken over by slumlords or mismanaged and banks faced with declining property values and non-payment of bonds started to redline the areas.

Nearly one billion people—one in six on the planet—live as squatters in the world's cities. Within a generation, their ranks are projected to swell to two billion. Then almost half the people living in cities will be squatters. These new urban pioneers come in search of jobs. They could not afford anything on the housing market, so they build homes themselves on land that isn't theirs.

Squatter life is precarious. Most of the world's squatters live in overcrowded shantytowns, or slums. Many squatter communities lack safe drinking water, toilets and sewers, and thus are breeding grounds for disease.

A well known feature of cities is the 'slum'. The UN-HABITAT attempts at a definition by describing a slum household as "a group of individuals living under the same roof that lack one or more of the following conditions: access to safe water; access to sanitation; secure tenure; durability of housing; and sufficient living area.

According to the UN-Habitat, Sub-Saharan Africa hosts the largest proportion of the urban population residing in slums (71.9 per cent); 166 million out of a total urban population of 231 million are classified as slum dwellers. The region has the second largest slum population in the world after South-central Asia, which has 262 million making up 58 per cent of the total urban population in that region. UN-Habitat estimates that 924 million people worldwide, or 31.6 per cent of the global urban population, lived in slums in 2001.

Growth of the suburbs

The suburban areas have long since grown dramatically. This was assisted in some cases by transport developers. There were houses often built by the Metropolitan line to sell to new commuters who used their services. Goldthorpe suggests that in many cases people living in these areas place much more emphasis on home than on local activities. Friends are more widely spread than in the traditional working class areas. This would seem to be in line with the observations made by Wilmott and Young.

Standardised and crude death rate

The crude death rate is measured by the number of deaths in a particular year divided by the thousands of population. However, this is not necessarily a satisfactory measure. If we look at different regions or towns, some may have a much larger proportion of elderly people, and therefore in turn, a much higher death rate than another town, where there may be relatively few elderly people. For this reason therefore, one can often have a standardised death rate, which looks at the typical population as whole and sees what the death rate is.

Sociologists would also be interested in the difference between death rates of different socioeconomic classes as well as other categories. The death rate amongst the working class is higher than amongst the middle and higher classes. We can think of some factors that are perhaps inherent in the system if pollution is a major killer, then it is likely that pollution will be worse around working class homes rather than elsewhere. In many cases the working class lives much nearer smoking factories, than the managers or owners do. Some sociologists would suggest that lack of access to healthy foods would be part of the problem. However, available data does not clearly show this to be the complete picture. If we look for example at health guidelines on eating fruit and vegetables portions per day, it seems likely there is little correlation between socioeconomic class and this type of diet. It could also be argued that different classes are better or worse educated in terms of healthy eating. In smoking, we find significant differences between the classes for men rather than for women. The so-called couch potatoes are no longer entirely confined to the U.K. or other Anglo Saxon countries.

During the Second World War, when rationing was introduced in countries such as the U.K., foodstuffs were scarce, since many of them had to be imported. Therefore the then government tried to encourage people to use what there was within the country. In turn, it meant that they tried to get people to eat food, which they would have otherwise not eaten. One of the best-known cooks of the time, Margaret Patten, was employed by the Department of Food to try to encourage people to eat healthily. Food such as sweets was strictly rationed and there was less chance of obesity from this cause.

Successive governments have looked slightly more at primary care. This means that they have tried to look at how to prevent illnesses and only how to treat them. The obvious example here would be that of smoking which is still a major cause of death, globally. One of the problems of primary care is that in most cases, local health officials are more likely to be aware of the particular problems, which arise in their area, and these might not necessarily be typical of the country as a whole. They may also be able to make separate provisions. In some cases they may encourage good parenting, which may have effects not just on the likelihood of children contracting diseases, but also have additional benefits in terms of better behaviour and less social disorder.

SELF EXAMINATION QUESTIONS

1. What is meant by the term 'death rate'? What happened to death rates during the 20th Century? Were the changes similar for all social classes? Why might this be important to know for a sociologist? Why are there some disagreements about the causes of changes?

2. What is meant by the term 'crude death rate'?

3. Why are there differences in death rates between different countries? How far is it only a consequence of differences in incomes? What other factors apart from health might influence death rates? (Hint. How far are suicide and road accidents important in this respect)? What influence has international bodies such as the World Health Organisation and the World Bank had on changes to death rates?

4. How far is it true that higher social economic classes have better diets? Do richer people always have a healthier life style? How could we test this concept? Are there differences between the genders in terms of smoking and drinking etc?

5. Why do some people suggest that the healthiest period for eating was during the Second World War, specifically in a country such as the U.K.? What happened to the minimum and maximum amounts of food that most people could obtain? Why did the U.K. government take an active interest in the way that people ate? Why did the U.K. government use people such as Margaret Patten, the well-known cook, to try to publish new recipes?

6. What has happened to the risk for mothers and children under the age of 5? Why was this considered to be the most vulnerable age for most children until recently? Why, were there arguments about the desirability of caesarean birth? (Hint. What are the costs of different types of birth and what are the physical risks)?

7. How far would more exercise help to improve death rates? What prevents people from taking more exercise? How far are there constraints imposed by the physical surroundings, for example, places where people can easily walk and how far is it just due to lack of self-control? What could local authorities and central governments do about trying to encourage people to exercise more?

8. How far does the provision of the welfare state mean that families no longer need to be big in order to provide for old age? In 2009 it seemed to be suggested that there was a reversal of a past trends towards an extended family, for instance, 3 generations living in the same house. What would be the effects of this on society?

(Hint. Why might it make a difference to the number of women who could go out to work.)?

9. What is meant by saying that the National Health Service should concentrate more on health rather than treating illness? (Hint. Why might it be cheaper to try to encourage people to live more healthily rather than to treat them when they are sick)? Should the government try to look at poorer rather than rich areas when trying to improve health? (Hint. Why are mortality rates different between the different groups)?

10. Why do men and women seem to be marrying at a later age than they did? Why might the provision of bigger houses in the early part of the 20th century have meant that newly married couples might live in the same house as their parents? What effect would rise in house prices have on the ability of newly married people to be able to obtain their own houses? What effect is this likely to have on the total population?

11. In May 2004, ten new countries joined the European Union and two more in 2007. What effect might this have on the number of potential employees and also on the number of people requiring Social Security and Education? (Hint. Is the age profile the same amongst these ten countries as it is in the U.K.)? Would the ten countries have the same level of unemployment as in the U.K. and also would the typical family size be the same?

12. What is meant by the term internal migration? Which areas do people tend to move to and which areas do they move from? Is this the same for all the different age groups and if not why might it differ? Why would it be important for sociologists to be aware of this and what are the implications for education, jobs and transport?

13. Why might the inner city tend to have more members of the underclass, compared with other areas? (Hint. Where are house prices highest?) Do the under class have the same number of cars as for example the middle class? Why might this be important when looking for jobs in certain areas)?

Chapter Eight

Health

Sociologists have been interested in the health of the residents of a country for a variety of reasons. One is that health is often related to social class with the wealthier classes living longer than the poorer ones do. We might assume that health is determined by a number of factors many of which overlap with areas of interest for sociologists.

Health and longevity is determined by availability of health care, access to a healthy diet and clean drinking water and regular exercise. Health is negatively impacted by such demerit goods as tobacco, drugs and alcohol. External influences to health include reduced risk of pollution whether in the home, from traffic, an industry or at work. In most developed countries, the Government provides health care including doctors and hospitals. The U.S.A is a glaring exception to this general rule with the state leaving much health care to the private sector and insurance companies. In most of the developing countries, access to health care remains an issue. To use Kenya as an illustration, although good health is a pre-requisite to socioeconomic development, public budget allocation to the health sector has hardly been enough over the years in per capita terms.

Most countries have a bureau of standards whose purpose of existence is to ensure that products meet standards of conformity towards quality, free from defects and contamination.

Government provision of health care in the U.K.

The National Insurance Act 1911, which was enacted by the then Chancellor of the Exchequer Lloyd George for the Liberal government, is sometimes referred to as the nine pence for four pence (9d for 4d) Act. This is since employees had to contribute four old pence, just over 1 ½ pence per week, whilst the government and employers gave the rest of the contribution. This Act as, the name implied, set up a system of National Insurance. Although the name "national" was used it could be argued that it was slightly misleading, since only some employees gained from it, whilst people outside the workforce did not do so. The term National Insurance still applies to taxation contributions, though at this stage there is very little connection between the amount collected and the amount distributed in the way of benefit. The term National Insurance, however, originally meant what it said, i.e. it was like a government policy for the community as a whole, which was probably cheaper to collect and administer than for rival private insurance companies to try to do so. Prior to this mortality rates for the different socio economic classes had been quite different. However since there are many factors affecting health, it is not clear how far this was due to better medical services available to the rich and how far it was due to better diet, housing conditions and working conditions. The 1911 act is important since it was the first time that a U.K. government had been involved directly to get health improvement. It could however be argued that other legislation in the 19th century such as acts about town planning and even Chadwick's reforms in the 1850s may have had just as much effect. Poor town planning as written about by Friedrich Engels accounts of life in cities such as Manchester show how poor conditions were in the early part of the 19th century.

The National Health Service itself was set up in 1946 immediately after the Second World War. In spite of general support in the country, many doctors, particularly consultants, opposed it. This was partly at least because consultants did not relish the thought of having to work for the government. The First World War had shown the lack of health of many recruits to the army, who had to be fattened up before they could be sent to fight. The original assumption with the National Health Service was that once money had been spent to bring people to a reasonable state of health, that then National Health Service expenditure would fall. In practice this has not happened, but it is not quite clear what the explanations are for this. One is that people have higher expectations, e.g. in many poorer countries, if people contract a particular disease, e.g. breast cancer, it is assumed that they will die from it, whereas increasingly since the Second World War, great efforts have been made to keep people alive, sometimes through surgery, sometimes through medication, etc. The NHS also followed on, not entirely coincidentally, from the Beveridge Report in 1942. Beveridge was briefly a Liberal MP in the coalition government, but he is perhaps better known for his work at the London School of Economics. His report, which set up the welfare state as a whole, is sometimes said to be able to help people from the cradle to the grave.

The NHS has had criticisms from the public, although they seem to approve of it as a whole even if their individual experiences are not necessarily very good. The Conservative governments from 1979 to 1997 introduced the idea of the competition of the internal market. It was suggested that being able to buy in services from different health authorities would make the whole service more efficient. Critics argue that in practice it just led to more red tape and more form filling, since prices had to be established in an area where prices were not usually charged. The present Labour government since 1997 has set a series of targets, e.g. waiting list times for patients should not exceed a year. The problems are that such targets can easily be manipulated. This would be in line with Weber's concerns about bureaucracy. If the government insists that people should not, on the whole, wait for more than one year, then may be a temptation for doctors and others not to put forward names until later than necessary. Similarly, if the government just looks at the volume of people treated, then doctors and others may well concentrate on less crucial cases where it is much easier to get through a series of treatment for many patients rather than concentrating on sicker patients where treatment including operations will take a lot longer. Similarly, even the concept of mortality rates for different hospitals and surgeons may well lead to doctors being willing to treat people with lower rather than high risk, since this would show a better result. As always with statistics, care has to be taken to compare like with like. In February 2004 the government announced that it was considering the problems of too many targets not just for health but also education etc.

Government provision of health care in Kenya

Access to health care is a challenge for this predominantly rural population. With a population that is over 31 million people; the death rate is estimated at 14 deaths per 1000 people, annually. The major causes of death in Kenya are from communicable (and vaccine-preventable) diseases and malnutrition. The structure of the Kenyan health system and the inadequate physician supply do not support the needs of the populace.

Kenya's health system is faced with obstacles such as political corruption, a high incidence of AIDS, widespread public issues such as the need for sanitation and water purification, and increasingly high birth rates (32 per 1000). Provision of health care services is primarily curative, not preventive. Research shows that 70% of health care costs in Kenya go to emoluments and not service.

Furthermore, development of health infrastructure has not kept pace with the population growth rate. In particular, many health facilities lack the necessary equipment and medical supplies.

Medical personnel, trained by the government at public expense, are leaving the public service in large numbers for better opportunities in the private sector and in other countries.

The health sector reforms that have hitherto taken place (including introduction of National Health Insurance Fund, free health services, cost-sharing, exemptions and waivers, etc) have all aimed largely at addressing affordability and access to health care services. Spending to promote access to health care is crucial, given also that Kenya is a signatory to the WHO Abuja Declaration. The latter requires member countries to spend at least 15 per cent of their national incomes (GDP) on health. In the last national budget (2007/08), only about 4.9% was allocated to the health sector.

National Hospital Insurance Fund, Kenya (NHIF)

National Hospital Insurance Fund is a State Parastatal that was established in 1966 as a department under the Ministry of Health. The original Act of Parliament that set up this Fund in 1966 has over the years been reviewed to accommodate the changing healthcare needs of the Kenyan population, employment and restructuring in the health sector.

As at 2005, the fund covered only about 20-30 per cent of the population and was more skewed in favour of the formal sector, leaving out the population categories in the informal sector.

In terms of accessibility, NHIF has offices in less than half of the current 72 of Kenya's administrative districts, and about 400 accredited health care providers (for in-patient services), which are unevenly distributed. Access to NHIF services in the rural and, in particular, remote areas has been minimal due mainly to poor infrastructure and long distances to the Fund's offices. Thus, the initial intention of NHIF reaching out to all, by making the scheme accessible to as many Kenyans as possible, has not been attained.

The Fund offers an affordable package, given the nature of services provided. Monthly premiums (ranging from Ksh 30 to Ksh 320) are low, as compared to those of the conventional insurance schemes, which are actuarially determined. However, even with the low contribution levels, many Kenyans have not been able to join NHIF, mainly due to the high poverty levels. In relation to the benefits offered, NHIF has no provision for exclusions. As such, all medical conditions are covered, including maternity cases. There is also no limit as to the number of a beneficiary's dependants. The NHIF Act No. 9 of 1998 provided for both in- and out-patient cover. But up to now, only in-patient benefits are offered.

National Social Health Insurance Fund (NSHIF)

Due to the weaknesses of the NHIF, the National Social Health Insurance Fund (NSHIF) was conceptualized for implementation, with a view to enabling more effective provision of health cover to all Kenyans, at both in- and out-patient service levels. In contrast to the private/commercial health insurance plans where premiums are actuary based (higher risk individuals pay more for their medical cover), a social health plan contributions are based on members' ability to pay but access to services depends on individuals' health care needs, hence a socialized concept, with emphasis on community spirit of solidarity.

Unfortunately the National Social Health Insurance Fund (NSHIF) Bill 2004, tabled by the Minister for Health in 2005 was not debated and subsequently lapsed.

Health, class and gender

In the last century it is very noticeable that deaths due to some serious diseases such as polio and smallpox have fallen drastically or totally been eradicated, respectively.

There are diseases that tend to be associated with poor living conditions, such as cholera although middle classes people have died from it as well. All the same there are those that do not know the demarcations of class, for example cancer of the cervix. This is one where theories can be reasonably tested, since cancer of the cervix is not usually observed either amongst Jewish women or amongst nuns.

In other cases we can see relationships between people's habits and disease. Heart disease has become a major killer, and is mainly related to bad diet and lack of exercise. Whilst heart attacks are often associated with middle class men, particularly executives, this is not necessary the case. In addition, the number of deaths from male lung cancer (a consequence of smoking) in the U.K. has fallen, presumably because of the decreasing number of men who smoke, but female lung cancer, on the other hand, has risen.

Life expectancy has generally risen on a global level. In some of the Sub-Saharan African countries -such as Kenya and Lesotho, maternal education has been accepted almost unanimously (together with other important elements) as a major socioeconomic factor in infant and post-infant mortality. 3 principal interpretations have been that educational level is an indicator of living standard and consequently determines access to goods and services that influence mortality; that formal education permits acquisition of knowledge and modern standards in the areas of hygiene, child care, health and related domains that affect the level of mortality; and that education measures the degree of breaking with tradition.

Access to good health facilities and necessary drugs has been associated with social inequalities, with the people in the middle and high class bracket being able to access while those on the lower cadres of society are not able to access them. In addition people in long-term unemployment are equally unable to access health services and may have more ailments than those who are in employment. Studies show that people in the unskilled working class visit the doctor more often and for a wide range of ailments, than those in professional occupations.

Problems of defining health

One of the main problems of health, which is rarely identified, is how we define health in the first place. Sometimes it is merely defined as the absence of disease; others suggest we need to go further and define the term to mean the ability to carry out certain tasks such as the ability to walk without problems. Lower targets can be set, for example 'the ability to be able to get out of a chair unaided'.

Some sociologists view health as mechanistic; where health care is seen to be necessary in order to carry out repairs. However, this approach seems not to pay enough attention to mental characteristics. There are some purely physical needs like breaking a leg when skiing. In such a case it is reasonable to assume that this is a physical problem.

In many other cases with irritable bowel syndrome and some cancers, there is a link between mental and physical well being. Until very recently, doctors were not trained to look at psychology at all, even though the link between mental and physical health has been established for many years. In some cases, the conventions of the time and societal environment are taken into account in assessing health issues. It is often assumed that in a society which seems to rush around – mainly in urban centres - people tend to be fatigued.

Different approaches to health

There are different sociological attitudes towards health. One non-mainstream view from Ivan Illich is that the population would be better off if the medical profession did not interfere so much in the first place.

The Marxists would argue that doctors are there to help the employers by having a workforce that is sufficiently healthy to be part of a productive work force. Some Marxists would also argue that doctors are there to sign sick certificates ensuring that people do not make money out of the companies unnecessarily.

The supply of doctors in developing countries

Medical personnel in the developing world more leave their parent countries in large numbers for better opportunities in other countries. The World Health Organization observed in 2006 that the shortage of doctors and nurses in the developing world is causing furtherance of disease and death as they look for jobs in richer countries.

On average, 25 per cent of doctors and five per cent of nurses trained in Africa are working in developed countries. 29 per cent of Ghana's physicians are working abroad, as are 34 per cent of Zimbabwe's nurses. Africa has 24 per cent of the world's disease burden, but just three per cent of the health-care workers and accounts for less than one per cent of global health-care spending. The WHO reported that more than four million more health-care workers are needed in 57 countries, mostly in Africa and rural parts of Asia, to fill the medical gap.

Medical drugs

The concept of drugs and how they should be paid for is one that is fraught with difficulty. The Royal Statistical Society in its journal of '*Society Statistics*' suggested that in many cases, drugs are only tested on perhaps 6,000 people before being released for public use. Where drugs are used for people who would otherwise be terminally ill, this number may be sufficient with no worry about possible side effects. On the other hand, there have been examples, perhaps noticeably the thalidomide tragedy - a birth control pill that was manufactured by a Distillers company subsidiary - where many people were born with defects, amongst them being born with no limbs.

Feminist view of health

Feminists argue that some health problems such as anorexia are largely manmade diseases. Young girls have much stronger views about the ideal weight than boys will, as a result of what is touted to be beautiful say by the models of the catwalk. This is not helped by the fact that girls are perhaps less willing to take exercise compared to many boys who would be quite happy to play sport. This could also be a result of stereotyping.

Feminists would also argue that even childbirth which has often been encouraged to take place in hospitals is not always helpful. There are obviously some cases where the women may be at risk in which case hospital births might be desirable mainly because of the proximity of medical equipment and qualified medical personnel. Qualified medical personnel have largely contributed to the low mortality rates that have been achieved over the years on a global level. However, women are at liberty to choose where they wish to have their children if there are no obvious risks.

The role of the media and health

The media is known to be quite vocal in reporting on the problems of drugs. Recently, one of the local television stations in Kenya ran a series on hard drug use at the Kenyan Coast. Yet more people die of smoking than those who die of drug use. Nevertheless, though the media will report very widely about deaths caused by certain drugs, such as heroin - and one would feel sorry for the parents in such cases - the much bigger risk is continually ignored. This is perhaps because the media seems quite happy to have advertisements from the tobacco companies in their own newspapers. Other risks such as alcoholism and its associated risks are also usually ignored by the media.

Unemployment and health

There seems to be a linkage between mortality rates and health even if we allow for the likelihood that unemployment is class related and that different age groups are likely to have higher rate of unemployment.

Suicide rates seem to be higher amongst the unemployed. Evidence from studies done shows that the unemployed people go through several stages: In the short term, unemployed people may well find that being unemployed gives them an opportunity to get away from the rat race and to catch up with tasks, which previously they had not had time to do. After this, many people get into a stage of stress. Whilst work causes stress the isolation which is often caused by unemployment, for instance , being unable to go to entertainment spots, church and other activities, does not help because the socialisation process is often more difficult when one is out of a job.

Jobless people are increasingly likely to lose self-confidence which further contributes to them not being able to obtain jobs.

SELF EXAMINATION QUESTIONS

1. Discuss the different approaches to defining health.
2. How do sociologists relate health to social class?
3. There are certain health matters that are dependent on the gender of an individual. How far is this statement true?
4. What kinds of challenges are associated with the period and manner in which drugs are tested before being released for public use?
5. What is meant by 'man made' diseases?
6. What role does the media play in ensuring a healthy society? How can this be improved?
7. Suicide rates seem to be higher amongst the unemployed. How true is this statement?
8. Sociologists have advanced the theory that people who are unemployed go through certain stages once they are unemployed. Which are these stages and how are the individuals affected at each stage?
9. How true is it that the socialization process is often more difficult when one is out of a job?

Chapter Nine

Education

British Education System and Immigrants

Marxism suggests that there are underlying problems for immigrant children. The main one would be economic deprivation; this would arise partly because power is almost entirely in the ruling class that is not found in the ethnic minority. With this power and wealth, the ruling class are in a strong position to pay less to ethnic minorities particularly in the case of a monopsony buyer of labour, say, if a firm is the major one in a relatively small town. Therefore, the children in turn are likely not to go to the independent sector, in Britain this comprises about 7% of the total number of children.

The public schools would usually claim that one of their advantages is that they offer better facilities, which is hardly surprising when charges in the early 2000's were often about £12,000 per year. They also offered smaller classes. Smaller classes would mean that they have more opportunities. Apart from this direct association with money, which is comparatively rare even for the white population, they would also be mostly assimilated in the urban areas, particularly in the inner cities. Sociologists such as Marxists might well argue that a report in September 2004 to pay more money to teachers working in poorer schools would be welcome. The resources given in many cases to schools in the poorer areas, not withstanding Educational Priority Areas (EPAs), have certainly in the past been less than elsewhere. This is particularly true in the 1960s, where various educational reports showed that they did not get the resources awarded to the grammar schools.

People coming from more deprived backgrounds, including the ethnic groups, would have less access to the latest technology, such as computers, and this in turn would mean that they would get lower marks. This would be especially so where the syllabus assumes, implicitly or explicitly, that they have access to such facilities. In many cases the immigrant children may feel alienated, since there would be more emphasis on the values of the ruling class, for example, reference to classical music or British pop music, but none to reggae. Similarly, the authors studied, sometimes referred disparagingly as 'white dead men', such as Shakespeare, will not relate to the experience of the immigrant children. Marxists would probably conclude that the system was geared to the needs of firms rather than to the needs of individuals. Functionalists on the other hand might well suggest that children should be integrated into the British system as a whole.

Some Marxists would also suggest that the aspirations of parents are low, although this differs widely between the different ethnic cultures and there are significant differences in their educational performance. Other writers would suggest that the whole language of teachers is likely to be different, using their extended language, whereas parents of immigrants may often use a more restricted language. Some Marxists may suggest that some teachers themselves are hostile to immigrant children, although authorities such as the Inner London Educational Authority in the 1980s did its best to stamp this out, though not necessarily in an efficient manner. However, successive Conservative governments were hostile to what they saw as Black Studies. The National Curriculum has reverted back to a more traditional setting.

Functionalists would assume that children should be assimilated into the British way of life. This would cover a wide area including British music and literature. According to functionalists there are often hidden values within the school curricula, which need to be explored. They suggest that there should be a way of achieving a value consensus. This might be relatively easy to achieve in some cases;West Indian children would often be more aware of Christian traditions than many children who are white British.

In addition, functionalists suggest that, education might take a long while to achieve the desired effects, partly because the norms would take a while to evolve. Socialization would always be important. This may well be achieved by ensuring that schools are relatively large, so that there is little chance of schools becoming exclusively white or exclusively black. The functionalists would probably reject the concept of teaching languages for the ethnic minorities. They would probably regard this as unnecessary anyway, and would insist that if it had to be done, it should be done within the family setting.

It might be more difficult to gain consensus about the use of single sex schools. Some Muslims would welcome this, since it is easier to maintain modesty as they see it in a single sex school, particularly at secondary level. Functionalists would probably not see this as part of the assimilation process. Part of the problem with the assimilation process is that most minority groups are not looking to be assimilated but want to be respected as equal members of society as seen in the Swann Report 1985.

The integrationists by contrast would want to work out why ethnic minorities did not do so well in the first place, assuming this was the case. They might look, as would the Marxists, at measures of deprivation to see whether exam results could differ because of this; there is obviously a link between social class and educational results. They would also look to other factors which might relate to ethnic groups, for example occupation, although most evidence seems to suggest that ethnic groups are not highly represented in any one industry. There may be exceptions as it is in Leicester, where non-whites are probably a majority and there is a considerable degree of employment within the textile industry. They also want to look at factors from the educational system itself which might explain why minorities do not do well. These factors could include perception where, for instance, teachers may regard West Indian children as less capable and stereotype them on this basis. This may not be confined to ethnic minorities.

Racism and ethnicity

Many of the early sociologists, such as Karl Marx and Weber, were interested in equality. Equality here related to ethnic differences or differences in income and opportunities between the genders. However, in more recent times there seems to be more focus on the effects of immigration as well as racism.

The concept of immigration is not new. Most people talk about the native British, although it is not too clear what is meant by this, since the very term 'Anglo-Saxon' refers to people who came from relatively small tribes from what is now Germany. There were immigrants already in the 18th century, mainly because of slavery. In the 19th century immigration occurred particularly from Ireland, which then was not divided into two parts, particularly following the potato famine in the 1840s.

Perhaps racism came more to the fore when it was easier to classify people as immigrants, partly because of the colour of their skin and the languages they used. Jews, for instance, as well as other groups, often fled to Britain to escape the excesses of Russia under the Tsar in the 19th century as well as in the early 20th century. Immigration has always taken place due to what sociologists might describe as push and pull reasons. The push reasons would include religious or political persecution, for example intolerance towards Protestants by the French led to emigration by the Huguenots in the 18th century.

Interestingly enough, the same pressures occurred in the early 2000s with the NHS encouraging doctors and others to come into the health service.

Sociologists have often been divided about whether immigration should lead to assimilation; that eventually there will be little difference between the so-called natives and the immigrants. There are at least two problems about assimilation. One is whether people already living in a country want to help to assimilate people coming in, while the other problem is whether people coming wish to be assimilated. There are a considerable number of racists, who regard people from other countries as inferior. It is difficult, however, to be precise about the people who in some cases would seem to be racist in principle, but in practice would treat individuals fairly well. Some sociologists have suggested that there are problems with dealing with immigrants with different religions, but this hardly explains hostilities to people from the Caribbean, where on the whole their heritage is a Christian one, and as far as one can judge it, the number of church goers amongst the Caribbean people is probably higher than that of the native population in the U.K. There may be some cultural differences, although it should be noted that since the ethnic groups are by no means homogenous, this too is subject to debate. People coming in from a Muslim background will often have a more puritan outlook towards sex outside marriage and homosexuality than the so-called liberals within the U.K. Paradoxically, the people associated most with hostility towards immigration may well have similar views about sex outside marriage and abortion.

It is never completely clear how far the British are racist. There are often jokes which would seem to be racist, not merely about black people, but also about Welsh, Irish and Scottish people. The number of people voting for outright racist parties has been relatively small. In many cases the racist parties have adopted policies at the local level concentrating on welfare issues rather than stressing their racism. The assumptions about immigration have not been helped by the lack of knowledge about immigrants. Surveys have shown that people vastly overestimate the number of immigrants living in the U.K. as information on this is often second hand. Although there are statistics carried out by different bodies, most people do not have accurate information on which to base judgements, and the concept of rationality, which was an assumption of many of the early sociologists, has not been the basis for decision making.

The assumption of immigration, particularly from the New Commonwealth countries, essentially meaning not white, for instance India, Pakistan, Bangladesh and the Caribbean countries, has been slowed down by a variety of immigration acts. The assumption by many people that all immigrants are black ignores the differences, even in a city such as Bradford, between the people of Pakistani origin and people of Indian origin, where there are differences of religion as well as social class.

Some sociologists reject the concept of assimilation and assume that we should instead look at the differences which exist, and where there are some common values, celebrate the results. It could be argued that the former Inner London Education Authority in the 1980s tried to do this by encouraging people to study a variety of different cultures rather than concentrating on what would seem to be mainstream subjects.

If we look at the history from the Second World War onwards, the number of non-whites living in the United Kingdom around 1950 was probably about 100,000. This was a representative figure of 1 in 500 of the population, which would have meant there was virtually no contact for many people in ordinary life between white and black. At the present time the figure is much higher as seen from publications such as '*Social Trends*'. The British economy grew after the Second World War, partly due to Keynesian demand measures, and partly because there was an increasing demand for many goods and services which had not been available during the Second World War. Additionally, a great deal of construction work was needed in order to build new houses and factories to replace those which had been destroyed during the war. Therefore, far from discouraging immigration, the government, as well as large employers, often encouraged people to move to this country.

During Atlee's term as Prime Minister from 1945 to 1951, most of the immigrants were from the Caribbean as well as from India and Pakistan. There were immigration acts in 1962, 1968 and 1971, the first and the last under a Conservative government and the other under the Labour government of Harold Wilson. Though this restricted immigration, it did not stop the entry of dependant relatives. The 1971 Act meant that most people migrating to the U.K. needed work permits, but these were granted relatively easily, especially for work that the native population did not want to do. They included work in hotels, where the wages were often low, and the National Health Service, where working conditions were not very good and nurses were badly paid. However, as unemployment grew to around the three million mark, the number of work permits tended to decline. Permits, instead of being given for manual work were given for professional work.

Britain entered the European Community in 1973 and under this Union there is free movement of labour between the different European countries. Therefore, the pattern of immigration has changed from the New Commonwealth to a pattern of migration from the European Community, which by the late 1980s was about one quarter of the total. The total from the Indian Subcontinent and other New Commonwealth areas is also about a quarter.

The issue of immigration is often linked with colour, since people from the New Commonwealth countries were predominantly non-white, perhaps 80% of them, whereas those coming from the so-called Old Commonwealth, Australia, New Zealand and Canada, were predominantly white.

The immigration patterns have also become more complex. The British population is an aging one. In the early 2000s the number of over-65s was more than that of the under-16s. The portion of people coming from the Indian Subcontinent is totally different; dependents normally follow the male head of the household and there is a much higher proportion of young people. The proportion of males amongst immigrants is also higher compared to that of the white group.

If we look at the disadvantages which ethnic groups might suffer from, we can see this would be related to the job that they do. The male ethnic groups are very strongly represented in the transport industry. This is probably partly because when there is relatively full employment few people want to take on the lower paid jobs, which are often also associated with shift work. The textile industry is another one, particularly in Leicester, which attracts large numbers of immigrant workers, with not-so-good working conditions (the so-called sweatshops) and low pay, particularly before the introduction of the National Minimum Wage. Male ethnic groups are also found in other manufacturing industries which have been subject to severe decline. Ethnic minority women have jobs which are not dissimilar to those of the white population, with the exception of the National Health Service, where one could argue that the original pull and push practice of the NHS, finding it difficult to recruit staff and being better paid compared to overseas, has perhaps contributed to this.

Perhaps more importantly for the ethnic groups are not so much the jobs which they do but the level of their jobs. As one might expect, black people generally have been over-represented in less skilled manual occupations. This has been partly due to differences in qualifications, although this could change quite rapidly with changes in the educational system, and increasingly higher proportions of children, particularly from the Indian Subcontinent, wanting to go to university. One could also argue that there is a second generation aspect; whereas people from the Indian subcontinent have to conform to the stereotype of shop-keeping, the second generation will often not want to get into the family business and will instead seek to have jobs in the professions.

There are significant differences between ethnic groups of Caribbean origin and those from the Indian Subcontinent. One of the noticeable features about people from the Indian subcontinent is the relatively high proportion of self-employment compared to the white population. There are also differences in earnings between white and black. The differences are greater between men rather than women. As already mentioned, ethnic groups are often more involved in shift work, though it is not quite clear whether this is due to a desire to work unsocial hours to make up for low pay, or whether it is because of the industries in which they are in. The differences in age profile may also account for some differences, since generally older people earn more than younger ones, particularly in white-collar occupations, but also in manual occupations, where supervisors will get more money than operatives.

In periods of high unemployment as in the 1980s and the early 1990s and now the rates of unemployment for the black community were much higher than for whites as seen in the data obtained in '*Social Trends*'. There were differences between the different ethnic groups. It is not clear how far this is due to racism and how far due to other factors. Some industries are much more prone to unemployment, particularly manufacturing and construction, compared to other industries which are said to be recession proof. It may also reflect differences in the regional balances of unemployment. London and the South East have lower unemployment rates than the West Midlands, particularly since the 1980s.

One can also look at housing. The ability to be able to borrow money is partly related to present income, as well as future income. The quality of housing may also vary according to the location. The white population are less likely to live in terraced houses or flats, but Asian communities prefer different types of housing, partly because of the extended family system, whereby several generations may live in one house. This would in many cases be comparable to the situation existing in the U.K. until the 1930s or slightly later, when different generations lived in the same house, before the growth of suburbia from the 1930s. There are also differences within ethnic groups, with West Indians being more likely to live in what was Council Housing but increasingly Housing Association type of housing, compared with the people of Asian descent, who in many cases favour owner occupation.

The health patterns are different between different ethnic groups, with infant mortality rate being much higher for the black rather than for the white population. This is perhaps due to the lack of care available from the health service and it could also include other factors such as class differences.

Sociologists are in many cases interested to discover and explain how the differences arise. In many cases the disadvantages of ethnic groups are correlated with their position in society. People at the lower end of the socioeconomic range will tend to have lower life expectancy, whether they are white or black. It is also not quite clear how far there might be differences between first and second generations. It could be that if we had sufficient evidence we could show that if assimilation takes place - and it seems likely that the children from ethnic minorities want to become assimilated, particularly to join the professional classes - then some of the differences will disappear.

Part of the problem may reside in the ability or inability to speak Standard English, which is not the same as literacy in the conventional sense. Some of the media tends to suggest that this is partly the people's fault, that is, they do not enter the mainstream culture and instead prefer to keep within their own culture. There is some evidence from the U.S.A. that people do prefer to work with their own minority groups, though it is not clear whether this is a retreat from racism or is in itself racist behaviour.

Marxists would tend to assume that these problems are simply an extension of the problems of the class system and that if we remove them, the rest of the problems will be done away with. Sociologists have often used the word 'norm' to denote the values of society. The word 'deviation' has negative connotations, implying that anybody who does not comply with the norms is inferior. Again, the assimilation model in some respects seems to assume that there is a native culture that others should belong to and that belonging to it is better than rejoicing in difference. There have sometimes been reactions to this, for example the slogan 'black is beautiful'. Differences in approach spill over into education.

Some sociologists would suggest that black people should become part of the white British life by learning in their educational system, not merely to obtain the conventional qualifications, such as GCSE's, A levels, degrees or professional qualifications, but also to have the same cultural values, which will enable them to fit in. This will not only be in the educational system, but also in the job structure.

There are a number of different factors affecting educational performance. One may be the family pattern. There seems to be a higher proportion of Caribbean extraction children who come from single parent families. It would need to be seen if variations in performance are related to this. Clearly, in turn, this could be correlated with lack of income. Douglas, for example, in his well known studies of education suggests that some parents are much more supportive than others. It is not clear whether children coming from an Indian Subcontinent background will receive support in reading within the family.

SELF EXAMINATION QUESTIONS

Chapter 9

1. The Marxist school of thought observes that the education system in the U.K. may alienate the immigrant children. Explain how they arrive at this observation and possible measures to change this.

2. According to the functionalists, how does socialization impact the education system with respect to achieving a value consensus in schools?

3. How do the difficulties faced by ethnic groups in the education system impact on the kind of jobs they get and the levels of management they can rise to?

4. What have been the main causes of immigration into the U.K. for various ethnic groups? How have the patterns of immigration over time?

5. How is education in deprived neighbourhoods affected by the lack of or minimal resources (such as technology) available to the schools in these neighbourhoods?

Chapter Ten

Religion

Sociologists are mainly concerned with how the observance of religion, or its absence, affects society. The word religion is difficult to define. It would usually invoke the idea that there are stronger powers than mankind within the universe we inhabit. Most societies seem to have some belief systems although Lenski and Lenski suggest that in hunter gatherer societies and also in horticultural societies, it was unusual and the concept of a supreme being is much more common in agricultural societies.

Sociology and religion

One of the reasons for studying religion within a sociology framework is that religion or its absence is likely to have an effect on the society. Some sociologists seem to have dwelt on the prohibitions that some religions impose on sexual behaviour, while others - especially some of the functionalists have seen it in a wider context; that it can produce a shared set of values which brings society together. Part of the problems with studying religion within sociology is that almost everyone will have their own preconceptions.

People who have no religious faiths are likely to assume that everything about religion is superstition while people within one religious faith often have limited ideas about other religious faiths. Even within one religious faith people often have very limited or distorted ideas about other people of different parts of the same religion. This may be particularly true of countries divided on sectarian lines as for example in Northern Ireland where in many cases there is little social interaction between the Protestants and Catholics, who are of the same religion. Stereotyping is likely to occur as with many other differences of opinion. After the attack on the Twin Towers in New York in September 2001, there have often been assumptions that all Muslims are likely to be violent. These stereotypes are nothing new; the Jews were often treated as pariahs in Europe in mediaeval times.

It is also more difficult to study religion since the definitions are often vague, for example, how do we define whether anyone is of a particular religion since there is not usually any reason to have an accurate figure.

There are also a number of terms used within a religion such as *Christianity* and these can often cause confusion. Terms such as evangelical, Anglo Catholic, fundamentalist, liberal, conservative are often used without any clear cut idea of which people might be of this particular persuasion. In many cases the terms are used as one of abuse rather than with any precise meaning. There is even less reason usually to count how many people would belong to one of the factions within a particular denomination. Many people would probably have no clear idea of which faction they belonged to.

Sociologists and religion

Weber thought that as people became better educated and therefore more rational, it would lead to a loss in religious beliefs. Marx thought that once classless communism has been established then religions would disappear. His assumption was that religion was used to oppress the masses. In practise, even though atheism was established as the national religion in Russia and then the USSR, the number of worshipers went down, but did not disappear. Whilst atheism is the state religion in China there are still many people of different faiths including Christianity and Islam. Other people have assumed that as people get richer and more attention is paid to efficiency and production, religion would become less important.

Marx, Religion and the ruling class

Marx defined religion as the opiate of the masses. Some Marxists have developed this argument much further and suggest that the ruling class have used religions to legitimise their own power. In the U.K. the monarch of the day has a coronation in Westminster Abbey, where the Archbishop of Canterbury, usually regarded as the head of the world wide Church of England takes a major part in the ceremony. This gives rise to the myth in Marxist eyes that the monarch is part of God's plan for the world. They would also suggest that religion supports the status quo and this helps in many cases to exploit the poor.

The truth about the rules and the monarch is more complicated. There are many countries, which have a Christian heritage, and not all of them have a monarchy. The U.S.A is an obvious example of a republic. Similarly within the British Isles the Republic of Ireland is as its name implies a republic although in this case the heritage is predominantly Roman Catholic. Many countries in any case have a constitutional monarch which means that the monarch has very limited powers. In the U.K, some Anglican bishops sit, as of right, in the House of Lords and are therefore part of the parliamentary system. This has caused controversy partly because the Anglican Church is by no means a majority within the Christians in the U.K. and partly since there are more people of other faiths now such as Islam, Hinduism and Sikhism within the U.K. These faiths have no representation as of right within the houses of Parliament. There is also opposition from some of the people who have no religious beliefs at all.

In contrast, in many other countries there is a clear-cut distinction between church and state. France, since the time of the French Revolution in 1789, would regard itself as a secular society although the Roman Catholic Church is still quite powerful.

The U.S.A. was built on the separation of powers and also on separation of state and religion particularly because many of the 17th century settlers were fleeing from religious persecution but there has often been government intervention which reflects the views of religious people. This would apply to the prohibition era in the U.S.A. when the sale of alcohol was forbidden during the interwar years of 1920 -1933, that is, between the ending of the First World War in 1918 and the beginning of the Second World War in 1939.

Russia and religion

Marx also believed that in a truly socialist society, religion would disappear. In spite of the Communist revolution in Russia in 1917 religion did not disappear. There have been many suggestions that the number of Christian believers in Russia is probably now proportionately greater than in many countries in Western Europe.

In Russia, after the 1917 Russian Revolution, there were limits on religious activity. Whilst the 1936 Russian Constitution guaranteed freedom of worship, in practice, Christians were sometimes persecuted. Many Russian Orthodox churches were closed down, particularly during Khrushchev's term of office in 1958 –1964. How far religion has been tolerated depends to a large extent upon the individual leaders: President Mikhail Gorbachev President of the Soviet Union in 1988 –1991 and general secretary of the communist party of the USSR in 1985 –1991 who introduced Glasnost roughly translated as "openness" was more relaxed about religion. Indeed, on one famous occasion he described himself as an atheist, although a baptised atheist.

Marxism, Religion and Poverty

Marxists have often taken the view that religion makes life bearable; therefore, there is much less desire on the part of the working class to change. In the Marxist view, people would have religious beliefs supported by the middle and upper classes, which helps to prevent revolution. This attitude towards religion was sometimes of eternal bliss or sometimes referred to, sarcastically, as pie in the sky by and by. This would lead in turn to what is sometimes described as an other-worldly attitude, that is, not to be concerned too much about this life since the life afterwards is so much more important. This is one of the many reasons why the Charity Christian Aid which spends most of its money in the poor parts of the third world has chosen the slogan "We believe in Life before death" as a counter to this view.

It is difficult to see how Jesus telling his followers to sell their possessions and give the proceeds to the poor can be construed as a man made religion made up by the rich. It could equally be said that not many Christians seem to take much notice of this text. Nuns within the Roman Catholic Church take a vow, which commits them to poverty, chastity and obedience. The monasteries, which thrived in the U.K. until their dissolution by King Henry the Eighth in the 16th century, were also bound by similar rules but in practice often became very rich and powerful. This might seem to lead to credibility of Weber's ideas, which we mention elsewhere, of the church going from a radical approach to a bureaucratic one. Ironically as with Marxism, there seems to be a great deal of discrepancy between the founder of the traditions and the institution, which has been set up in the name of the individual. Weber suggests that in many institutions such as Christianity, the period of a charismatic leader is followed by one of bureaucracy. It could be argued that this might easily be true of revolutionary regimes, which start off with ideals and eventually become bureaucratic.

Haralambos and Holborn in their book *"Sociology, Themes and Perspectives"*, quote part of the hymn "God made them high and lowly and ordered their estate". This is part of the well known tune "All things are Bright and Beautiful" which was sang in many churches. The hymn is from Mrs. C. F. Alexander a Victorian hymn writer. Whilst the Victorians might have used such verses to justify their own position, it does not appear in most modern hymnbooks. Haralambos and Holborn do not quote the rest of the verse, which is "the rich man in his castle, the poor man at its gate, the Lord ordered their estate". This of course gave to the rich a conclusion which was in their own self interest; that if God had given them prosperity then they must be good people.

Marxists often suggested that capitalists had used the Bible to support their own status. We might notice here that in the present era this seems much more likely to be true in the U.S.A. than in the United Kingdom. In the United States, the Reverend Pat Robertson has stood several times for the U.S.A. presidency. He is one of a group of people referred to as televangelists, who have spread what is sometimes called the prosperity gospel, that is, if people prosper God must be on their side, whereas if they do not then it shows that people are not in line with God. Another clergyman, the late Rev Jerry Falwell (1933-2007), formed the moral majority concept in 1980 which is meant to be a political body but draws very heavily on fundamentalists. It has made considerable amount of broadcasts and owns many radio and TV stations. Again within the U.S.A, the fundamentalists and the New Christian Right have often supported the Republicans generally and in particular to get the late former U.S.A President Ronald Reagan to power. More controversially, they also got George Bush Jr. into the presidency when he came to power in 2000 following a disputed election ballot. Attitudes may have changed with the election of Barack Obama in 2008.

Durkheim's attitude towards religion

Durkheim was on the other hand concerned with how religion affected the integration of society. Durkheim, for example, in his book *"Elementary Forms of Religious Life"* studied practices in what he believed were religion in its most primitive stage as with the Australian aborigines.

In this, he drew the conclusion that religious worship was in reality the worship of the community from which people were a part. He suggested that beliefs and practices, which looked at the concept of the sacred, contributed to communal values. He felt that religious activity helped to bring people together. This seems to ignore the views on the sects some of which are world affirming and others are world rejecting.

Weber's attitude towards religion

Weber and monotheism

Weber thought that the concept of monotheism had arisen in Israel because of the dangers that beset Israel as a relatively powerless tribe, which was very subject to foreign domination. According to Weber the prophets of the Old Testament explained the problems of Israel as worshipping false gods. The Old Testament Prophets whilst saying this, on many occasions also condemned the Jews of their day for not helping the poor; they complained bitterly about the use of false scales and other practices which were often against the interests of the poor.

Weber, society and capitalism

Weber was concerned with how different religious belief affects change in society and rationality. He thought that Calvinists had formed the majority of capitalists and sought to explain why this might be true. He saw Calvinism, and therefore Calvinists, with their emphasis on self-discipline and abstinence as helping to create the Protestant work ethic. He contrasted this with other types of capitalism where money had simply been spent on buying consumer items to show off ones wealth. In contrast, the Christian Capitalists tended to regard wealth as a sign of virtues and would often plough the money back into the firms. This attitude towards investment would be likely to give a greater Gross National Product than for nations, which had a smaller share of investment.

Furthermore Weber saw that the ascetic protestant capitalist would wish to go on gaining profits. Many ascetics would not wish to do anything that distracted them from work. Physical training and sport would be fine if they promoted health, but not if they were only used for pleasure. Going to public houses or theatres or gambling would be condemned since they did not add to the wealth of the individual or society. Since Weber's time and before Nonconformist churches ascetics have often been opposed to what they see as excesses. These excesses would include not only drinking, but also in some cases, gambling and smoking. Whilst they have presently modified their restrictions, drinking would not usually be allowed on Methodist church premises. It is also noticeable that Methodists were encouraged not to buy shares until the 1920s; the logic behind this was that people should not be encouraged to obtain money, which they had not worked for.

Weber's views on vocation

Weber did also point out that Calvinists saw vocations to not only include those of the clergy, nuns and so on, but of all professions and were taken to believe that success in such vocations is an indication that God is pleased with the individual. If nearly all occupations, except those which are considered as harmful to the community, are regarded as vocational then we will get to the spirit of work hard, play hard, which in the 19th century was often regarded as part of the protestant work ethic. It could be argued that this was the forerunner of what is often thought of as the modern prosperity gospel. Critics however would point out that this concept of capitalism was there before the Protestants anyway. Others would argue that in the modern era, particularly in a country such as the U.K. and many other countries where few people go to church, capitalists do not need religion as a cover for what many people would regard as money grabbing. Capitalists will carry on without any pretence that this is connected to religious beliefs in anyway.

Weber also suggested that the emphasis on vocation helped towards the concept of specialisation or division of labour, since it will help to produce more long term profits and also fits in with the concept of vocation.

Weber assumed that charismatic organisations - in which he included the early Christian Church, with Jesus as the charismatic leader - would not usually last long in their original format. Once the original charismatic leader(s) has left, then we would tend to get a bureaucratic organization. He assumed this applied to Christianity. This has certainly been one of the criticisms of many Christians in the 20th century and early 21st century about their churches. The comment is often made that they seem to be more preoccupied with setting up committees rather than with anything else, like saving souls.

Functionalism and religions

Functionalists have often regarded religions in the same way as Marxists in that they have regarded religions as a conservative force, that is, on the side of the status quo. Religion, by concentrating on shared beliefs, helps individuals to cope with problems that might otherwise have an impact on society.

We can see instances, however, where the church has played a major part in opposing the rulers of the day. In Northern Ireland when the Protestant majority often gave undue preference to job allocation like in the shipbuilding yards such as Harland and Woolf, the Roman Catholic Church often gave its support to people who fought this discrimination. Similarly in South Africa the former archbishop of Cape Town, Desmond Tutu has often spoken out against oppression by the former white minority with its apartheid regime. In Kenya, the church –through the National Council of Churches of Kenya (NCCK) – was also at the forefront of the fight for democracy during the oppressive political regime of the 80s and 90s.

The General Synod of the Church of England which consists of the laity as well as clergy and bishops was often opposed to measures undertaken by the Conservative Governments of the 1980s and 1990s which it saw as being harmful to the needs of the poor.

Post modernism and religion

Some post modernists have suggested that the idea of science as being the answer to all problems is no longer true. Therefore people might revert back to traditional religious beliefs since science can not provide all the answers.

Distrust of science

The idea that science is all important, and will always be helpful would have been an odd idea given the history of Nazi Germany where many scientists seemed willing to take part in horrific experiments in the concentration camps during the Second World War without worrying too much about the ethical considerations. The idea of value free physical or social science can be questioned. We might also notice that in more modern times there has been some distrust in science, for example, on the effects of Genetically Modified Crops, cloning and perhaps more unreasonably about the effects of vaccinations on small children in the U.K. The publication in one of the medical magazines *(the Lancet)* of an article about the effects of triple vaccines aroused great controversy and fear amongst parents of young children, such that there has been a drop in the use of the triple vaccines with their alleged link to rubella.

The General Medical Council in 2010 censured the doctor concerned with the report.

Prince Charles has suggested that more attention should be paid to homeopathic medicines in an article in the Guardian in February 2004. There seems to have been more interest in traditional remedies and some people would suggest that this is reasonable since medicine has been too concerned with the physical and not enough with the mental.

Scientists have been slightly divided over the issue of Global Warming. Many people would feel that this is of overriding importance since if some of the assumptions were true, it would lead to major natural disasters such as wide scale flooding, which would require more attention than many other issues.

Other people have been distrustful of science since the thalidomide affair in the 1960s where many children were born deformed because of insufficient attention in looking at the side effect of drugs.

Monotheism and Polytheism

The term *'monotheism'* is used to denote religions such as Islam, Christianity and Judaism to mean the belief in one God. These three faiths have one root, that is, Judaism. Other major religions which are also monotheistic include Sikhism. Sikhism has its roots in Islam and Hinduism.

In Islam, Christianity and Judaism the major assumption is that this life is the only one on earth. The idea that God is good is accepted by the four monotheistic religions mentioned but is not necessarily an accepted part of other faiths. For example, with the ancient Greeks, their gods were not always good and also were not concerned with earthly affairs. Other religions such as Hinduism believe in many gods and this belief is known as *Polytheism.*

The assumption that this life is the only one on earth is however not true for the Hindu religion. Here, the concept of reincarnation is accepted, that is, people come back to earth after death but could be in the form of another human being or as an animal depending upon behaviour in this life. The concept of reincarnation is likely to influence people's behaviour and also influence people's attitudes toward animals.

Rise of fundamentalism.

The term *'fundamentalism'* has often been used in a derogatory manner. It has been increasingly used in recent years either to denote those of the Christian faith or those in the Muslim faith. Sociologists would argue that there are also fundamentalists in other faiths, most notably in India where there is reassertion of Hindu values as they would see it. It has been used to establish the Hindu Nationalist Party (B.J.P) as a strong alternative to the Congress party, which had dominated India politics for many years, since it gained independence.

Within the Christian community fundamentalists would claim that they believe literally in the word of God, that is, the bible as being infallible.

The connection between the fundamentalists of different religions is that they would usually assert that only they have the truth and that all challenges to their authority should not be tolerated. They will be conservative in that they would wish to return to what they see as traditional values. This might well mean social change accompanied by political change. However, in the U.K. political challenge is much less common than in the U.S.A. where Christians have often used the term *moral majority* - usually with right wing views - to suggest that their values are the right ones.

Professor James Barr is one of the few theologians to have looked at the growth of fundamentalism from a theological perspective. He suggests that because people are less tied to one denomination as they may have been at one time, for example, the 19th century, people within that denomination or another would tend to stick together because they saw it as important to serve that particular denomination as opposed to others. However, as people felt freer to be cross-denominational or have less church boundaries, then Christian theology became more important to the members. He also confirms that statistics show that there is truth in the stereotyping of fundamentalists and social conservative viewpoints. He also suggests that theology leads towards the psychology and not the other way round as many people have often thought.

The Taliban in Afghanistan were ironically assisted in their struggle against the Russians by the Americans. They would also insist that education for women was wrong although many Muslims would dispute these interpretations of the Qu'ran and Islamic teaching. Similarly, in Iran, whereas the government of the Shah prior to 1979 had often been associated with slightly more liberation for women the revolutionary government reversed this.

In Nigeria, in the north there have been arguments about how far Islamic law should be enforced. This move towards Islamic law is partly because there was a reaction against the endemic corruption of successive Nigerian governments. There was international controversy when a court imposed verdict of death by stoning, for a woman who was found guilty of adultery. Even some Muslims who supported the sentence did not understand why only the woman faced the penalty. She was subsequently pardoned.

In the U.S.A. fundamentalism has often been associated with the idea that only creationism should be taught. It also has been very much associated with the anti abortion lobby.

Creationism is the belief that God created the Universe at one time. From the bible some calculations have suggested that this was in 4004 BC. Most scientists do not accept this point of view. In the U.S.A., after the well known debate in the 1920's called the 'monkey debate', in some of the states, particularly in the South only creationism can be taught. Most scientists at the moment believe in the Big Bang Theory, but this has not always been the case. Fred Hoyle, a very prominent scientist, believed in the steady state universe, where the universe was not expanding or contracting.

Similarly the term '*fundamentalist*' has often been used in the Muslim religion to denote those who would interpret the Koran in a very orthodox way. This might include those who would suggest condemning people to death for committing adultery.

Whilst some people have suggested that there are links in the way fundamentalism is treated in the major religions not all people accept this view. Muslim fundamentalism is often associated with a reaction against western society excesses as Muslims and others see it. This would include both lax sexual behaviour as well as much of the greediness of the West. Christian fundamentalism on the other hand is perhaps more connected with individual behaviour in terms of sex but, say, in the U.S.A. it is not against western style capitalism. Giddens does, however, in his book *"Sociology" (1989)* suggests that both types of fundamentalists have a strong nationalist element and both want to have a strong nation as they see it, by getting back to strong religious and cultural values.

As with the rest of sociology it is often helpful to distinguish between what the founders of the religion or a set of beliefs said and how the followers of the religion have interpreted it. This is equally true of what some people call the quasi religions such as Marxism or Fascism. In many cases, people's attitude towards the quasi religions may seem similar with religions to those outside it. In the late 1960s, there were many protests about the war in Vietnam with such countries as Australia fighting on the South Vietnam side to combat the North Vietnamese side lead by Ho Chi Ming who had managed to get rid of the French from Vietnam. Many people who were pro North Vietnam as it then was would go round chanting from Mao's little red book which in many ways seemed similar to those people chanting from the religious books or hymns. Chairman Mao was the leader of communist mainland China.

The original sources

We can see what the prophet *Mohammed* has to say about Islam in the Qu'ran and what Jesus has to say in the New Testament. There is no one founder of Judaism, but Judaism, Christianity and Islam would agree that Abraham usually referred to as Ibrahim in the Muslim religion would have been regarded as one of its founders.

Durkheim, often regarded as one of the founders of sociology, thought that religion was about both beliefs and practices that united people into communities. Some of the sociologists thought that religion provided a set of values, which would help knit people together. Unfortunately as in Northern Ireland it may indicate widespread differences, which have divided the two communities.

Definitions of terms

One of the problems of studying religions within sociology is that almost everyone will have their own preconceptions. This may be particularly true at a time of tension, where some of the media seem intent on stirring up religious tension, for instance, about people from the Muslim community. Television images tend to show the more militant Muslims, the more extreme orthodox Jews or extreme fundamentalist Christians, emphasising violence rather than the more moderate position. From the information given by the media one cannot know how far people are usually like this and whether what they show is representative of the whole. This is made more difficult since definitions are often vague, for example, how do we define whether anyone is of a particular faction since there is not usually any reason to have an accurate figure.

The term *'High Church'* or *'Anglo Catholic'* means people within the Church of England often called high church people, who will carry out some of the rituals of the Roman Catholic Church.

The term *fundamentalist* means people in the Christian religion who believe that the bible is literally true. In the U.S.A. it often seems to be associated with people who have right wing views on social issues, are anti abortion and in some cases belong to the gun lobby, which would restrict the use of guns. The term *evangelical* might reasonably be construed from ordinary English as anyone who wanted to share his or her faith with others. However it was used in the 19th century to denote those such as William Wilberforce (1759 -1833) within the Church of England who wanted to engage in social reform. He was very prominent in the anti slavery movement. It is often now used to mean those who usually from the Protestant churches, who are mainly concerned with gaining people to their faith. *Liberalism* is another phrase with many different meanings. Nathaniel Micklem defines it in his book *"The Theology of Politics"* as meaning those who see all people as potential children of God and therefore of some importance. However, it is often used to mean those who do not take the bible literally. Nathaniel Micklem was in the hierarchy of the then Liberal party as a Vice president as well as being a leading member of a training college of the then Congregational church now part of the United Reformed Church. In other cases the word liberal is used (particularly in the U.S.A.) to mean people with no strong moral views at all and who would be tolerant of most practices.

Religious Information and Religious Decline

Problems of obtaining adequate data about religion

If we compare data on religion with, say, data on politics, we have more accurate figures on politics than of religion. Before the coming of the secret ballot there was a voting register so that it was possible to see how anyone had voted. We can therefore speak with some confidence about how people have - as a whole - voted.

When discussing the increase of secularisation, we have far more difficulty in saying how many people belong to a particular church, go to a church on any one day and even less about what people believe because there is not usually any reasons on why records should be kept. There are some exceptions, we can look at the number of church weddings as this will be part of a legal requirement. There have been some attempts to have a census within particular churches, for example, the Church of England, but this is comparatively unusual.

We rarely, if ever, have an idea of how many people belong to any of the factions within the church. Also for the first time in the U.K., the census in 2001 did attempt to ask people about their religious views or their absence, but this is comparatively unusual. We might however be fairly suspicious, for example, about the 390,000 people who say that they belong to the Jedi (the Jedi appear in the Star Wars movie series).The Christian handbook *"Religious Trends"* edited by P. Brierley is useful as a source of information but even this tells us to treat the figures with some caution as many of the figures are estimates.

There is probably general agreement about loss of church membership and attendance, but there is probably less agreement about how far there has been a decline. We will probably find that no church has any need to count the number of people at any one service. There is no equivalent of a school register. Some churches have a large number of members following a confirmation service, when people are committing themselves to the church. Churches, however, will not usually take people off their list of members unless they are notified, for example, of the death of the member or the member notifies the church that he/she is moving to another church. In many cases therefore, churches may have outdated church membership lists.

We can also in some churches, such as the Church of England, look at the fall in numbers of people who have been confirmed or baptised as well as the ratio of clergymen to the number of people. Some people feel that children ought to be baptised or christened even if the parents have no intention of coming to church after that. Many members of clergy have tried to prevent this from happening.

People still seem to indicate that they have religious belief but do not seem to believe that this has much to do with church going. Other people would claim to be religious, that is, they believe in God without any need to attend a place of worship. Many people do not seem to see the point of going to a church where hymns are sang in old-fashioned language. Some churches have tried to overcome this perception by having much more lively services which do not rely on church organs but is rather similar to a lot of pop music. Some people would also regard most of the people in the church as hypocrites. Some other people would also say that they can find God within the countryside and other places.

If we are looking at the number of people who attend church on one day, as part of the evidence of secularisation we have a number of problems. The proportion of elderly people is higher within the churches than among the general population, so that we would expect fewer of these people to be able to attend church service on a Sunday, although in some cases the church may go to them. In many cases churches will hold services in old people's homes or hospitals. It is unlikely that church services, which occur in many old people's homes, will appear as part of any census about worship.

In other cases older members may simply watch a religious programme on TV. Some people may attend more than one church service in one day, so there may be double counting. However allowing for all the difficulties of measurement, it is reasonably clear that there are fewer people being married in church, being confirmed or in other way entering the membership. Also there are less people going to church weddings and getting children christened or baptised. This is particularly true of the Church of England.

Decline in importance of the clergy

We can look at number of baptisms and the number of clergy as evidence about secularisation. This may not apply to all denominations as some denominations or sects - for example the Quakers - do not have clergy. The name given to the clergy differs both within the same church and between different churches. For instance the name of the person who leads the services may be priest, pastor, vicar, or Father. This partially reflects the roles which they are expected to take.

Role of the clergy and the laity and numbers involved

The minister or vicar will nearly always be licensed to carry out such activities as weddings, funerals and baptisms depending upon the ritual of the church. Different parts of the church expect different things from their clergy. In the Roman Catholic Church the preaching will usually be done by the priest, whereas in the Methodist church there has been a system of lay preachers since Methodism was formed by the Wesley brothers (John Wesley 1703-91 and Charles Wesley 1707 -88) in the 18th century. The term *lay preacher* means people who are not full time servants or officials within the church community and will often have jobs elsewhere. They are not allowed to conduct some of the church services; they often cannot preside at a funeral, wedding, baptism or christening. The Church of England has had an increase in the number of lay leaders. Whereas in the past there has usually been one priest to one church, this has not been the current practice in The Church of England where - particularly in rural areas - the priest will be responsible for several different parishes.

Some people would see the moves toward more involvement by the laity as a move towards greater participation of the ordinary member and in particular increasing the role of women. Critics on the other hand would probably see it as a response to a crisis and therefore one that is reducing the role of the clergy as part of the secularisation process. Others would see it as part of a general movement toward some form of democracy or at least egalitarianism with not just a few people making the major decisions and taking all the key roles in the Church. Some sociologists would think that in the past, the church has tended to be too authoritarian and that getting people who are not part of the clergy to take on more roles is helpful.

Growth of the Ecumenical Movement

Professor David Martin in *"Sociology. Of English Religion"* argues that the ecumenical movement will increase the strength of Christianity and so will the ordination of women. The ecumenical movement aims to unite the Christian churches.

In many cases there are weeks of Christian unity when the church from nearly all traditions/denominations e.g. Roman Catholics, Anglican, Baptist, United Reformed Church, Salvation Army and others will come together in a given church during the week to share services. There are also a number of churches where different churches have joined together to form one church. In the case of Thamesmead in south east London which is essentially a new town of about 40,000 people the Roman Catholic, Anglican, Methodist and United Reformed Church have one church in which all of them will share the church buildings . This makes it even more difficult to assess how far there has been a decline in particular denominations since in many cases there are Local Ecumenical Parishes (LEPs).

Decline of church membership

We can get some information about this from books such as the Christian Hand Book *"Religious Trends"*, care has to be taken however in interpreting some of the figures, for example, whilst it would be true that there has been a decline in some United Reformed Church Membership, the figures of membership depend partly upon capitation, such as how much the congregation has to pay towards the central organisation. Therefore for any individual congregation there may be a time lapse between reporting the information and the time of the actual loss, the Roman Catholic congregation might be underestimated because of the capitation effect. The number of priests, vicars or ministers may have fallen for example, in the Anglican Church from just over eleven thousand in 1980 to just over ten thousand in 2000, but in many cases lay workers and lay preachers who have increased in number may do very similar work for example, in taking services as well as pastoral visits. It could be argued the other way; that they were only allowed to do these tasks because of the decline in the number of men and to less extent women wishing to enter the priesthood in the first place.

The Roman Catholics and the Anglican tend to use confirmation data, that if somebody has been confirmed, he/she will still be taken as a member even if they have not been at all active within that church. *Confirmation* is the word used to denote that they have taken a personal commitment to the church. In the Baptist Church 'baptism' - usually undertaken by adults - will also mean that the individual wishes to become a member of the church, and thus has the general meaning of 'confirmation' as it is in the Anglican Church.

In some smaller denominations such as the Quakers there seem to have been a number of people who attend meetings, but who do not wish to become members. Therefore it may be that people will attend more than one church.

Part of the problem in trying to define whether secularisation has taken place is that different sociologists have used different definitions. Some would think that worship is the most important aspect of being religious, whereas others may assume that it is the extent to which beliefs alter individual lives and others may see it as the extent to which it alters society as a whole.

Whilst most people think of churches in a sense of a religious building, many of the newer churches (sometimes called *the house church movement*) will worship in people's houses or sometimes in a school room. It will thus be difficult nationally to get an idea of the number of people worshipping in such circumstances.

There has been a drop in the number of marriages conducted in church, however it could be argued that in some cases people wanted a romantic setting, and that the laws allowing a wide number of buildings to be used for marriage could affect the number without implying that the couple and their families are not regular church-goers.

Changes in non Christian religions and numbers

There has been an increasing number of people belonging to other non Christian religions. It was claimed in 2004, that there are 300 mosques in the Birmingham area alone. There is also an increasing number of Sikhs; in 1995 there were three hundred and fifty thousand people claiming to be Sikhs. This was more than double the number of people claiming to be Hindus.

Apart from sects which are probably linked to Christianity, there has been more interest in other main faiths with the influx of people from other countries particularly the Indian sub continent. Partly because of the partition of India into Pakistan and India in 1947, Pakistanis are more likely to be of Muslim origins and Indians of Hindu origin. (At the time of partition many Muslims fled from their part of India to what became Pakistan and similarly many Hindus fled from what became Pakistan to other parts of India.)

This has meant that it is much more common to find a mosque in the 21st century in the U.K. than ever before. The only 19th Century mosque was the Shah Jehan Mosque in Woking built in 1889. Similarly in other areas it is possible to find Hindu temples or Sikh Gudwaras. Jewish synagogues have been in the U.K. for a long while.

Steve Bruce's views

Steve Bruce has said about secularisation that whereas in the past the church applied to the whole of life, it has lost its central influence since even in church-ran organisations such as schools, there is little difference between these schools and the ordinary state schools. Bruce would also argue that Youth Clubs and others, are similar to those run by other organisations, and therefore there is little distinctive role.

Bruce seems to ignore the change in other beliefs. Many people are at least vaguely attracted to new age beliefs even if they are not well defined.

Surveys suggest that many people believe in some kind of sprit even if they do not belong to a conventional Church. Bruce also believes that since we are more egalitarian and no longer deferential, people will refuse to believe in something more important than what man does and that God can do things, which man cannot.

Bruce's ideas are very questionable for example; during the 1980s in the United Kingdom data from Social Trends would not indicate that we have become more equal, in terms of income. He also assumes that social classes mix more; we may live in a society of different races but many people still live most of their lives both at work and at home, mixing mainly with people of one class or ethnic group and do not really know much about people in other groups. When we look at the importance of star signs (Zodiac) to some people , then it is difficult to believe that we are really living in a scientific age.

Some sociologists have believed that efficiency and profitability have become all-important. This is not necessarily very rational. Profitability of firms could be at the expense of the environment as for example, has happened with the oil firms.

Bruce also makes the point that if there is no general community where people do not know their neighbours, we can hardly expect the church to represent the community. He assumes that the industrial revolution led to the development of Methodism. It seems this is partly possibly because the Anglican Churches were more numerous in the country rather than in the town. It may however also be as the Wesley brothers (John and Charles) both looked at the social problems of the day including heavy drinking, which created problems particularly for women and children. The Methodist Church, appealed on such issues to some of the working class as well as to reformers in the middle class. It might also be noted here that the Wesleys' original intention was not to form a separate church.

Bruce also argues that the experience in Ireland and Scotland is different to that of England, the newcomers in Ireland were Protestant Scots who would have had very different religious viewpoints to that of the native Irish. In other cases, the landowners would have been of a different nationality to that of the native population and this may be one of the reasons why the Protestant Catholic divide has been much greater in Ireland than it has been in England. Also, though Bruce does not say this, the partition of Ireland into the Republic of Ireland and Northern Ireland in 1922, was not the historic division between Ulster and the rest, but was intended to ensure Northern Ireland would always have a Protestant majority. Scotland still has a more pronounced Roman Catholic/Protestant divide that can be seen too readily if one looks at football matches involving Celtic (traditionally a Roman Catholic side) and Rangers (traditionally a Protestant side).

In Scotland, the Church of Scotland does not have Bishops, and is generally assumed to be more interested in society as a whole, than the Church of England has been. Bruce argues that if there are several religions, this will remind people that they have a choice, and therefore might lead to fewer people going to church. However, sociologists like David Martin have argued that in countries such as Sweden where the church is more connected with the state, attendances are low, because of the single church. It could of course be argued that in Sweden there is less need of the role of the church as a social provider because the state carries out most of these activities that have traditionally been associated with the church.

Bruce argues that the New Christian Right which have been very important in the U.S.A. have not in fact won general support for their puritan attitude; these attitudes would include being anti abortion and anti divorce laws. One of the main churches which is associated with the New Right is that of the Southern Baptist and generally the New Right has been more important in the South of the U.S.A., than in the more liberal North.

Lack of observation of religious festivals

We may also look at the ways in which people observe festivals. There has been an increasing trend in the last few years for Christmas day to become a day on which the supermarkets have opened, which has annoyed not just religious groups, but others who want to be with their family on Christmas day.

Christmas has become a time when many commercial firms find that they can sell more goods and services. At one time it was estimated that about ¾ of sales of personal computers were in the fourth quarter of the year. What is very clear is the commercialisation of Christmas and its affiliated ideals such as 'Father Christmas'/'Santa Claus'. Easter by contrast, which is more important for most Christians, is comparatively less celebrated except for the sale of Easter eggs or hot cross buns.

People often are more inclined to go to church after a major incident either in their life or nationally, for example, in the U.S.A. after the destruction of the World Trade Organisation, more people were recorded as going to church. They may also go to church after bereavement.

Churches as focal point for community

Churches have often been used more for social services such as playgroups until the recent legislation about providing more nursery places with state funding through tax allowances. Churches both in the Christian religion and most others have a golden rule; to love God and to love our neighbour as ourselves.

This is not a distraction from the main purposes of a religious faith and neither is it a new role. The central halls of the Methodist church such as the Central Hall in Westminster provided not just services of worship on Sunday or on other days, but also medical services such as nursing before the days of the National Health Service was very important. They also provided a social service, which was more important before the introduction of the welfare state. The idea of special organisations such as the uniformed ones like the Boys and Girl brigades mainly in what was the Congregational Church, now part of the United Reformed Church, dates back to 1883 for the boys and 1893 for the girls.

The scouting and guides movement dates back to the early part of the 20th century. This happened after Sir Robert Baden-Powell 1857 -1941 returning from the Boer war (the war between the Dutch usually called the Boers and the British in South Africa) saw the need for a movement to train the youth of the day in an informal setting on how to build themselves spiritually, mentally and physically. The Scouting movement was therefore formed in 1907 by Lord Baden Powell and the Guides in 1910 by his wife, Olave.

Patterns of church membership

Church membership has several patterns.

In most churches, the women outnumber the men even though until recently most clergy were men in nearly all the denominations. In the Roman Catholic Church, women are still not allowed to be priests. In the Church of England there are no women bishops in England but in the U.S.A. there was the first woman bishop in 1988. Churches have been used by predominately either the young or the elderly but relatively few people in the 30- 50 age range.

Churches are to be found more often relatively in rural rather than urban areas. Some people suggest that this is due to the anonymity of urban life. There is no peer group pressure to attend church in the towns whereas in a small village it may very much be present.

In towns, there is often little connection between the different roles that people play. People may live far away from their work place and in many cases will go to a shop or have an entertainment pattern where they are not known. In contrast it is often felt that people within the rural community will know each other more.

Decreasing respect for the clergy

Some commentators have suggested that there is less respect for the clergy in the sense that people are presently less deferential. However, it could be argued that it might be partially a result of more widespread education. In the 19th century and until the major changes in the 1870 Education Act, few people could read or write and in many cases the working classes would hardly have had time to read even if they were literate. Books were also expensive and there were fewer (other) sources of information.

Times are different now and there is almost bound to be more questioning of ideas. Others have suggested that greater knowledge of science and technology has made faith redundant. Nonetheless, it is easy to find distinguished scientists who are members of a faith as well as equally distinguished scientists who are atheists or agnostics. Whilst we live in an age where science and technology may dominate our lives to say that we live in a scientific age seems to be implausible; relatively few people know very much about science to, say, an A level standard.

Leslie Paul in his book *"The Church by Daylight"* found that there were few young clergy within the church. However this may be slightly misleading since in many churches the emphasis is now on people who have been employed on a large number of specialized areas who then go on to become priests or ministers (the term often varies according to the denomination or church). The average age of people becoming ministers in the United Reformed Church is now about 50 and so obviously the average age of ministers will become greater.

The book by Paul was confined to a fact finding approach solely on the Church of England, yet there are differences between different strands of the Christian church. In the early 2000s it was argued that though the United Reformed Church was short of ministers the Baptist church was not.

Others such as Martin have mentioned apathy as a problem not just affecting the church but nearly all other major voluntary organisations. He describes this as part of the loss of community in society as a whole. Although he does not say this, it is very noticeable that the political parties that often had quite large membership in their youth wings in say the 1960s have since lost this.

Loss of traditional practices

Some traditionalists are said to have been alienated by the reform within the church. Some people found the Roman Catholic Latin mass helpful and did not approve when it was changed in to the native languages. Others in the Church of England will not approve of services, which they do not see as having the majesty of the 1662 Prayer Book. They will regard these moves as part of what is often called "dumbing down". This is to mean, instead of expecting people to use their brain, the church has succumbed to the same temptations as secular society and given people something which is nice and easy. Others find the 17th century language archaic and will suggest that in a multi cultural society where English is often a second language for many of the citizens it will be difficult to attract people to church services with such old language. They would probably argue that part of the purpose of the Reformation in the 15th and 16th centuries was to bring the church closer to the people.

Some secularisation theories think that science will be the main form of knowledge and other forms of knowledge become relatively unimportant. What is fairly clear is that though people sometimes assume that science led to the decline of religion, it seems unlikely that many people having looked at scientific beliefs have then concluded that religion has nothing to offer. It does not seem to be the whole of the picture, since church membership is much higher in the U.S.A. than in the U.K. and there is little reason to believe that the U.S.A. is less scientific than the U.K. It is also not clear how we can test this idea, for example do we find that at universities, people from a more scientific background will be less likely to attend a church than people from, say, an arts background? Does it mean that science explains ideas which could not be explained before? However, science itself can be a matter of faith since most people do not have enough knowledge to be able to test scientists' views. Some people would suggest that we need more than science, since for example in the Nazi era scientists were often willing to carry out horrific experiments in the concentration camps in the 1930's. Post modernists might well suggest that science itself needs to become more scrutinised. Other people have suggested that the apparent lack of faith by some leading theologians, for example the former Bishop of Woolwich, John Robinson with his book *"Honest to God"*, and also the former Bishop of Durham, David Jenkins with his ideas about God, seem to make it more acceptable to doubt basic ideas. Such people would probably claim that they were trying to explain about God in modern terms rather than using out-dated ideas.

Bryan Wilson and Secularisation

The late Bryan Wilson is one of the main writers on secularisation. He has used Weber's ideas and assumes that with rationality and technical efficiencies, if this was all-important, then we are in a world without enchantment. Wilson assumes that there are many non-scientific forms of meaning in society, but this is evidence for the decline of religion.

Bryan Wilson suggests that the church has generally become less powerful. During the abdication crisis in 1936 when Edward VIII was deciding whether to marry Mrs Simpson an American divorcee, the church was listened to. Eventually King Edward VIII decided to abdicate as it was felt that the Church represented Christian public opinion meant that a king could not get married to a divorcee. Similarly, when the late Princess Margaret was wondering about marriage to Captain Townsend, the church was also influential. But in most cases, the church is generally not listened to. Bryan Wilson points out that in many cases, Lady Thatcher while Prime Minister was too busy to see the Archbishop of Canterbury. He also points out that the wages of a clergyman are far less then many unskilled manual workers and wonders why it is assumed that religion requires no expertise.

In July 2004 there was a debate in the Synod of the Church of England about whether its entire clergy should be paid the same, but this was defeated. This would have given a rate of pay, which was less than £20,000 per year to everyone including bishops and archbishops. Other more egalitarian denominations such as the United Reformed Church do pay the same to all their ministers even if they are the elected Moderator (the head of the particular denomination for the year).

Bryan Wilson also points out to the decline of baptisms. In 1950, 66% of children in England were baptised in the Church of England, but in 1973 this figure was 47%.

He also suggests that in a multi racial society, Christianity just becomes one more religion amongst others. Since he wrote this it has often been claimed that there are now more Muslims in the U.K. than people who belong to the Methodist church.

He suggests that the churches themselves have a much more secular attitude to both sex and to marriage. He points out that in most cases babies are born as a result of decisions about family planning. This would be in contrast to the older view that babies were a gift from God. One could however criticise this approach and say that the Roman Catholic Church has still remained opposed to abortion or even officially to family planning.

He points out the decline in the number of children who attend Sunday school; in 1953, 18% of children between the ages of 3 and 14 attended Church of England Sunday schools. This figure has dropped at present.

He observed that the work place is an area where religious values do not seem to matter and efficiency does not allow for personal values. It could however be argued that though the work place itself may have become increasingly secular with more technology, there have been some positive movements towards ethical investment since the time of his writing. The Co-operative bank says that it will not lend to businesses which engage in what it regards as immoral activities and a much smaller bank registered in the Netherlands, Triodos Bank will only lend to businesses which it believes have positive ethical values.

Other sociologists

Some philosophers like Nietzsche have propounded the idea that God is dead. Wayne Ellwood points out that even by 1851 only 45 % of the population-attended church and in the slum areas the percentage was much lower at about 10 %

Michael Foucault (1926 -1984) suggested that power is used to achieve domination for particular groups. Prior to modern industry life people were dominated by religion, and social life used these concepts.

Festivals and their impact on society

The truth or otherwise of the festivals is not the concern of sociologists. We can see that most Christian churches will have Sunday as their day of worship. Some of the more puritan churches will try to insist that the day of worship is not used for entertainment or commercial purposes e.g. there were restrictions on flights to some of the Scottish Western Isles on a Sunday because of this.

The idea of the Holy Day in Christianity and Judaism goes back to the ten commandments, which both Jews and Christians would regard as having been given to Moses by God where people are supposed to observe the seventh day as holy. The Jews have always taken this to mean Saturday, whereas most Christians who believe in the resurrection of Jesus have taken it to mean Sunday.

In 2003, the licensing authority gave three public houses in Strornoway (the main town in Lewis) the right to serve alcohol on Sundays. Prior to this the free Church of Scotland, which had one of its strongholds in the Western Isles, had managed to keep Sunday dry. The decision meant that Harris - one of the other Western Isles - is now the only place in the U.K. which will not sell alcohol on Sundays.

The observation of festivals and holy days has an impact on other commercial activities, for example, in the times that shops in the United Kingdom are allowed to open on a Sunday by trade unions often for secular reasons, opposing the religious principle to have Sunday as a day of rest.

Some festivals such as Christmas are used by commercial firms to sell far more goods. On the other hand, many workers even if not particularly regarding Christmas as a religious festival will resent working on Christmas day. In 2003, the government was set to introduce legislation to prevent larger stores from opening on Christmas day if it falls on a Sunday. The definition of large stores was if they were over 280-sq. metres 3000 sq. ft. 97 % of responses to a consultation exercise in 2003 including business had wanted Christmas Day to be observed by the larger stores. The stores themselves said they did not want to open on Christmas and would welcome legislation since they felt that they would have to open on Christmas day if one of their competitors did. The puritans in the U.K. during the Cromwell regime in the U.K. (1649 –1660) had abolished Christmas celebrations.

Until the present time nearly all state schools had Easter time as part of the Easter holiday though this is changing with proposals for 5 or 6 school terms in the U.K., depending partly upon local councils' preferences.

Historically Lent (the forty days before Easter) was a time of abstention from overindulgence. This seems to have fallen into abeyance apart from the minor example of Shrove Tuesday, more often known as Pancake Day, which is when some Christians used to eat up many things before Ash Wednesday and the period of abstention.

Jewish and Muslim holy days

Other religions have different holy days, the Jewish Sabbath is taken to be on Saturday although to be more accurate it lasts from Friday sunset to Saturday. Muslims have Friday as their holy day.

The Muslims have Ramadan as their month-long time for fasting during the daytime. Unlike Christmas, Ramadan is not the same date each year. In a multicultural area this can well affect other factors such as the shopping programme.

Attitude towards sacred and unclean things

Both Jews and Muslims regard pigs as unclean animals and so do not eat pork and its products. Hindus on the other hand do not eat products from cows as they are regarded as sacred animals.

The differences in diet may be important to institutions such as boarding schools, hospitals and nursing homes which should take care not to offend people and their religious beliefs. There were proposals by the European Union to ban killing of animals in certain ritualistic ways such as kosher killing by some Jews and Halal meat observed by some Muslims. This was because it was felt that the ritual killings were cruel to the animals.

In most religions there are things that the believers would regard as sacred. Within the Christian religion, the Roman Catholics would regard communion as sacred; similarly in Islam Muslims would regard the Qu'ran more often referred to in the West as the Koran (the book which Muslim regards as having been given to the prophet *Muhammad*) as sacred; orthodox Jews would regard the Torah (the scroll versions of the first five books of the Old Testament) as sacred and so on. Even within a religion, however, there are often differences of opinion. Within the Christian Religion, the Salvation Army do not have a separate communion service and the Religious Society of Friends more often referred to as Quakers do not have a communion service as they regard all meals as sacred and do not require a ritual. In France in December 2003 there was considerable controversy over the proposal endorsed by the French president that Islamic headscarves worn by many Muslim girls at school together with other large symbols such as the Christian cross should be banned from the classrooms because France, since the French revolution in 1789, had prided itself on being a secular state.

Some critics thought that the motive was less secular than racial seen to portray the Muslim community as outsiders and was politically intended to be electorally popular with many people with racist tendencies. Others more supportive of the proposal suggest that Muslim women were in some ways being victimised by having to wear the scarf.

Other non-religious beliefs

There also seems to have been more interest in astrology. Many of the tabloids have, as a regular feature, a column with signs of the zodiac and their predictions. It is difficult to know how seriously astrology is taken, apart from romances where some people seem to believe that different people from different star signs will be more compatible. On television there are invitations to phone in at premium rates to have a personal star reading.

Religion and Society

Some people have suggested that a religion always involves believing in a supernatural power. This is not necessarily true of all religions.

Many religions have a set of rules, both the Christian and Jewish religion has the Ten Commandments as part of their rules. These will tell people not to steal, not to kill and not to commit adultery, not to covet amongst others. Most religious groups including many in the Christian faith will have songs, which are called hymns, and prayers with which people can identify with.

Some sociologists have suggested that religion helps to unite society. Though it is sometimes said that the church plays no part in modern life, at the time of the war with Iraq in 2003, most of the bishops were opposed to the war and said so.

Roman Catholic attitude towards vocations

In the Roman Catholic tradition, the role of the priest or the nun as the case may be, was regarded as a vocation, whereas most other jobs were not regarded as vocational. It might be noted here that in many cases, nuns - then as now - would help for example in teaching and running of schools as well as in hospitals, so that a nun was capable of jobs. This applied to the open orders of nuns. This means that nuns do not spend all their time within a convent, where they communally live. Perhaps the most famous nun in the 20th Century was Mother Theresa (born Agnesa Gonxha Bojaxhiu 1910 - 1997) who having been born in a poor part of the Balkans near Kosovo spent much of her time working amongst the poor in the poorer cities of India. There are however also closed orders, where the nuns spend all their time within the confines of the convent and its grounds.

The New Christian Right and capitalism

The followers of the New Christian Right have often been associated with more military spending whether to combat the fear of communism, or more recently in the battle against terrorism following the World Trade Organisation tragedy in 2001. They usually emphasise in contradiction to communism, that capitalism is important. This seems rather ironic given that when one looks at the Bible they would see that the prophet Amos condemns very strongly the people who oppress the poor. It is also ironic given that Jesus very strongly suggests that people who do not help the poor will not be called his servants irrespective of the religious practices that they indulge in. The assumption that all Christians are right wing and support capitalism is in strict contrast to people such as the late Martin Luther King. He was subsequently assassinated due to his unhidden pursuit of a vision of a United States of America, which was united by race rather than divided by it.

The Marxist criticisms do not seem to be universal since in the United Kingdom's Evangelical Alliance, which is formed of fundamentalists, will be conservative in respects such those of sex, but the Alliance does condemn aspects of capitalism such as greediness. The former Pope, John Paul II (Latin: Ioannes Paulus PP. II, Italian: Giovanni Paolo II, born Karol Józef Wojtyła, 1920 –2005) as leader of the Roman Catholic Church too was often regarded as conservative on sexual matters such as contraception and abortion but he also strongly condemned the greediness of unfettered capitalism.

Limited roles of women within the Church

One of the criticisms, which the Marxists also make about Christianity, is the limited role for women. Jesus himself often uses the word 'sinners', which does not as - many people think - refer to people that are bad, but the marginalised people of the day. It is very noticeable that the disciples were sometimes surprised when he spoke to women. The restrictions on priests marrying were not there in the first era of the Church but were imposed in the middle ages, often for financial rather than religious reasons. Roman Catholics would claim that the first Pope was St Peter who was married.

The criticism of the limited role for women might be thought by feminists to be rather ironic given that in most of the communist states, women have been noticeably absent from the major leadership roles. We might therefore conclude, not unreasonably, that the patriarchy dominated both religious and non-religious countries. In 1977 the Sacred Congregation for the Doctrine of the Faith declared that women were not able to be admitted to the Roman Catholic priesthood. The assumption made was that as Jesus did not call any women to be his disciples, this would be true for all time.

Conservatism and Christianity

Marx thought that Christianity would be a conservative force. One of the problems with using the word 'conservative' is that it has several different meanings; for example, in ordinary English it would mean someone who did not wish to have changes. This could apply within the church framework though often the word 'traditionalist' is used to describe people who do not want a change in the way in which church services are conducted.

The term 'liturgy' is often used to describe people who support the Prayer Book Society, that is, they like a service in which the 16th century prayer book is used. The term conservative is also used often to describe people who do not like changes in which they see religion being watered down, in the Roman Catholic Church they might be opposed to any changes in divorce laws, or changes in re-marriage within a church or to the idea of women becoming priests. It might also be used in some of the fundamentalist churches to mean those who oppose the idea of homosexual priests.

In 2007 and 2008, there was a lot of argument about this issue both in the U.K. and also in the U.S.A. One celibate homosexual was offered a senior post in the Church of England, but subsequently turned down the post because of the amount of hostility.

Within the Jewish community, the orthodox Jews may have an interest in keeping the style of dress the same and would be generally opposed to the idea of women rabbis. The reformed strand on the other hand will have women rabbis. Many of the differences within the Jewish community are similar to those within the Christian community like disputes about homosexuals.

Church and society

Some churches have been much involved in social issues, with the Salvation Army featuring high in most people's estimations. Amongst other things they run hostels for people who can not be able to go to the government funded ones, which ranked above those of the Salvation Army.

Internationally, the late Mother Theresa is perhaps one of the best known religious figures on the social responsibility side. She was a Roman Catholic nun. She died in 1997. Her work in the slums of Calcutta received a great deal of admiration from many people irrespective of their religious beliefs or absence of them.

Christianity and oppression

Unfortunately for Christians there are too many instances of the opposite being true, for instance, the Dutch Reformed Church in South Africa propped up the religious beliefs of Afrikaners by insisting that the division between black and white was part of the bibles' teaching. It therefore supported the concept of apartheid, that is, literally the separation of white and black with separate homelands for the blacks but in practice it was more that the blacks were to be subservient to the whites. In the

"*Long walk to Freedom*" by Nelson Mandela, 1994, it is easy to see how religion has served to oppress people. In that book, Nelson Mandela who later became the first black President of South Africa shows vividly the tensions that existed between the races. Rowan Williams - the present Archbishop of Canterbury - made this point about oppression in his Christmas sermon in 2003 when he was trying to reconcile some of the practical problems that have meant that Judaism, Christianity and Islam are often seen to be at loggerheads with each other.

Religion and the poor

In South America, quite a number of Roman Catholics are either Marxist or have views which would be regarded as left wing especially as the concept of liberation theology is heard. Some Marxists suggest religion promises heaven to people who have nothing on earth. This probably ignores the extent to which the bible criticises the rich, as with the prophet Amos for ignoring the needs of the poor. The poverty and justice bible lists approximately 3000 references to poverty and justice in the bible as a whole. There have been examples of theology, such as 'prosperity gospel', which seem to support the rich particularly in the U.S.A. with the Tele evangelicals such as Pat Robertson.

Capitalism has also been full of scandals such as those of Enron where the auditors, far from being a separate independent force, were also part of the consultancy force, and therefore they did not act as an independent arbitrator. There is no suggestion in many such cases that the people in charge were affected by religious beliefs. More recently many people have been offended by the way that the largest financial institutions particularly those affected by the sub prime mortgage market pursued profits without any ideas of the risk partly many people suspect because of the bonus culture.

There are also opposite examples Traidcraft and the fair trade mark - both founded by a Christian, Richard Adams - have tried through fair trading of cereals, chocolates as well as clothing to help the poor to get a fair price for their work. Shared interest which claims to be run on Christian principles borrows money at a rate of interest (usually 4 % below base rate) and lends money to entrepreneurs in third world countries, which are engaged in ethical enterprises at rates well below the rates which would usually be charged commercially. Base rate means the rate at which the bank of England announces each month and which most other borrowers or lenders take their cue to set their own interest rates.

The reasons why Shared Interest does this is that in many case the entrepreneurs in the third world countries especially if they are running a small enterprise, will not be lent money by the banks but in most cases will otherwise have to resort to borrow money at extremely high rates of interest from local moneylenders.

Other fundamentalists such as Richard Sider in the book "*Rich Christians and the*

Hungry World" would be very concerned to see how Christians, through a simpler life style, could support people in other poorer countries.

Judaism and Islam attitudes

In other religions such as Judaism, many of the early settlers in Israel, after its inception in 1948, shared together their possessions in what would seem to many people to be more of a socialist society; the *Kibbutzim*.

Within Islam there is the need to give to the poor. This is called *Zakah* or charity and is one of the five pillars of Islam. The concept of Zakah is that it purifies people from their greed or selfishness and will help the people grow into the type of people that Allah wants them to be. The minimum amount of money that Muslims are expected to give is 2 ½% after allowing for their own family needs. The richer Muslims will usually expect to give more.

The overthrow of the Shah in Iran was due to radical Muslims. Indeed the 1979 revolution, which got rid of the Shah, is often called the Islamic revolution.

Some Muslims would claim to believe in theocracy; that the word of (Allah) God is more important than democracy. This is not unique to Islam however. How far the theocracy was helpful or not came to the fore in the earthquake in Iran of 2004 when about 40,000 people died. Some people who did not like the Iranian government of the day suggested that the Iranian government, which partly claimed to be a theocracy, had been too preoccupied with personal morals. It had not paid sufficient attention to the needs of well constructed houses in an area that was known to be in an earthquake zone. This partly accounted for the large number of casualties when compared with the effects of similar earthquakes in other countries such as the U.S.A.

Many Muslims have condemned the practice of usury, which means lending at high rates of interest. Some would go further and deny that people should lend at any rate of interest. This has caused problems with the provisions of loans for students' grants since some Muslims feel that they should not take such loans.

Historically the Christian church did not approve of usury. This is one of the many reasons why the Jews unfairly depicted in Shakespeare's Shylock were depicted as moneylenders since Christians were not supposed to do this.

Islam and women

There has been common understanding by many people that the Muslims have subjugated women. It is well known that the Taliban refused to let women attend schools in Afghanistan. This was the reverse of the policy during the dominant Russian influence. In 2009 there was considerable comment about whether veiling is helpful or unhelpful to women. Some have suggested that this looks at the role of women merely as sex objects whilst others see it as a form of male dominance.

The French lower house overwhelmingly endorsed plans not to allow religious objects in school whether they were the crucifix from the Christian churches particularly Roman Catholic or headscarves from the Muslim religion. This was done because France was a secular society. Pakistan besides having a very strong Muslim background elected a woman as President. The late Benazir Bhutto was the daughter of a previous President. The subjugation of women seems therefore, not to be true of the Islam faith as a whole, but rather only to the ways in which some people interpret their faith.

Islamophobia

This term has come increasingly important after the tragedy of the World Trade Organisation in New York in 2001, when perhaps 4,000 people were killed. In the U.K the MP for Rotherham, Denis McShane, who was one of the European ministers, has questioned how far the Muslim community has condemned the acts of terrorism. This perhaps reveals partly that people do not understand the structure of the Muslim community where Imams, roughly the equivalent of priests, are often doing other jobs as well and are not paid officially.

The Muslim community is divided into two main strands; the Shiite and the Sunnis. There does not exist the equivalent of, say, the Archbishop of Canterbury for the Muslim community. Some of the media have queried the value of Islam in general. Robert Kilroy Silk – a former Labour Party MP - did this in an article in the Sunday Express. The Muslim community unsurprisingly suggested that it was very insensitive and observed that had the comments had been made against other groups, there would have been uproar.

It is very noticeable however that Rowan Williams, the Archbishop of Canterbury and The Chief Rabbi in England, Dr Jonathan Sachs have gone out of their way to try to reconcile some of the differences between the religions of Islam, Judaism and Christianity. It is perhaps easier in the U.K. and other "white" populations to stir up hatred against Islam since many of the Muslims will be of different complexion or colour to the rest of the population. For scapegoating to take place, an easy form of identification is helpful. 'Scapegoat' is the term used to denote people or groups of people who are unjustifiably blamed for the problems of society as a whole. The term itself was used in the Jewish tradition of finding a goat that was sent into the wilderness to take away the guilt of the people.

Judaism and anti Semitism

In the 13th century in England there were massacres of Jews in York and elsewhere. The Jews, like many other puritans, including what Weber observed of Calvinism, are often noted for hard work and are more likely to be prosperous than people of a more easy going disposition. Jealousy of the Jews was partly based on the wrong assumption that all of the Jews were rich. This can also be found in the 20th century with Hitler proclaiming that the Jews were mostly to blame for Germany's problems in the 1930s. Hitler, like many other dictators and those of an authoritarian nature, managed to find scapegoats.

There is some truth in the sense of Jewish people looking after their own community. In the debate on ethnic minorities and how they are underrepresented in parliament, observers often left out those of Jewish origin such as the former leader of the Conservative Party Michael Howard. The most famous politician in the U.K. of Jewish origin was almost certainly Benjamin Disraeli 1802 -1881 who became Prime Minister twice in the 19th century.

Churches and capitalism

Lutherans follow Luther's (about 1483 –1546) ideas. He is often thought of as the father of Protestantism His original ideas were to challenge what he saw as some of the laxity of the then Roman Catholic Church rather than to form a separate church. It is sometimes said that his ideas led to the creation of modern capitalism. It seems more likely that the truth is more complex; several countries including England under Henry the Eighth became Protestant for a number of reasons. It seems likely that the merchant classes, partly because of national pride and partly because of the desire of freedom, supported the Protestant church. The merchant class of the day often regarded the Roman rule as abhorrent when the rise of nationalism seemed to be important for many countries. This is one of the many reasons why even philosophers such as Locke in the 18th century who advocated religious tolerance would not have seen this applying to Roman Catholics as they owed allegiance - as he saw it - to a foreign power.

Luther married and had 6 children. The concept of married priests is mainly associated with Protestant denominations as the Roman Catholic hierarchy does not generally approve of married men as priests. There are some exceptions to the Roman Catholic rules about married clergy, when Anglican clergy have converted to Catholicism.

Luther is regarded as conservative in his attitude compared with other more radical elements such as the Anabaptists; his translation of the bible into German also had an effect on German as a literary language.

Sects and cults

Most people mainly use either term to mean something derogatory and often in a hurtful way. It is perhaps best to define them in a way that says that they differ sufficiently from the mainstream religion such as Christianity so that they are not recognisable to the defenders of the mainstream. Part of the problems is therefore that the sect or cult in question will often not describe or regard itself as a cult where many of the mainstream religions will. The Collins Dictionary of Sociology suggests, for example, that Shakers, Quakers and Amish Mennonites would be examples of sects. This may not be correct since whilst the Mennonites are living a life which tends to be world rejecting, that is, they do not approve of electricity and other such amenities this is untrue of the Quakers. The Mennonites will also often dress in what others would regard as old fashioned clothes.

The Mennonites were founded in the Netherlands by Mennen Simons (1496-1561) they believe in adult baptism and also in pacifism. There are about ½ million Mennonites in the U.S.A. The Amish who are a conservative branch of the Mennonites are well known for their anti modernism. The same is not however true of the Quakers. Whilst they used to wear plain clothes rather than joining in the fashion of the time the same is not generally true nowadays. The Quakers included Elizabeth Fry in the U.K., the well known 19th century prison reformer. Joseph Rowntree and Cadbury the well known chocolate manufacturers who were Quakers would have been regarded as part of mainstream Nonconformist Christian at the time even if their views differed. In the U.S.A. William Penn whose name is commemorated in Pennsylvania was one of the Quakers who ruled that state until the American War of Independence when the pacifist principles, which still generally prevail amongst Quakers, meant that they could no longer hang on to that state and as such they gave up control voluntarily.

Why do people join cults?

In sociology, we are not concerned with the truth or otherwise of people's beliefs but in why people join the sect. We are also concerned about what, if any, is the practical impact of the religious beliefs on the rest of society and to a lesser extent on the believers themselves.

It is important to avoid the stereotypes that seem to be inherent in most of the media, such as the belief that people only join the cults or sects because they are brainwashed by the often charismatic presence of the sect leaders who will in most cases tell them to do what they would not do in ordinary circumstances. Professor Eileen Barker, perhaps one of the best-known sociologists in this field did not find this to be true, say, of the Moonies. The assumption that they are all clones would be disputed even by those who think that they are not part of the Christian community and would wish to convert them to what they see as the proper Christian faith.

In the book *"Evangelising the Cults"* by James A. Beverley a professor of theology tries to answer the question "Why do people join the sects"? He would dispute the idea that they do not love. He suggests they may want to have social contacts who will love them as they are. Commentators have for example said that the Moonies have often been very loving to one another.

Spiritual needs not fulfilled

Many people over a long period have thought that there is something beyond them and have believed that religion fulfils a particular need in them. In many cases, particularly in the U.S.A. people have been dissatisfied with the church they have attended and have turned to sects instead. They may have found the sects more loving than the church they have previously attended.

Personal crisis

Psychologists have drawn up a list of stress factors such as divorce, bereavement amongst other factors, which seem to be reasonably true for many people in western society as one of the reasons why people join cults and sects. At times like this, particularly with a society that many people feel is impersonal, it is common for people to look elsewhere to find solace. This is in line with sociologists' concept of association to denote what happens in modern society. It is perhaps even more common to see where this need arises with bereavement since whilst society has become - at least in theory - much more open about sexual matters, death seem to be a big taboo subject. Many young widows in particular have felt shunned after the sudden shock of a funeral. In the U.K. many people will not be church members and so they will find a friendly face helpful. This is even more likely with a nuclear family than with an extended family where family members live near each other and could help at such times.

Stability

In a period when many things such as employment patterns change rapidly and when the media can bring us more news about tragedies such as wars extremely rapidly, an authoritarian approach which seems to explain all this is very welcome. The Jehovah's Witnesses scenario often uses this approach on a door to door basis when trying to give away their journal "*the Watchtower.*" They will often start their greeting along the lines "Do you feel that we need a solution to the world problems?" The founders or chief people with the cults often have very strong personalities and their absence of doubts about themselves will probably appeal to many people.

Social needs

Nearly all of us have social needs. Maslow in his well-known hierarchy of needs identifies some of these and Aristotle the Greek philosopher who lived about 2500 years ago also came to the same conclusions. Whilst some of us find this in our work, the changing patterns of employment, long distance or long time commuting and working at home patterns all tend to make this more difficult. Attending a cult where people are often welcoming even if only to evangelise may well be more helpful to many people than the impersonality they find in much of daily living like supermarkets which look similar and are very impersonal. Some churches have not always been welcoming particularly to people who are regarded in some ways as being different so the sects may appears to fulfil more of the social needs.

Status reasons

This could include such status reasons as scientology. It was founded by the late Ron Hubbard (1911-1986) who was born in the U.S.A. and who during the 1930s and 1940s was a science fiction writer. He formed the Church of Scientology of California in 1954. Before forming the church he had published information about Dianetics, which used a theme based on the science of the mind. He also had a church of scientology headquarters in the U.K. in East Grinstead in Sussex.

The Church of Scientology gives different awards as people progress in the hierarchy of that church. Giving people different grades of memberships as they progress will appeal to people who need status which they may not obtain in their jobs. Some of the sects rightly make people feel that they are important and not just a cog.

Intellectual reasons

The Christian Scientists founded by a woman – Mary Baker Eddy which is unusual for a religion - a denomination or a sect has published a newspaper *"the Christian Science Monitor."* It is widely read and respected even by people who find the Christian Scientist beliefs bizarre.

Publicity

The Beatles, perhaps the best known British pop group of the 1960s, visited the Maharishi and he became known as the guru (teacher) of the Beatles. This made him far better known than would have been the case with any ordinary Hindu.

The Unification Church

The Unification Church followers are often described as the Moonies after the name of its founder; the Rev Moon who was born in what was then North Korea in 1920. He was imprisoned under the communist regime of North Korea because of his anti communist beliefs and showed great courage which won him admiration from many people. He went to the U.S.A. in the 1970s and publicly defended Richard

Nixon, the Republican President who subsequently became the only president of the U.S.A. to resign his presidency. He has been very media conscious especially due to his church's mass weddings. The Rev Moon also met Mr Gorbachev, then the Soviet Union leader, privately, which will have added more to the Moonies status.

Millenarianism

This refers to the religious beliefs that are often mixed with political beliefs that a messiah will return and bring in a new millennium (one thousand years) around the time of the end of the second millennium. This was often mixed with the idea that the year 2000 held special significance. This seemed very odd since most theologians believed that whilst we have our years in the West after the assumed date of the birth of Jesus (AD standing for the Latin words Anno Domini, meaning in the year of our Lord) in fact it seems more likely that he was born in the year which we would now refer to as 6 BC.

Distinction between church, denomination, and sects

Sociologists have often tried to draw a distinction between the three terms. They would suggest that *church* would include the longer established ones such as the Roman Catholics and the Church of England. *Denominations* would include relatively newer ones such as the Methodist, which was founded by John and Charles Wesley and grew out of the Church of England in the 18th century. Both John and Charles Wesley were ordained ministers of the Church of England. A *cult* may be defined as a religious group held together by a dominant, often charismatic individual, or by the worship of a divinity, an idol, or some other object. The term often suggests extreme beliefs and bizarre behaviour. A *sect* is generally a small religious or political group that has broken off from a larger group from a large, well-established religious group, like a denomination, usually due to a dispute about doctrinal matters. In its historical usage in Christendom the term has a pejorative connotation and refers to a movement committed to heretical (unorthodox) beliefs and that often deviated from orthodox practices.

Both in developed and less developed countries the influence of cult has arisen. These may be in some cases very similar to other religions, there may be cults within the Christian church. In nearly all cases there is a leader who is charismatic; in the Waco tragedy in 1993 the leader David Koresh was certainly charismatic. In this case the cult was what most sociologists would call world rejecting since the sect had predicted the end of the world. The siege ended with many of the people dying through a fire when the federal authority eventually stormed the Davidian headquarters in Waco.

In many cases cults would stress certain texts within the orthodox religion more than looking at the religion as a whole. In one extreme case, several thousand people died as the result partly of snakebites obeying one of the more disputed texts of the New Testament. It is common to find within a cult that people make a positive choice to become very involved with the sect, often giving up family ties. Partly for this reason some people have concluded that the cult must have brainwashed the people to join them.

Perhaps the most famous study of cults was that of Professor Eileen Barker, who destroyed the common view that Moonies were from way out families. It seems likely that cults thrive most where there is either a very rapid social change, as in some parts of the U.S.A., or at times of high unemployment or political stress. One of the problems with cults is probably the nomenclature. People are likely to call other ideas sects if they do not approve of them. Some sociologists would regard the Quakers as cults whereas many other sociologists would not regard them in this way even though the Quakers have no religious ritual such as communion.

It is difficult to obtain accurate figures about the sects, partly because in the census of 2001, which asked people about religious ideas for the first time, there is no reason for a central authority to carry out any sort of census on sects. In some cases, some groups, such as the Brethren, often called the Plymouth Brethren, would have what most people would call a church meeting, in an unmarked place, so that others would not be aware of it. In other cases, as we have mentioned, such as with transcendental meditation, (which whilst having Hindu origins does not proclaim this) it is difficult to see what we would mean by someone claiming to have been influenced by TM unless we have asked them.

There has also been more interest - at least anecdotally - in the sects such as the Seventh Day Adventist (the Mormons) as well as the Jehovah's witnesses or the Moonies.

Communitarianism

This phrase which originated in the U.S.A. led to a movement with the same name. It has often been associated with the right wing Christian fundamentalists. Communitarians believe that there has been a breakdown of the community with continued movement toward excessive individualism and consumerism.

They would like people to be able to monitor other peoples' behaviour if these people fail to live up to the rest of the community's standards. Generally, they would also associate a lack of community with a decline in moral standards and the general loss of the traditional family system. They would also want a return to gender roles in which presumably the men would go out to work and the women would stay home to look after the children.

Critics would suggest that they are too preoccupied with middle class values. The nuclear family system is relatively new. The extended family system would have been more of a traditional system and it is a patriarchal system that would obviously disadvantage women. Communitarians would say that this would lead to a better upbringing of the young; this would be in line with Murray's views which are noted elsewhere.

There is of course always a problem, of trying to distinguish between nostalgic romanticism and reality. The Victorian era in the U.K., seen by some as a period of widespread church attendance and therefore a more model society, was one in which social problems such as excessive drinking were widespread. This is one of the many reasons why General William Booth (1829 -1912), the founder of the Salvation Army, preached forcefully in the temperance cause which advocated giving up alcohol entirely. Other nonconformist churches occasionally set up temperance hotels in order to counter the menace of alcoholism as they saw it. Joseph Rowntree, one of the best-known Quakers set up chocolate factories partly in order to give alternative employment and also to give an alternative to alcohol. At that time chocolate and cocoa were thought to be part of a more healthy diet. It is also far from clear whether families were happy and some observers feel that sexual abuse within the family was fairly common. Josephine Butler (1828 -1906), who was one of the great social reformers and also a Christian feminist, had to fight very hard in order to get the age of consent for sex to be raised from 13 to 16 in the 1880s. She did this partly because many young girls at that time became prostitutes before the age of 16 and also had had coerced sex with employers.

Some nostalgic people long for a return of the good relationship, which they assume or think they remember, existed in the Second World War. Research from the Mass Observation Surveys do not always suggest that this always existed. Before the Second World War, the East End of London was often torn between supporters of Sir Oswald Mosley (the leader of the National Union of Fascists which supported the rise of Hitler) and the large number of people (not just from the Left) who were often violently opposed to him.

Figures on crime may be misleading. There were streets around parts of London which were unlikely to have recorded crime in the 1930s since police rarely visited them, or if they did they would have gone in pairs because these streets were quite unsafe.

Overall view of Communitarianism

However even people who do not accept the basic concept and underlying theories of the Communitarians about the "good old days" might feel that it would be better if people could, keep neighbourhood watch schemes which have become fairly common in this country usually in middle class areas. They might also feel that neighbourhoods that let people see what children are doing while outside were desirable and might let children lead a freer life than that of being confined to their own gardens or being part of the chauffeur driven service with their parents always having to escort them to activities. This would preclude children becoming mature and taking responsibilities for their own actions. Whilst the term dependency is often used pejoratively by the middle class usually in reference to the working class, it can also happen with middle class children. It might also help to avoid the problems of obesity for both the adults and the children if there was a closer link within families so that people eat together rather than having hurried snacks in order to, say, watch television.

Loss of community

The media commented considerably about the loss to the community when farmers became bankrupt as a result of the mad cow disease BSE in the early 2000s. The tourism industry which suffered far more than the smaller farming community and often had no compensation was largely ignored. The media had often seemed less sympathetic to the plight of the coal miners in the mid 1980s, perhaps partly because of the personality of the miners' leader Arthur Scargill. Social research has shown that in many cases miners did not obtain full time jobs afterwards having become redundant and the close knit nature of much of the mining community was often lost. An article in the Guardian in February 2004 showed the huge financial cost of the break-up of the mining industry following the miners' strike in the 1980s. The social cost is however more difficult to calculate.

Even in the very urban areas, activities such as hop picking seemed to give some Eastenders - the name given to people living in the east end of London which has traditionally been very poor - amongst others, the opportunity for a type of holiday. This often meant that some people could get away from the east end for sometime away from their homes.

The church is often expected to help the community to have a focal point. This has been true perhaps more so in the rural areas and also in areas such as the Welsh valleys with the miners.

The concept of the golden age

The supporters of secularisation sometimes seem to point to a golden age from a religious point of view when people went to church and believed in such concepts as hell and contrast that with the present time. We have very little data about church attendance before the mid 19th century. In some cases there were penalties applied for not attending church or for going to a different church such that we are certainly not looking at the free choice to which we have become accustomed to in the western style society.

Religion and politics

Religion has hardly figured in the election leadership in the main parties in the U.K. except in Northern Ireland. In early 2003, Duncan Smith, who was the then leader of the Conservative Party, was a Roman Catholic as was Charles Kennedy the then leader of the Liberal Democrats. Tony Blair, the former Labour Prime Minister was an Anglican, but has now converted to Roman Catholicism. He was thought of as an admirer of Roman Catholicism partly because his wife was Roman Catholic and because of his choice of school for some of his children. It is doubtful, however, whether the electorate and the media were very much influenced by the religious convictions of these leaders.

In the U.K. in the 19th century the Church of England traditionally supported the Conservative Party whereas the non-conformists (churches which are Protestant but not Church of England) tended to support the Liberals. The Labour Party has sometimes been said (e.g. by Morgan Phillips a former general secretary of the Labour party in the 1950s) to owe as much to Methodism as to Marxism. In the late 20th century and early 21st century, however, there has been little connection between voting behaviour and religion or its absence in most parts of the United Kingdom. This is not however true of Northern Ireland.

In the U.S.A. this is less true, with the fundamentalists generally supporting the Republicans.

In Latin America the term 'Liberation Theology' has often been used. This emphasises the nearly 3000 texts in the Bible, which suggest that support should be given to the poor. In some cases prominent members of Liberation Theology have been assassinated, although this has been rare. Supporters of Liberation Theology have been contrasted to other parts of The Roman Catholic Hierarchy who often seemed to be on the side of the oppressors. Liberation Theology would certainly be different to that of the former Presbyterian Minister, Paul Hill, who was executed in the U.S.A. in 2003 for killing an abortionist. Ironically, protests against his execution were limited to a few liberals and some fundamentalists who did not want to see a fellow fundamentalist executed.

Although the Church has sometimes been oppressive, there have also been many cases where schools and hospitals have been founded out of care for the community by it. Indeed until the welfare state was established, partly during the Liberal government of 1906-14, and partly during the Labour government periods of 1945-51, the Church was often the major form of welfare.

As we see in the section on education, the churches were for a long while involved very much with education. They were often also places where people could obtain some sort of basic health service.

Some rulers, notably Hitler, did not try to use the church very much in order to gain power. Joseph Goebbels (1897 –1945) the Nazi minister most responsible for propaganda rightly predicted - with what is often called privatised religion - that providing the churches could carry on with services of worship, they would not normally worry too much about politics. There were some exceptions since Dietrich Bonhoeffer (1906 -1945) was a German Lutheran pastor and one of the leading German theologians who was hanged for his part in the abortive attempt to murder Hitler in 1944.

Religion and egalitarianism

Much however depends upon the hierarchy within the churches. The Quakers have been more egalitarian, since George Fox (1624 -1691) generally thought to be the leader of the Quaker movement, used both men and women to preach in the 17th Century. The same is true of other major religions as well, within the Jewish religion, the Reformed tradition has had women rabbis since 1972 and Rabbi Julia Neuberger is probably one of the best known of rabbis, apart from the Chief Rabbi Lord Dr. Jonathan Sachs. Whilst the term Chief Rabbi is often used there are three major strands within Judaism and he is only Chief Rabbi of one of them. Rabbi Dame Julia Neuberger became a peer, that is, a member of the House of Lords in 2004 having been nominated by the Liberal Democrats.

Religion as a progressive force

A Polish Pope was often instrumental in demanding reforms.

In some cases, churches have been associated with nationalist movements. In Poland, the Roman Catholic Church was part of the resistance in the 1980s, particularly under Lech Walesa, and he subsequently became Prime Minister of Poland, backed by the Roman Catholic Church.

Similarly, in Rumania, on at least one occasion, leaders from all the main religious groups, whether Orthodox or Catholic or Fundamentalists staged demonstrations against persecution. Various surveys in the Soviet Union, including the now independent countries such as Latvia, Lithuania and Estonia, suggest that religious beliefs are perhaps stronger in many ways in those countries than in countries such as the United Kingdom.

Other views of church and State

The Anabaptists in the 17th century believed that the earthly institutions were corrupt and therefore whilst they were usually peaceful they disputed the basis on which civil government lay. For this view they were often persecuted. We can see some parallels to this attitude at the present time not just from the Anabaptists but from many of the rightists in Federal U.S.A. who fear the powers of the State very much and stress the need of individual decision making.

Other aspects of religious tolerance

The arguments about religious tolerance are not confined to the history books. In the wake of the World Trade Organisation tragedy in 2001 and the Iraq war since 2003 show how far people of different religion or none have respect for each others beliefs has become of more importance. This is not confined to the Muslim/Christians divide only, but also the Muslim/Hindu divide between India and Pakistan. In May 2004, following the surprise announcement by Mrs Gandhi of the Congress Party not to seek the prime minister position in India, a Sikh (Dr Manmohan Singh) became prime minister of India for the first time.

Christian Socialism

This term was used in the 1840s by many people who formed a group - including the well-known author Charles Kingsley – that was as critical of some of the bad effects of capitalism as Karl Marx had been. In 1889 the British Christian's Socialist Union was formed in the U.K. on the assumption that many of the existing churches were more supportive of capitalism and they wished to counter this view.

Churches as influences on legislation

Churches in the U.K. have generally regarded themselves as non-political except in the case of Northern Ireland where voting has been on sectarian lines with the exception of the Alliance Party and a few other smaller parties.

Churches have tried to influence legalisation and government policy; towards 2000 many Christian bodies as well as secular bodies such as Oxfam tried to probe the idea of debt relief on the poorer countries that owed to the richer Western countries and financial institutions. Often the poorer countries of the world paid more in interest on their debts than they received in aid.

The Church of England still has several bishops who are appointed, as of right, to the House of Lords. This has aroused slightly more controversy than usual especially as at the time of writing most of the hereditary peers have been forced to give up their seats in the House of Lords. 'Hereditary peers' means those who are in the House of Lords due to gaining their titles from their parents, usually their fathers. Some people feel that in a secular state that no one should be part of the legislature because of their positions within a religious body. Others feel that the Church of England should not be in a unique position and there should be representatives of other persuasions within the Christian church and possibly from other faiths such as Judaism or Islam. In 2003 most of the Anglican Bishops opposed the war with Iraq. Thus though they might have been part of the establishment (the name is often given to the people who comprise what some people think of as the main fabric of British society),they were not in line with most of the establishment such as the majority of Labour and Conservative MPs who supported the war.

It seems strange to many people that the Prime Minister, who is not necessarily part of the Church of England, should have the duty of appointing bishops in the first place.

The Queen is still the head of the Church of England in England and Wales. In Scotland she is head of the Church of Scotland which is theologically nearer to the former Presbyterian Church than the Church of England. The Church of Scotland does not have bishops.

The term Episcopalian means churches, which have Bishops as with both the Roman Catholic Church and the Church of England. The Pope is said to be the Bishop of Rome. One of the problems with trying to unite the churches is the role of the Bishops and this has been a stumbling block to discussions between the Methodists and the Church of England.

Church and domination

Authoritarian people have always wanted to dominate other people. The idea of running other people's lives often seems to have appealed as well to puritans in a variety of different religions. This has particularly applied to sex where the Roman Catholic Church has been opposed to birth control partly because of a text in the Old Testament on this and partly because of tradition. The Roman Catholic has generally been opposed to abortion. If the logic is to be pro-life then it would seem also logical that one should try to keep people who live in poorer countries alive, where the death rate for children is often very high and ensure provision of adequate aid and fair trade to these countries. This does not seem to have been the case and is one of the criticisms of some fundamentalists.

In the Southern parts of the U.S.A. the church was often again used to prop up white domination.

Distinction between Religion and Politics

It is often assumed that religion can be kept separate from politics, but in practise religious views must over-lap with political ones, in 2004 the hierarchy of the United Reformed Church told people that they should not vote for the British National Party, since the party was a racist group opposed to the ideas which the church believed in. In 2009 both the Archbishop of Canterbury and the Archbishop of York said that Christians should not back the BNP for the European elections.

In modern society however, doctors and scientists have taken over the role of priests in defining what is normal and what is deviant.

Foucault suggests that history is defined by discourses, which rise and fall and this causes social changes.

Bryan suggests that religion has declined because the production of goods has become important, and other aspects of life have become less important.

Turner assumed that religion's main importance was to control sexuality. Once this was no longer important for economic reasons then religion automatically declined. Turner assumes that the fact that there are more marginalised religious organisations indicates religious loss of importance, and is part of the secularisation process.

Country's income and religion

It has often been assumed that as people get richer they will turn less to religion.

In this respect it seems at first sight to have been true of countries such as the United Kingdom and Sweden, but does not seem to have been true of a country such as the U.S.A. Other countries however in the Far East for example South Korea and Singapore have had rapidly expanding Christian churches, although it is not quite clear whether this is at the expense of other religions or whether these people had no formal religious beliefs before. If it was at the expense of other religions then the concept of secularisation could still apply. If it was not at the expense of other religions then the concept of secularisation can hardly be claimed to be universal and we would need to have a theory which accounted for the different experiences or perhaps a set of theories to account for different countries experience. Since countries in the Far East (The Tiger Economies) have been growing in economic terms more rapidly in the 1990s than almost any other country, then the idea that more money automatically leads to less religion would not seem to be proved. Post modernists might argue that as we move beyond modern capitalism, and even state capitalism, as the all-important alternatives, people might need other things in their life, including religious faith.

Secularisation

This refers to the main modern societies in which it is assumed that religious organisations will tend to lose influence. This is partly because it is sometimes assumed that scientific knowledge, as with Darwinism, has been said to disprove religion.

This is partly because, as people become wealthier they tend to assume that they will have less need of some sort of divine intervention in order to improve their position in society. It is not always true that church membership has declined. In the United Kingdom the number of people taking baptisms, weddings, funerals, has declined. This is sometimes known unkindly as hatched, matched and dispatched. However, it is difficult to find accurate figures for the number of people who would still believe in God or would claim to be of a particular religion. How can we measure this if we look just at church attendance? Who measures the church attendance anyway? There is not usually any member of the congregation who would have to do this .There may well be people who are away on an appointment or that are too old to attend. This is particularly noticeable in many churches where church membership consists of the elderly rather than the young.

On the other hand, one cannot be sure that all the people attending church would necessarily adhere to the ideas of that church. Following the World Trade Organisation building being destroyed on September 11th 2001 more people seemed to go to church in the U.S.A., but it is unlikely that all of them would have adhered to religious values. Similarly, even within the U.K., church membership will be much higher in Northern Ireland, perhaps because of the sectarian divisions. If people feel threatened they may be more likely to assert their own identity by going to church. Some people have suggested that U.S.A. has higher church membership partly because it is in practice, an amalgamation of many races and cultures.

In the United Kingdom, and perhaps more so in the U.S.A., there has been a decline in the major churches, to some extent offset by the increasing number of people joining the cults and sects. There are also, partly because of immigration, more people who belong to other religions, noticeably Muslim, Hindu, Buddhists as well as Sikhs.

There have been a number of ideas about secularisation. Peter Berger suggests that it has been more important for men than for women, for urban areas rather than for rural areas and for people in mass production than in other occupations. It is certainly true that far more women are in church than men. This could however have a number of different explanations; women are often more introverted and it may be that introverts are more likely to feel that they need something outside of themselves. For the age pattern it may be true that there are more time pressures for middle aged people than retired people who have much more time. People who have a choice and then go to mass production jobs may well be people who do not want relationships in the first case.

Other people have suggested - particularly from the fundamentalists' side - that the more liberal churches such as the United Reformed Church have lost, in percentage terms, far more people than more Conservative Churches. This does not however explain why the Quakers (Society of Friends) do not seem to have lost so many members, or why the Salvation Army has also lost many members. The opposite argument would be used, for example, that if in many cases the churches do not seem to be interested in what goes on in the society around them, both at home and abroad then the privatised religion would have little meaning to most people outside the church. Certainly some people have suggested that both Liberals and Fundamentalists are in practise, unconcerned about the world.

Other people have suggested that as people get richer, they have more choice about activities and so will tend to find other things to replace church going. This however does not explain why some countries which have become much richer, such as South Korea or Singapore have had an expanding church membership. It also does not explain why the percentage of church members in the U.S.A. is so much higher than in the U.K. It could be argued however that relative poverty may make people more inclined to go to church and this could be one the reasons why the black churches have thrived more in U.K. Other people have argued that since church going is no longer respectable, it is no longer necessary to go to church. For this reason the people currently within the church, have a much stronger set of beliefs than people in the previous age.

Some churches, which do not belong to any organisation, seem to have thrived. One explanation of this is that in many cases there are a few people worshipping in a large church, so that most of the energy goes to maintaining the fabric of the church rather than being used to attract people in.

Many sociologists as well as social scientists from different fields have talked about secularisation. Weber assumed that as the economy became more industrialised, scientific ideas would mean that there would be the end of traditional beliefs. However, how do we know what the truth is? Many people have commented that church attendances are smaller than in the past in the U.K. This is almost certainly true however it is extremely difficult to tell why people go to church. In the Victorian era (1837 –1901) the middle class rather than the working class went more often to church. The "golden era" seems not to have existed in modern times in the U.K., even in 1851 only 40 % of the population regularly attended church. This might have been partly due to peer group pressure, that is, appearing to go to church was the right thing to do. For some occupations such as members of parliament there was for a long while the assumption that all MPs would belong to a religious faith. Charles Bradlaugh fought against this as did John Wilkes who was elected several times in Middlesex.

Similarly, many training colleges belonged to the different denominations.

Going to church for non-religious reasons

We may find this strange, but there are comments made in the media and elsewhere about parents who want their children to go to Church of England school for secular reasons. Some of the reasons include the fact that they may have a better reputation or that they have more prestige as seen in some areas as being white. It is therefore not uncommon to find that some parents of, say, 10 year olds, will go for a while to the local Church of England so that their offspring go to the school of their choice and disappear after this time. There were in any case fewer alternatives for example watching Sunday sport would have not been available for most of the era.

Some sociologists have now suggested that going to church is a leisure time activity which has to appeal more than the alternatives such as watching television, going to sports fixtures, shopping or even carrying out do-it-yourself activities which have grown partly because more people own their own houses and so have more incentive to improve their houses as they see fit.

Within the U.K., however there are different patterns of church going with much higher proportions of people going to church in Northern Ireland and voting on generally sectarian lines. This was shown in November 2007 when in voting for a possible devolved parliament the biggest parties were the hard line parties of Ian Paisley and the Democratic Unionist Party on the Protestant side and with Sinn Fein on the Roman Catholic side. The main non sectarian party, the Alliance party got about 7 % of the total votes whilst the more moderate parties on the unionist side, the Ulster Unionists and the Social Democratic and Labour Party (SDLP) on the Roman Catholic side, did worse than the hard line parties.

SELF EXAMINATION QUESTIONS

Section 1: Definitions

1. What is meant by a 'belief system'? How far do belief systems affect modern society?

2. What might cause belief systems to change in society? How far, would an influx of people with different cultural backgrounds cause the values to change?

Section 2: Why study religion

1. Why have sociologists, especially Weber, been interested in the influence of religion?

2. What problems might there be in judging how far religious beliefs alter society?

Section 3: Data

1. What was meant by the 'Golden Era' for the church in the 19th century? Which social classes would have gone to church in the 19th century? Why did working class people often not go to church? Why might not everyone agree that it was a Golden Era? (Hint: Would people have gone to church because it was a respectable thing to do?) Why might it have been convenient for some people to believe that God established the different classes in their different positions?

2. What are the problems in trying to obtain adequate data about church membership etc? Why, if there is a central membership which churches have to pay towards, might churches want to under estimate their numbers? Why might it be difficult to get up-dated membership lists in many parishes?

3. Are there similar problems in obtaining other data, for example, the number of people being treated by a doctor? (Hint: Do all people who have left an area get taken off a doctor's lists?)

4. Why has there been a decline in Baptisms and Christenings. Are there differences in approach ,why might some clergy refuse to accept people for christenings if their parents have not previously attended church?

5. How can we tell whether people take astrology seriously? Do all people who look at their star signs and information in the press take it seriously? Why might it be more difficult in this case than with telling whether people take other religious beliefs seriously?

Section 4: The concept of the sacred including festival books

1. Why might sociologists wish to investigate the concepts of festival and religious rituals? How far do the festivals perform a unifying force in society?

Section 5: Sociologists and religion

1. Why did Weber assume that more scientific ideas would lead to the decline of traditional beliefs? How can we measure the advance of science if at all? How much does the average U.K. citizen know about scientific ideas? Why might a greater knowledge lead to a questioning of ideas?

2. Does the fact that there are prominent scientists, such as Stephen Hawking, who are opposed to church ideas mean that religion is outdated? If we find other prominent scientists who do believe in religion does this prove that religion is correct?

3. Why do people send their children to Church of England schools for non-religious reasons in the U.K.? Why might school rules about girls wearing trousers, help to ensure that some church schools were more likely to have white children than non-white?

4. Why did Karl Marx assume that religion made life bearable for the poor? What, if anything, might this say about the system of beliefs? What, if anything, might this say about the people claiming to practise the system of beliefs?

5. Why did Weber assume that religious institutions would have a charismatic leader followed by one of bureaucracy? How far has this been true of the major world religions of which you have knowledge? Does it also apply to any other system of beliefs?

6. In what way might people use religion to dominate different groups in society? What would Karl Marx have thought about this? Does the fact that the Monarch is the head of the Church of England mean that people will automatically assume that the church blesses him or her? Does the fact that other churches, for example,

in the U.S.A. that do not have a monarch as head in any way, affect their religious practices or system of beliefs?

Section 6: Church and society

1. In 2004, it was suggested that school fares would no longer be paid for children if they travelled over 3 miles. Why might this affect the number of children going to church schools? If the government refused to pay for children who wanted to attend a church school that was not nearest to them, would this be fair?

2. Some Roman Catholic schools have insisted that parents put forward their child's name to go to a church school, before the age of 3 so that they do not get last minute applications from parents who suddenly decide that the Roman Catholic school is the best one. How far is this fair?

3. Some Church of England schools use criteria such as whether the parents attend the church, whilst other use other criteria such as distance from the school and whether siblings already attend the school. Should there be one set of criteria for all the schools?

4. How far does more immigration lead to a greater number of people in different religious faiths? From which of the major religions are the people from the Indian sub continent more likely to belong to? Would it be sensible to have state Muslim schools, in the same way as there is Church of England or Roman Catholic schools? Should this also apply to people of other religious faiths?

5. How far is Northern Ireland an exception to the general religious patterns of the United Kingdom? How far does religion influence voting patterns in Northern Ireland, and how far does it influence voting patterns in the rest of the United Kingdom?

6. How far does religion affect voting behaviour in the U.S.A.? What issues in particular might different religious attitudes affect voting?

7. Do differences in cultures explain why some black churches have had the gospel services with more emphasis on gospel singing etc? How far does psychology of the individual reflect in the types of religious service they might wish to attend? How far do different types of religious service affect the individual and his or her systems of beliefs?

8. What is meant by the term 'Liberation Theology'? Why has it arisen and what are the effects? Does it disprove the Marxist hypotheses that religion is always there to oppress people?

9. How far have religious beliefs helped to prevent revolution? (Hint: When might it have been used to remove despotic governments?)

10. Has the church always propped up the power of the ruling class?

11. What is meant by the term 'Conservative' when applied to religion? Is the church always conservative? Why might it be difficult to prove or disprove this hypothesis?

12. Does the fact that Christianity often has had limited roles for women, mean that it should be criticised? Does the fact that many denominations now have women clergy prove that the church has become more egalitarian? Why do more women attend church than men in the first place?

13. Why might there be a difference between some more egalitarian churches and other more traditional churches? How far do the changes towards egalitarianism in some churches reflect the views of society and how far do the changes influence society toward greater egalitarianism?

14. Does the fact that in the Roman Catholic Church priests can not normally be married, means that they cannot understand women's problems? Would your answer be the same if we looked at secular organisations such as the president of the U.S.A., who has always been a man?

15. Why in Eastern Europe was the church sometimes regarded as a progressive body? How has it managed to remain in spite of the state religion, in some cases, being atheism?

Section 7: Sects and cults

1. What does a 'sect' or 'cult' mean? Why is it difficult to obtain accurate information about the number of people within a cult?

2. Why might sociologists be interested in the average time between which people enter and leave a cult?

3. What are the main reasons for people joining a cult? What is meant by the term 'World Affirming' or 'World Rejecting'? Would the same type of people join either type of cult?

4. Why did Doctor Barker launch *'INFORM'* in 1987? Why has there been limited accurate information about cults?

5. How can we judge whether someone belongs to a particular church or sect?

Section 8: Secularisation

1. It has sometimes been suggested that church is just another leisure time activity. Is it true that it has simply declined because people have a wider range of choice? How far do such activities as sports affect church going? Does the correlation show that more sport has resulted in less church going, or could it be the other way round, that less church going has resulted in more sport activities on a Sunday? How far can sociologists help to find the solutions to this, and why might they be interested in doing so?

2. What is meant by 'secularisation'? How can we tell whether the U.K. has become more secular? How far do changes in Baptisms or church weddings or attending church at Easter give us conclusive proof as to what is happening? Are there any other statistics, which we might want to obtain?

3. How far would old people watching a religious programme on television such as *Songs of Praise* mean that people are involved within the community of the church? In an ageing population why might the answer to this be of some importance to views about secularisation?

4. What do we notice about the age and gender profile of most churches within the United Kingdom? Why do more women than men go to church? Does the different age profile for men and women i.e. women living longer than men partly account for this?

5. Why do people seem to go to church more in the rural rather than the urban areas? How far is it true that there will be more peer group pressure in the rural areas? Does this prove that the ideas of the Communitarians have some truth in them?

6. How far is it true that a greater knowledge of science has made faith redundant? What particular scientific beliefs have an effect on people's religious views?

7. Does the fact that there are fewer young clergy prove that the church is declining? Do all churches have clergy? Why might the advent of women clergy make a difference to the ways in which people view religion? In what ways would an influx of clergy who had previously worked in secular occupations affect the traditional role of the clergy?

8. What do people mean if they say that loss of traditional practises has led to people being alienated by the church? Would authoritarian or liberal people be more concerned about loss of traditional practices? What were the advantages of having Latin as the main language for Roman Catholic services, particularly if people were likely to move from one country to another?

9. What problems might immigrants, in particular from non-English speaking cultures, find with a typical church service? (Hint: Why might such people find it difficult to cope with 17th or 18th century English?)

Section 9: General

1. How far is it true that the main importance of religion was to control sexuality? Why has there been much more debate about abortion in the U.S.A., rather than in the U.K.?

2. What do we notice about the role of women in the Marxist states?

3. Why might sociologists be interested in how far children should be allowed to have religious symbols within a school framework?

4. Why was Durkheim interested in how religion affected the integration of society?

5. How far would an emphasis of self-discipline be true of people within different religions? How far, in turn, would this affect the ways in which they viewed work and also savings?

6. What is meant by the term 'theocracy'? What would be the problems of this in a country where people belonged to more than one of the major religions?

7. How far does a belief in religion mean that people want to help the poorer people of the world?

8. Why is it more difficult to see how far changes in religious practises and ceremonies have an effect of people's lives than to judge other effects such as class or income?

9. Why might it be helpful in some cases to see what the founders of a religion say, rather than to observe what the believers practice?

10. How far is religion a unifying force within society?

11. How far do festivals and their observance show that people take religion seriously?

12. How far do churches help to solve people's social needs? If they solved these problems, does it prove that the churches are successful?

Chapter Eleven

Globalization and Power of the Large Firms

There is often much talk about the world's largest economies. Less attention has, however, been paid to the power of the transnational corporations. Of the world's biggest 100 economies the balance is almost equally divided between countries and corporations. Organisations such as General Motors, Wal-mart and Exxon each have larger economic outputs than the 50 least developed economies.

These large organisations are well able to move their resources between one country and another. This, however, partly depends upon the industry. For General Motors the time taken to build a new car or to launch a new type of car would be quite considerable. On the other hand, Wal-mart may be able to take over an existing supermarket chain fairly quickly. Wal-mart will have much economic power and it is unlikely to want political power –in equal measure, except when trying to influence planning decisions in its favour. Exxon, on the other hand, will be much more aware of different political changes since the price of tax of petrol is to a large extent determined by the amount of tax that governments impose. It is therefore more likely to want to lobby governments, or in the case of U.S.A, to get it to allow new prospecting in places such as Alaska which might be viewed unfavourably by different governments.

One of the features of globalisation nowadays is that information is very quickly available across all the major, including less economically important, countries. This can be easily seen in the money market where everyday on television we can see the differences in the exchange rates. We can also see changes in the major stock exchange prices whether in Japan, the U.S.A. or the U.K.

The power of the money market was readily shown when Britain left the European monetary system (EMS) in September 1992 and interest rates in the U.K. rose from 10 % to 15 % in one day.

At the time, many people, irrespective of their feeling about the desirability or undesirability of the EMS, seemed to sense intuitively that the ability of speculators to force government to carry out economic polices was undesirable. What is certain is that the concept of national economic sovereignty in an era of free exchange markets is very dubious. If people can switch currencies quickly then it is difficult to see how very different interest rates can apply in different countries. This would occur when there are very strong reasons, for example, people are very concerned about the strength of that particular currency whether for economic or political reasons. OPEC countries which gained vast amounts of money as a result of the increase in oil prices in the early 1970s have often had hot money, that is, money which is looking for the highest safe rate of interest. George Soros who made a name and a fortune for himself by his ability to both forecast currency fluctuation and also by being an active player in it was accountable to no one but himself. There have been suggestions that there should be a small tax on large-scale currency movements. The Tobin tax named after the economist who devised the idea is such a tax, but it is difficult to see how this could be applied. The effects of globalisation can be seen more dramatically on many third world countries where if interest rates go up for domestic reasons in the U.S.A. or the western European economies, the citizenry will have to pay large amount of money as they repay their debts to the West.

Whilst successive governments have talked about the need for research and development, most of it is defence orientated and most of the academic research done is directed towards the needs of the multinational firms. The money spent on defence is rarely scrutinised in the same way that money for example spent on social security will be and it is noticed that most economists' books do not scrutinise the money either. In some cases the multinationals have endowed chairs, that is, the name given to the way that a department or sometimes a professor may be appointed within a university.

The events of September 11th 2001 in America shows that there is vulnerability in our societies that needs to be addressed. If a relatively small group of people can distort an economy so easily we may have a choice between either trying to deter them almost entirely by force of arms or alternatively trying to find out what causes the radicalism in the first place. It is unlikely that the sociologist or indeed anyone else can stop the people who are likely to be suicide bombers. On the other hand the amounts of sympathy that such people might have might well be diminished by taking a more constructive view of what people feel aggrieved about and then acting accordingly.

Intelligence vs. arms

Unless one takes a purely pacifist line it is likely that intelligence, that is, investigating what people are going to do is as or more important than trying to deter violence by force of arms.

Global warming is recognised by many people, including scientists and businessmen, as a chief concern for the 21st century.

Bias in present research

A great deal of research meets the needs of the capitalist system. Many of the modern management methods taught in business studies courses assist the larger companies rather than the smaller companies. More business courses are also geared towards helping firms to become more efficient; there is hardly any countervailing power to help consumers to be more aware of their rights, though many people feel that large firms not only exploit the workers but also neglect the needs of the consumers.

In December, 2003, it was reported that Microsoft was being sued by one of its rivals over anti competitive behaviour. The rights and wrongs are not really important. What is important is that even the largest companies should be subject to rules ensuring that they do not go against consumers' interest in an illegal way. In other cases, it is usually a case for unfair competition between companies. In Kenya, Celtel, one of the two mobile service providers in early 2007 appealed to the Communications Commission of Kenya over what it termed as unfair competition from Safaricom, the other mobile service provider in that country.

Successive governments in the U.K. have talked about the need for an enterprise culture.

In many cases, apart from occasional television programmes or probing journalists, we are much less likely to be aware of the conditions that poorer people live in. On the whole, we see more about producing items of luxury for the richer countries of the world, whereas the needs of the poor in the Third World get less publicity, apart from Third World charities such as Oxfam and Christian Aid.

Criticisms of Globalisation by Professor Mary C. Grey

Mary C. Grey, a professor at the University of Wales who describes herself as an ecofeminist liberation theologian shows in her book *"Sacred Longings; Ecofeminist Theology and Globalisation,"* that it is often women who have suffered as a result of globalisation. She cites the case described by John Pilger of a factory of women in Saigon in Vietnam who work from 9 am to 7 p.m. for the equivalent of £12 per month and have a hygiene card which they are allowed to use for no more than 3 times a day for not more then five minutes. She also suggests that we have become almost entirely anthropomorphic, that is, believing that only human beings matter and that we are indifferent to almost every other living creature in life. People often seem to show no compassion for the way in which animals were slaughtered in the BSE scare in the early 2000s or the ways in which animal are put in very inhumane conditions for the sake of factory farming. There are some exceptions, people seem to be worried about the fate of their pets or of the whales or seals and other animals which somehow seem to project a cuddly image.

Oil companies have often been ruthless in their request for more oil. Many of the tensions in the current world have been exacerbated by the quest for oil. It seems very unlikely that the late Saddam Hussein would have gained the same notoriety if his country had not had oil.

The book about the Taliban by Ahmed Rashid, shows how the oil companies have been interested in oil, with pipes going through Afghanistan and neighbouring territories. Much of the positioning by the U.S.A. government, amongst others, seems to have been basically amoral.

Prof. Grey also suggests that learning is devoted towards skills learning rather than to learn to value things for their own inherent value. There does seem to be a paradox here. If as they do, the multinationals are responsible for the production of music CDs, then education is thought to be good if it enables us to do this more successfully. However appreciation of music or other arts is thought to be a luxury subject. How then do people get taught about the value of the arts in the first place? Her criticism of education as being geared to the needs of capitalism is very similar to that of Karl Marx in the middle of the 19th century.

She also suggests that some of the World Bank projects have been unhelpful for example the construction of dams such as the one at Narmada. This and the Gandhi canal, which is meant to solve the problem of Rajasthan, have actually helped to produce more salinity and even malaria in an area that has not previously suffered from the disease. Rajasthan is a desert area in India.

It is often claimed, but more difficult to prove that the World Bank tends to look at projects from the point of view of richer countries rather than from that of the poorer ones. It is also claimed that it ignores the externalities of its projects, which are important.

There has been a growth of animal rights protests, such as testing on animals for cosmetic purposes and companies do not usually do this now. There have also been protests about the transport of cattle and sheep from the U.K. to the continent. We might note there are some hours' restrictions but it is unclear that they are always obeyed

Differing national attitudes

Prof. Grey is not the only one to point out that the provisions of cash crops has often meant greater demand for water than crops grown in a subsistence economy where people produce mainly for themselves and sell any surplus in local markets. *Friends of the Earth* have also commented unfavourably on global markets, which mean that foods are grown and transported over great distances at the expense, quite often, of local producers. Selling in the overseas market would be subject to the problems of the cobweb theorem if the market were one of perfect competition. This means that prices can fluctuate violently. This was what Durkheim thought was wrong with modern industrial society as we mention elsewhere. In many cases there are often monopsonies (literally a single buyer in the market) and in other cases there are oligopsonies (few buyers in the market who can force the price to become lower than if the market was a competitive one). Due to international barriers to trade by the richer countries it is more difficult to export food products for the third world countries. This would be true of cocoa products in West Africa or coffee growers in East Africa. In both cases, the price of chocolate and coffee is high while the price of the cocoa and coffee bean is a very small part of it. For this reason, the Co-operative movement in the U.K. has announced that in future, all its own brand chocolate will be from fairly traded resources.

Also because of subsidies paid to farmers in the west particularly in America, farmers in other countries often receive a very low wage, this would be true of sugar cane which has an almost perfect substitute with heavily subsidised sugar beet.

Genetically Modified (GM) crops

One of the main scientific issues that has aroused controversy has been that of Genetically Modified (GM) crops. Supporters of the system of GM crops have suggested that we need GM crops to help the world's larger numbers of poor to have food. As we usually have food surpluses and the EU has set aside policies, that is, paying subsidies to farmers not to grow foods this seems dubious; the poor of the world do not have to suffer from food shortages, they just need resources to be able to afford them. Critics on the other hand suggest that particularly if there is a terminator seed, that is, seeds that will not be self perpetuating but will come to an end of their life that this will give even more power to that of the mass producers. They also argue that there will be cross-pollination so that people who for example would want to take part in the small but rapidly growing organic market will find that they cannot do so because their crops are contaminated. It has been difficult to find areas in the U.K. that are willing to go ahead with trials of GM crops. Critics have also suggested that far from the government remaining in a relatively neutral position on the issue and weighing up the costs and benefits has been very biased. Opinion polls in the United Kingdom suggest that the public as a whole seems to be against the concept of GM crops, whilst in the United States of America there is far less discussion. This may reflect differences in culture. The U.K. generally seems to have a more sceptical culture compared to the optimism in the U.S.A.

From a sociological point of view the issue is not so much the rights and wrongs but the ways in which different groups react to an issue. We have the supermarkets on the whole against GM foods whereas the large food producers such as Monsanto are very much in favour. In this case capitalists are not conspiring as a whole and this is not unusual in present society. More of the small farmers are against it than the larger farmers are. We see that groups are far from homogenous in their opinion on many issues.

Free Trade

Though many people have criticised the market system it should be noted that in many cases there is no free market. Many countries have often protected their own products from overseas competition. The European Union has aimed at self-sufficiency in temperate climate products. This means that other country products such as those from the British Commonwealth such as New Zealand and Australia that produce some temperate climate products have suffered. In other cases, the Caribbean countries which grow sugar cane, as does Australia have suffered as the European Union has subsidised the use of sugar beet in the EU countries.

There often seems to be confusion of free trade and capitalism lobbying. Free trade can be optimal given a number of qualifications. There is very little economic theory to support the idea that monopoly capitalism can deliver this optimal solution. A much freer trade which does not place restrictions on the exports from poorer countries or give heavy subsidies on American or European food, might well be helpful.

Different possibilities of the 3 stage world economies

It is doubtful whether it is possible within the confines of one social science discipline to be able to fully understand a concept such as globalisation. Clearly, we need to have some idea of historical development to see how globalisation has arisen. Also, given that commercial organisations will have their main aims as business targets such as level of sustainable profit and turnover, we will need to borrow at least some of the economists' tools. This could include looking at economies of scale which we might summarise as the advantages of big versus small operations. We may also need to have some idea of psychology since managers' preferences may include prestige, status, and power. How far managers and firms are risk averse or risk takers is also important when we look at the restraints if any on the major firms and organisations. Political influences such as the effect of wars, moves toward intentional co-operation including world institutions such as the World Bank and regional economic groupings such as the European Community, COMESA and SADC will also play their part. We would also need to examine how far Governments have encouraged or discouraged larger firms through monopoly legislation, implementation and enforcement of these laws. There may be a difference here; since the 1890 Sherman Act in the U.S.A., there have been legal constraints on monopoly in the U.S.A. However monopolies have arisen in the U.S.A.

The sociologist may be able to assist in the analysis by evaluating the ways in which society has as a whole evolves. The sociologist may also be able to examine the differences in culture and the way in which these are changing to. The cross-disciplinary approach should not surprise us. Whatever one might think of Karl Marx he had to use a number of different disciplines in order to put forwards his theories about capitalism.

The early sociologists, including Karl Marx and Weber were very interested in the division of labour. Clearly, in global firms, division of labour can be taken to extreme lengths. Also in many cases, components are interchangeable between different products, which make it easier to swap the locations of factories. It probably becomes even easier in modern times, where the emphasis is less on heavy industry such as steel and oil refining and much more production is contained within relatively small industrial units which can be duplicated almost anywhere.

If we look at many of the major companies, most of them have an American base. Perhaps the best-known example at the present time would be Microsoft, formed by Bill Gates, whose products can be seen in computers virtually all around the world. Car companies such as Ford, General Motors, IBM, will all have some degree of monopoly power. This has changed with the credit crunch. The widespread use of the English language has made it easier for, first IBM, and then Microsoft, to be able to dominate the computer world along with, to a lesser extent, Apple Mac.

One of the best-known sociologists in this field has been Immanuel Wallerstein, born in 1930. He has developed world systems theories, which have aroused considerable interest if not necessarily overwhelming acceptance. In order to put forward a world systems theory he has had to use cross-disciplinary boundaries in his theories using parts of economics, history, politics as well as sociology.

He suggests we could have a number of possibilities for example; we could have a world empire. One of the longest lasting empires was that of the Romans which existed before 45 BC, when Julius Caesar first came to Britain and continued to about 400 AD. The influence can still be seen in the Latin languages such as Spanish and Italian. Though the English use the word 'Anglo Saxon' to describe their culture about 2/3 or more of the words they use have Latin roots. It does mean that even now it will usually be easier for an English person to be able to learn a Latin language such as French or Spanish more easily than a German language such as German, Dutch, and Swedish. Though Latin is often described as a dead language, it was widely used in the Roman Catholic Church services for a long while . It was therefore possible for Roman Catholics to be able to go from one country to another and still be able to follow the church services. The effect of the British Empire, one of the largest that there has ever been and now renamed the Commonwealth, can still be seen in the impact left by its language. The reason why India can obtain some of the service jobs e.g. call centre workers from the U.K. is that historically many of the Indian population will have English as one of their languages.

We can also see it in the U.K. roads where Watlng Street, which ran from

Canterbury to St Albans, is the main highway for much of the A2 in Kent which runs from London through Canterbury to Dover.

World empires

The American government does not have an empire in the formal sense that the British had until the 1950s and 1960s. The American economy is sufficiently dominant that a downturn in the American economy clearly has a great effect on many other economies. Even a change in one sector such as the tourism industry will have significant effects on other countries. This was shown internationally after the destruction of the World Trade Organisation building on September 11th 2001. Its effects reverberated in many countries of the world through travel patterns. It was also shown in the U.K. when many people from the U.S.A were deterred from visiting the U.K. because of exaggerated fears about the extent of so-called mad cow disease. The phrase; '*if Wall Street sneezes the rest of the world catches a cold*' may be slightly exaggerated but does have some truth. This was vividly shown in the 1930s when the so-called great crash of the American stock exchange market led directly to the great depression which affected many countries including the U.S.A., the U.K. and the Commonwealth. It has also been shown with the present recession.

There is a strong influence in terms of the language used in films as well as in the success of the keyboards and computer programmes such as windows which Microsoft has produced. A major possibility according to *Waters, 1995* is that of the world economies, we could argue that the European Union, which had 25 countries in 2004, and 27 countries in 2007 is in this position, as there will be free movement of people and goods and services. We can also see the U.S.A as a major economy in its own right irrespective of Canada and Mexico who also belong to the North American Free Trade Area (NAFTA).

Waters also saw semi periphery groups of countries that were largely dependent on the core countries. This would presumably include many of the poorer Eastern European countries including Turkey, which not only hopes to enter the European Union, but has also, had its citizenry living in Germany. Many of these emigrants will send back money to their native countries and Turkey, like many others, is heavily reliant on this. Other poorer Eastern European countries include Bulgaria and Rumania, which entered the European Union in 2007

In February 2004, Tony Blair announced that he was setting up a commission, which would look at the problems of Africa as a whole. One of the commissioners appointed would be Bob Geldorf, who was partly responsible for Band Aid in 1984. It could be argued, as always, that trade would have been better than aid, since better access for agricultural products by both the European Union and the U.S.A. would have had more effect.

The third group would be that of the periphery states. These states are very reliant on the core states. This would include many of the sub-Saharan countries, which in many cases have not had any significant increase in per capita income and generally lack economic growth and development due to such social ills as poverty and disease. The domination of the drugs market by a few companies usually from the richer countries has also had a disproportionate effect on these poorer countries where drug prices cannot be afforded.

The chemical companies would claim with some justification that in order to do expensive research, patents are necessary so that they can be recompensed for the research and development. On the other hand, because they seek generally to get the money back with an average cost pricing policy it means that the people who need drugs, which tend to be expensive on this method of pricing, will not receive the treatment. One possibility would be to have a lump sum paid by government, which would enable the drugs company to recover their costs whilst leaving the poorer countries to be able to get the drugs and then decide how it could be distributed.

Effect of broadly similar laws

The legal framework within the Commonwealth is often very similar, and whilst all countries have their own laws, they will again be reasonably comparable to the British, in terms of contract law and operations at the House of Commons (Parliament).

Susceptibility to changes in expectations

The tourist market is very susceptible to changes in the mood of American consumers. At the time of the Gulf War in 1992, many Americans feared travelling abroad and this had an impact on tourism, in many countries of the world. Sociologists often talk about the importance of objective rather than subjective data. Despite this, it might be noted that subjective data is what people act upon, thus, it may be more important than objective data. This particularly applies to the idea of risk involved in travelling to different countries.

World socialism

The Marxists have argued in the past in favour of world socialism. When Kruschev the then Russian leader in the early 1960s said, *"We will bury you"* it was not as some people think a threat to wipe out other countries by military force but by the domination of the Russians through economic achievement. The Russian space mission had destroyed some of the illusions of the west, and particularly the U.S.A. that Russia was technologically a backward country.

However the collapse of the Russian empire around the end of the 1980s and the transition of countries such as China into using capitalist methods even whilst remaining nominally communist means that at the present time it seems unlikely that world socialism will dominate.

It is often difficult to find out what has happened in some of the more secretive countries. At the time of the cold war we could find examples of propaganda in many different ways with some suggesting that Russia was a workers paradise while for others Russia had been moving backwards since the revolution in 1917.

Problems of the 3-state model

Whilst Wallerstein's model seems to have been influential it is not difficult to find examples of countries which do not seem to fit the model:

Albania, under its late dictator Hoxha was very isolationist and was not - as the three part of the periphery model would suggest - one of the countries which were reliant on other countries. The semi periphery states reliant on other countries for the trading do not seem very well to fit the model, for example, Japan. Do we assume that as in 1945 or before that Japan was a poor country by almost any standards that it has been exploited by the west? In practice it received a large amount of aid from the U.S.A. partly to combat the effect of what the Americans would have seen as a communist threat in the 1950s. It has subsequently become one of the major economies of the world.

The countries, which belonged to Comecon before the ending of the Russian Empire around 1990, were in theory economic partners of the communist union. They were in practice very much subservient to that of the Soviet Union. Countries such as Bulgaria, Poland, Hungary, East Germany and Czechoslovakia (now divided into separate countries, the Czech Republic and Slovakia) would have been part of this union. Some other communist countries such as Yugoslavia under Tito remained relatively independent, and Albania was generally more associated with China than with Russia.

The British Commonwealth is very much a free association of members and members are free to join, as was the case with Mozambique a former Portuguese colony, or to leave. It can reasonably be argued that the U.K. does not as with most rich countries not do enough to help the poor. Until the 1960s the sterling area was important with many countries having their currencies linked to that of the pound. This included most Commonwealth countries, except Canada, but also included the Republic of Ireland. It was partly for this reason that the British government was so reluctant to devalue the pound (Sterling) until it was forced to in 1967. The sterling area meant that because currencies were tied to a fixed exchange rate with the pound it was relatively easy to trade without the uncertainties that have existed since that time.

We could also argue that Marshall Aid after the Second World War which gave money to the countries which were defeated, that is, Japan and Germany, as well as countries which had been devastated by the war - often because of being overrun by the Germans - does not seem to fit with the model.

Some people might well feel that we need a new equivalent of Marshall Aid again. In 2006, it was argued that Darfur could have had peace for the relatively small amount of £100 million. Stability often seems to be linked to economic development. A country with low rates of unemployment is less likely to turn to force to overthrow its government if the majority of people who want to work can do so. There seems to be some truth in this assertion.

It can also be argued that with the possible exception of the U.S.A., most of the western countries including the U.K, France and Germany may be rich by other countries standards, but because of trade with other countries they are not able to make decisions on their own without reference to what is happening in other countries. In the early 1990s it became obvious that if the U.K. had very high rates of interest compared with other countries and there were no restrictions on foreign exchange, this would soon lead to a vast flow of money outwards from the country including the so-called hot money.

The model largely ignores conflicts which admittedly in some cases have been caused and used by western countries but in other cases seem to have been internal. These have economically depressed many countries in Sub –Saharan Africa and also some Asian countries such as Sri Lanka.

Experience of the original six members of the European Union

Whilst the original six countries of the European Community (France, Italy, West Germany, Netherlands Luxembourg and Belgium) had shared the same experience of being overrun at some stage during the Second World War, this was not true of some of the later entrants. Both the Republic of Ireland and Sweden had remained neutral during the Second World War. The original impetus for the European Union then was political. The founders particularly the politicians who had often experienced both world wars, were determined that Europe should not go through the same experience again. They thought that giving the Germans the opportunity to sell manufactured goods, the French the opportunity to have access to a large market for its agriculture and the Netherlands the opportunity to use its specialty in transport would mean that there would be sufficient commercial ties so that there would be no opportunity for war. Several of the 2004 members such as Poland and Hungary and the Czech Republic have been part of the Russian sphere of influence so their people have different memories of post Second World War history unlike those of the original six.

Turkey, which still wants to join the European Union, will be if and when it enters the first country, which has had a mainly Muslim culture.

Does global culture ignore all national boundaries?

It is sometimes argued on the other hand that a global culture will ignore all cultural difference. This does not necessarily seem to be true. McDonalds has to adapt if it wants to make inroads into a county with a mainly Hindu tradition such as India. Hindus regard the cow as sacred, thus beef-burgers can obviously not be part of the menu.

The book, '*McDonaldization of Society*', by Professor Ritzer of the University of Maryland shows how McDonalds - the fast food company - has not only become a world-wide institution, but also how its methods have become part of the global economy.

Professor Ritzer suggests that the main aim of McDonalds is to get food as quickly as possible. He also points out that the use of computers has helped to make everything more predictable. The main advantage of McDonalds is the consumers' belief that they get a lot of food relatively cheap.

Professor Ritzer suggests the same ideas have also applied to other institutions such as education, since even if students have, say, a tick list on how their professor is doing, it can well help the lecturers who do not ask too much of their students. It also means that in many cases since professors are judged by the number of publications it is better to produce a lot of material however badly written it is.

Culture

Though the word 'culture' is widely used, it is not obvious what it means and how far people identify with it. Whilst people on the defensive talk about British culture being swamped by immigrants; British society like most societies nowadays is an amalgam of many different cultures sometimes differentiated age groups, so that young people preferences will often be more similar across international boundaries than with the older generations. It may also be affected by class : subsidies to the arts have often been criticised as giving the middle class the opportunity, say, to get cheaper tickets to the opera , which the working class do not usually go to. The male voice choirs by contrast often grew out of the shared experience of mining communities where there would have been few other facilities for entertainment. Similarly the brass band often grew out of the mining communities which were very close knit.

It surely depends upon different aspects of life. For instance, in music those people who like classical music could probably identify in this context with being European since many standard classical music programmes will have pieces by J. S. Bach and Beethoven -both Germans- Mozart who was Austrian and Tchaikovsky who was

Russian. For literature however we will probably find that language is more of a barrier and so many people could identity with American and British writers but fewer people will have read Goethe who is probably Germany's best-known writer; or Ngugi wa Thiong'o of Kenya, who mainly writes in one of the country's vernaculars. For jazz the influence has been American both white and originally black.

There are increasing global influences such as TV networks like CNN and entertainment influences like Disneyland, there are still differences in other directions. Cartoons are expensive to make, but dubbing is comparatively inexpensive, so that this means that they can be shown across many countries for very little additional expense. Cable and digital television means that it is perhaps even easier to sell cartoons than in the days where most families only had one television.

Whilst McDonalds can be found in many countries, the idea of a long lunch break will be more common in the Caribbean than in Europe. Similarly the concept of a pub where the emphasis is on drinking alcohol without food will have its roots in England but is comparatively uncommon in African cultures. Some people have suggested that this is one of the explanations of binge drinking which received much publicity in 2009 in the U.K.

Differences between rural and urban cultures

There are, within a country, often major differences between what might be called the deep rural areas and the conurbations. The differences between the Western Isles of Scotland and London or Glasgow are deeper than the differences between many of the major cities such as London and Paris. By the deep rural area we mean those areas where many people live and obtain their money from the local primary activities of farming, fishing, and forestry or related processes like cheese or butter making. This would be in contrast to people who claim to be living in the country when in practice they just sleep in the countryside but obtain their living, do their shopping and get their entertainment from the conurbations or large towns. Some of the Scottish Western Isles will have a very strong view about Sunday as a holy day and thus have sternly opposed flights to and from the Isles on Sundays. They will also tend to have a much more puritan view of life than will be found in a cosmopolitan city such as London.

Differences in patterns of shopping

In the shopping sphere, though supermarkets dominate in most countries, they offer low prices partly because they pay less money to their employees. However, in many of the continental countries of Europe, the patterns of shopping seem quite different. People in Austria will more often use the local farmers market. They will use old-fashioned baskets to go shopping and to get bread daily. Supermarkets exist but have not dominated to such an extent as in the Anglo Saxon cultures. In many

European countries people will travel greater distances to get to the local markets particularly on Saturday where the emphasis is often on fresh good food rather than on the cheapest. This can also be seen in African countries, where they even have 2 or 3 market days in a week.

Economists have often stressed the concept of comparative advantage, but it is difficult to see how this applies to much of modern trade, where one has almost identical products, for example, 1100 cc cars in most of the Western countries. The concept of product differentiation, which is linked to marketing, seems a more plausible explanation of what is happening at the present time. We could argue, therefore, that much of what is happening is due to effective marketing rather than being due to comparative advantage in the sense that 18th century economists such as Ricardo had argued.

Global middle class and the missing working class

Whilst in the past there have been slogans such as '*workers of the world unite*' it is often easier for the middle class to unite than the working class. Many of the professions and their professional bodies such as the Chartered Institute of Logistics and Transport cover many professions mainly in Commonwealth countries. The link here is that transport is almost by definition an international business and therefore there are points of similarity even for people working in domestic transport systems. Other professional bodies such as those in the accountancy field will also straddle several or in some cases many countries. In many cases, consultants and managers in a given profession will be able to move fairly easily from one job to another irrespective of the countries so long as there is no major language barrier. The growth of the multinational companies makes this even more likely. Though not much progress has been made on the harmonisation of professional qualifications; professionals will often have the same jargon to tie them together. Common interests usually mean that international barriers are often easily broken. Many of the articles will be written about development in other countries as well as different emphasis on priorities of those countries. Advertisements in professional journals or on the web mean that it is relatively easy to obtain information about jobs in other countries for professional people. They may well have studied together since in some cases - particularly for older workers - there may have been relatively few colleges, which catered for some of the professional bodies. .

The harmonisation of regulation on many products within the EU means that it is much easier to comply and to be aware of the legal constraints than it may have been in the past. In some cases as with dangerous goods, the provisions have been laid down by the International Maritime Organisation so that they will be the same whatever country one is working in. This is obviously desirable since labelling of dangerous goods should obviously be instantly recognisable whether or not dockers can read at all well or in only one language. Bearing in mind that the captain of the ship may be from one nationality and the crew from many others, there were strong arguments to have the same regulations. This is why Russian and American experts amongst others, managed to agree on such measures even in the middle of the cold war.

Other organisations such as the International Air Transport Association (IATA) have also had similar regulations, as had the UIC (Union Internationale Chemin de Fer). The fact that IATA exists has made it easier for travel, since one airline ticket is usually easily recognisable to all.

The use of the Internet has made it much easier for people to be able to communicate with each other. Presently, it is more widely used by middle class rather than working class people for communication.

Unskilled workers migration

Unskilled workers can often find it easy to obtain jobs if they go from the very poorest countries to the richer ones since the local population will often not wish to carry out the menial tasks. This occurs in Western countries and some countries of the East such as Saudi Arabia and Dubai. There is however unlikely to be the same community of interest except where they form a large homogenous part of the population. For the working class there are more likely to be problems of finding suitable accommodation than for the middle class.

In some cases there may be illegal immigrants so that the menial jobs such as those in cleaning and in the building trades and fruit picking are paid cash in hand so as to evade tax and eventual detection.

The case of the Chinese cockle gatherers who died in February 2004 drew attention to both inadequate safety procedures and to the fact that people were receiving very low wages for a dangerous occupation. Ironically, because some of them had mobile phones, the tragedy received wide scale coverage more quickly than with many other accidents in different parts of the world.

The ageing population in the U.K. means that we need more workers or we have to radically alter our work patterns, or by working longer; having increased productivity or higher flexibility, but the status quo is not an option.

Similarities between Global Organisations

The oil companies

If we look at some of the largest organisations, the oil companies such as Shell or BP, are examples where research and development are important but the products are fairly homogenous. Petrol is much the same although there may be slight variations, for example, between unleaded and leaded. The research and development has often led to new uses for previously unused products. It has been estimated that there are now about 2000 derivatives of oil products. The effect of this was perhaps most widely seen at the time of the OPEC price rise in the 1970s, when more ordinary people, who probably did not associate plastics with oil, soon realised that an increase in oil prices led to much wider price rises than might be expected.

The cost of setting up new oilfields is enormous and can only really be carried out by either a large firm or possibly by some governments.

Boeings

Boeings has concentrated on aircraft manufacturing and has for a long time dominated the world market. Concorde was heavily backed by both the French and British governments when it was launched in 1973. However it was aimed at the small elite group of businessmen who would pay high prices to save some time. It seems strange that the subsidy which was given to produce the aircraft was not more widely criticised since it would enable a few highly paid people to travel in luxury. Most economists would have said that it was regressive; giving more to the rich than to the poor. It would seem that if subsidies were to be given at all to the aviation industry it would have been more sensible to cater for the mass market which has increasingly been that of tourism, visiting friends and relatives (VFR). The high costs of research and development in these fields have been offset by the economies of scale enabling them to sell to most of the worlds airlines as can readily be seen at any major airport. Ironically the Russian communist government at that time also tried to develop a similar aeroplane. Several European governments have joined together to form a consortium to enable the airbus process to go ahead since it is beyond the reach of countries such as the U.K. to go it alone.

The airlines themselves have gained from a favourable taxation regime compared with most other transport organisations and the private car .This has been increasingly obvious as the British government is trying to put forwards a long term view for airports which assumes that the favourable taxation system for airlines will remain for the next thirty years. The problem is more difficult as one country such as the U.K. cannot, alone, try to impose higher taxes on fuel or landing rights because the airlines would simply go elsewhere. If the problem is to be contained then international coordination would help.

Computers

The major giants in the technical field are IBM, Apple Mac and Microsoft. For a long while computers and IBM seemed to be virtually synonymous. However at one point it made huge loses and it is currently concentrating on turning these losses around by focusing on mainframe computers and consultancy.

Nestlé

Nestlé is in a field where research and development in the ordinarily sense is unimportant since items such as those made by Joseph Rowntree including chocolates and pastries could be made by many small firms .It has also grown through acquisition for example of Rowntree and also through the acquisition of Shredded Wheat which is still one of the major cereals eaten in the U.K.. The key here is marketing and customer knowledge. Critics have suggested that Nestlé has, as with most of the chocolate makers, paid very low wages to the producers of cocoa, which is one of the essential ingredients of chocolate. It is the biggest food firm in the world but has run into strong criticism about the way it markets its baby food. Nowadays Nestlé has become a major food corporation and has taken over other businesses such as Rowntree. It also has an interest in cereal companies such as Nabisco Shredded Wheat and Carnation milk. Nestlé has been widely criticised for promoting baby milk. This is because in many cases fresh water is not available so that whilst the baby food itself is healthy, the food given to the baby is not, so that breast milk would be much better. The concept of fair trade has come increasingly to the fore in the U.K. There have also been other developments such as the launch of café direct which on the coffee market will be probably only a minor challenge to Nestlé as it has its own giant in the field; Nescafe.

Proctor and Gamble

Proctor and Gamble have remained as one of the two giants in the detergent field competing with Unilever in the U.K. market. Here also, the key seems to be marketing since inherently there is little difficulty in making soaps. The term soap which is commonly used around the world to mean popular weekly televisions programmes, also known as telenovelas, such as *Neighbours* in Australia, *Wingu la Moto* in Kenya, *Coronation Street* in the U.K., got their names from the kind of television advertising that soap manufacturers such as Proctor and Gamble used to make. The intense advertising makes it difficult for new firms to enter the market but there has been increasing competition from the supermarkets' own brands (in the U.K.) since they have sufficient selling power to do this.

Giddens talks about the globalisation of the media. One of the factors in this is the growth of television and the media. In the first Gulf War many people watched coverage from some of the American TV stations such as CNN. In many hotels, the cable TV networks show American channels. Giddens writing his book in 1989 talks about the importance of British programmes since many of them are exported to the

U.S.A. Since writing his book, the BBC in particular has greatly extended its sales. This includes nature programmes, which will have a wide appeal since they are not devoted to any one culture. The BBC has also sold many of its comedy programmes to many countries. However, the U.S.A is by far the biggest producer of TV programmes.

In the U.K. and other Western countries except the U.S.A. there are National newspapers which in many cases have heavily relied on the Reuters organisation for their sources of information.

Types of Transnational Co-operations

Many of these are conglomerates. Unilever which makes detergents such as Surf and Persil; bread spread such as Stork Margarine and Blueband; Ice cream (Walls) and until it sold off the meat part was a major part of the meat industry in the U.K. Conglomerates cover different types of products and services. Transnationals can be sub-divided into those which Perlmutter calls ethnocentric ones where the head office is dominant and there is similarity in all its branches wherever they may be. On the other hand is what he calls polycentric whereby the individual firm's decisions are mainly made in the country by the local management with the role of the central organisation being to make major policy decisions. More recently however the large firms have often tried to move decision making to the centre, in order to take up the advantage of lower wage costs in other countries.

The Japanese companies often managed to export their management styles, thus altering many previously dominant management styles.

Giddens also draws attention to what is referred to as 'agribusiness,' which means that food production has been altered with large-scale firms processing the foods. This is nothing new, Levers originally had palm oil supplies for their soap and in turn Lever Brothers became a very large food business.

Sharon Beder from the University of Wollongong in Australia shows how the large-scale companies can in many cases manipulate public opinion. She shows how from the 1970's onwards, the media machine in the U.S.A. has become gradually more important. She also points out the meanings of the various think tanks, which then become part of the main sources of news. She suggests that the Heritage Foundation in the U.S.A. is frequently used as a method of getting information across. This has been particularly important for example in the attacks on the concept of global warming and also on the effects of dioxin. Part of the problem is that the public in many cases has little knowledge of science in spite of what the early sociologists might have thought.

Beder also draws attention to the fact that 98% of U.S.A cities have daily papers with no competition. Also, about six major corporations own most of the TV channels.

She points out the great influence of GEC (General Electric Company) which amongst other things is a major plastic manufacturer as well as a manufacturer of jet engines. She says that this can be used to give biased accounts of General Electric's actions.

SELF EXAMINATION QUESTIONS

1. What is meant by a transnational corporation? How far does their level of output indicate how much economic and political power they have?

2. Why might different methods of communication have an effect on the size of firms and upon a firm's ability to manage effectively? What effect does this have on the globalisation process and its efficiency?

3. How far is it possible for any one country to be able to control its own economy without being concerned about what is happening in other countries?

4. How far is it true that most university research is geared towards the needs of larger firms rather than the interest of smaller firms or consumers?

5. How true is it that globalisation leads to more problems for the poor and in particular poorer women?

6. What did Durkheim think was wrong with modern industrial society? In the light of your knowledge of your own or other countries, were his conclusions correct?

7. Why is it very difficult for Third World countries to be able to export many products, which would make them much more self-sufficient?

8. How much is public opinion important and how much can it be manipulated when considering issues such as GM crops?

References

http://findarticles.com/p/articles/mi_m1310/is_1992_Jan/ai_11921836

http://en.wikipedia.org/wiki/Urban_area

http://en.wikipedia.org/wiki/Rural_area

http://thattakedona.blogspot.com/2006/06/rural-urban-migration.html

http://www.fig.net/pub/athens/papers/ts12/TS12_2_Nabutola.pdf

http://www.hewett.norfolk.sch.uk/curric/soc/POSTMODE/post11.htm

http://en.wikipedia.org/wiki/Idealism

http://dealarchitect.typepad.com/deal_architect/2006/01/process_angiopl.html

http://www.tralac.org/scripts/content.php?id=2893

http://news.bbc.co.uk/2/hi/africa/1728875.stm

http://news.bbc.co.uk/2/hi/africa/5036398.stm

http://www.unu.edu/unupress/unupbooks/uu37we/uu37we0t.htm

http://www.globalissues.org/HumanRights/Racism.asp

http://en.wikipedia.org/wiki/Ethnic_group

http://en.wikipedia.org/wiki/Gypsy

http://en.wikipedia.org/wiki/Romani_people

http://www.umd.umich.edu/casl/hum/eng/classes/434/charweb/HISTORYO.htm

http://migration.ucdavis.edu/MN/more.php?id=1087_0_5_0

http://oriole.umd.edu/~mddlmddl/791/communities/html/africanmd.html

http://www.livelihoods.org/hot_topics/docs/eastAfrica.pdf

http://www.eldis.org/go/display/?id=18277&type=Document

http://www.unhabitat.org/content.asp?cid=2507&catid=5&typeid=6&subMenuId=0

http://www.un.org/Pubs/chronicle/2003/issue4/0403p19.asp

http://www.fordfound.org/publications/ff_report/view_ff_report_detail.cfm?report_index=567

http://ipsnews.net/news.asp?idnews=37411

http://www.sadelivery.co.za/best%20of%20DELIVERY/opinion_poor0311.pdf

http://earthtrends.wri.org/pdf_library/country_profiles/pop_cou_404.pdf

http://www.drh.go.ke/html/programs.asp

http://www.drh.go.ke/documents/Kenya%20DHS%202003.pdf

http://www.sit.edu/studyabroad/africa/ssa_ker/ker.pdf

http://www.wider.unu.edu/publications/dps/dps2002/dp2002-65.pdf

http://gateway.nlm.nih.gov/MeetingAbstracts/102194653.html

http://www.ipar.or.ke/dp60pb.pdf

http://www.ncbi.nlm.nih.gov/sites/entrez?cmd=Retrieve&db=PubMed&list_uids=12178524&dopt=Abstract

http://www.cbc.ca/health/story/2006/04/06/who-report-20060406.html#skip300x250

http://dictionary.reference.com/browse/cult

http://en.wikipedia.org/wiki/Sect

Kenya facts 2006 (www.cbs.go.ke)

Sunday Nation, July 8th 2007

Index

N

O

P

Q

R

S

T

U

V

W

Y